BERMUDA

MISS WORLD 1979-80
Gina Swainson

20c

INSIGHT GUIDES

BERMUDA

Edited and Produced by Martha Ellen Zenfell
Photography: Carl and Ann Purcell
Editorial Director: Brian Bell

APA
PUBLICATIONS

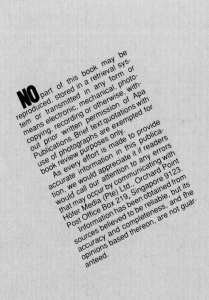
BERMUDA

First Edition

ABOUT THIS BOOK

Dust is not something commonly associated with the balmy island of Bermuda. Blues skies and pink beaches, the turquoise sea and the solid, distinctive shapes of the buildings are the impressions usually received. In spite of these potent images, which certainly do exist, it is dust which springs most readily to the mind of project editor **Martha Ellen Zenfell** when she thinks of this *Insight Guide: Bermuda*.

The first bout of dust came during a blustery month in England. An assignment came into the London office of Apa Publications, the company behind the award-winning series of travel guides conceived by photographer/designer **Hans Höfer**: let's do a book on Bermuda. Zenfell, editor-in-chief of Insight's USA CityGuides titles, leapt at the chance. A freelance editor and journalist with many assignments to her credit, Zenfell was intrigued by the idea of doing a book of nearly 300 pages on a destination of such diminutive proportions. Other Insight Guides have concentrated on countries such as France or Australia, but to achieve the same, in-depth coverage of just one island, rather than 50 (Zenfell's experience while editing Insight's guide to the *Greek Islands*), was a challenging prospect.

Repository of Wisdom

Her first task was to enlist the help of Apa stalwart and historian **Rowlinson Carter**. Carter writes now and again, and sometimes quite frequently, for British publications like the *Spectator*, the *Sunday Times Magazine*, the *Guardian*, the *Daily Telegraph*, *Tatler* and *Harper's & Queen*. Carter wasted no time in clearing out the books on Bermuda held in stock by the London Library, that repository of wisdom and dusty volumes located in St James's Square. Together they ploughed through the books, some nearly 200 years old, seeking out information about the place they would both soon visit. It wasn't until later they realised their good fortune. Bermuda's climate, ideal for sun-bathing, is unkind to rare editions, and the selection in London proved to be an important one.

The more Zenfell read about Bermuda, the more excited she became. Bermuda's Anglo/American culture is similar to her own, right down to opinions connected to the American Civil War. Her sympathies, like Bermuda's, lie with the American south, where she was born and raised before moving to Britain.

The important subject of photos was tackled by **Carl and Ann Purcell**. A successful photographic team who specialise in travel and travel-related subjects like hang-gliding in Rio de Janeiro and riding dolphins in the Florida Keys, Insight's standard brief – stunning photos combined with comprehensive coverage – posed a challenge even to this expert team. Battling poor weather and a dismayingly long list of topics, not to mention the difficulties of getting around (visitors cannot hire cars on Bermuda), the Purcells worked from dawn to dusk in order to produce this visual record.

No Insight guide can be completed without assistance. Our man in Bermuda proved to be the immaculate **Charles H. Webbe**, public relations manager for the island's Department of Tourism. A former reporter for newspapers in both Bermuda and Britain, he was persuaded to write the articles on food and music. In the end, though, it was Webbe's meticulous manners which saw the book

Zenfell

Carter

C. Purcell

A. Purcell

Webbe

through to completion. As requests grew numerous and more bizarre, Webbe's restraint in uttering the damning phrase "You want *what*?" became the primary reason this book is so comprehensive. Our sincere thanks to a tireless man.

Insight's policy of using local writers whenever possible was made easier by one visit to the desk of David White, ebullient editor of Bermuda's daily paper *The Royal Gazette*. Story ideas in hand, Zenfell solicited his opinions on who to approach to write what, then followed White's advice religiously. The outcome can be read on any number of pages: **Marian Robb** on art and culture; **Don Grearson** on life at the docks; **Nancy Acton** in a series of personality profiles; **Chris Gibbons** on sport, and **Rebecca Zuill** on flora and fauna.

Two other island writers were also approached: **David F. Raine** (architecture and sailing) and **David Allen** (Bermuda out of season). Raine, whose history of St George's can be bought in local shops, has connections with the National Trust building, the Bridge House, in the town of the same name. David Allen is the island's primary travel writer and also the shadow Minister of Tourism.

Writers and contemporary pictures taken care of, the second bout of dust came while searching for images to illustrate the book's historical chapters. Guidance through the collection held by the Bermuda Archives came in the form of **John Adams**, the custodian of the island's visual and printed heritage. Adams combed the files for suitable images; then, left to her own devices, Zenfell spent hours in the basement of the archives office, looking through historical works and family photograph albums to come up with a definitive selection. It was this marathon session which unearthed the picture of Mark Twain on holiday (see page 26).

A photo editing session back in London posed the next question: how to blend the black-and-white pictures and the delicately tinted postcards with the bold, graphic images of the Purcells and other photographers? Countless sifting and ordering of Zenfell's favourite images produced the results shown here. We hope you like them.

Great Catalyst

The contributions of the "home team" in London should not be overlooked. **Derek Brightwell** of Bermuda Tourism and **Pippa Grive** of Toby Oliver & Partners PR were immediate in their enthusiasm and attentions. Grive's initial, positive response to the book was a great catalyst. **Jill Anderson** marshalled the book skilfully through an array of Macintosh computers, **Berndtson & Berndtson** drew the maps, and **Christopher Catling** handled the proof-reading and indexing. **US Air**, the **Harmony Hall Club** and the **Lantana Colony Club** took care of the Purcells back on the island.

Dust thoroughly settled, Zenfell has only fond memories of this book and her trips to Bermuda. At times, though, she does wonder what it would have been like if she'd had the time to go swimming in that balmy, turquoise sea – at least once.

Robb

Grearson

Acton

Gibbons

Zuill

Raine

CONTENTS

TRAVEL TIPS

Bermuda has popped up in the oddest ways, originally as the result of a seismic shift in the Atlantic Ocean, and more recently as a synonym for a popular style of short trousers. Scholars might more readily associate the name with Shakespeare's *The Tempest* or perhaps with the lyrical flow of Andrew Marvell who, not alone among poets, wrote lovingly of Bermuda without even setting foot there.

One writer who did get there was Tom Moore, the 19th-century Irish poet. The object of his desire was, scandalously, the teenage bride of one of the colony's worthiest citizens. The latter understandably felt that Bermuda could manage without any more itinerant poets for the time being.

Naturalists might think of Bermuda in terms of the cahow, a bird as much the symbol of a unique environment as the dodo was of Mauritius. Gourmets once sang the praises of the Bermuda onion, arrowroot and even the potato. The arrowroot is now extinct on the island as the cahow almost was. Sailors will talk of Bermuda rigging, the thrilling Bermuda dinghy or of the mysteries of the Bermuda Triangle. It was in the last context that a pastor from California, having studied the Bible, proclaimed that Bermuda, in his opinion, was a signpost to one of two entrances to Hell.

No income tax: For tourists who do not wish to ponder such matters, Bermuda is an enduringly fashionable resort of magnificent ocean-going yachts, a sunny, temperate climate, brilliant beaches, championship golf courses and friendly people who routinely exchange cordial greetings with total strangers. To this list the permanent colony of expatriates would undoubtedly wish to add, in a whisper: "And no income tax."

The Atlantic Ocean all around "The Rock", as Bermudians call their island, is abysmally deep. The islands were created by a volcano which sent a needle of rock soaring three miles up from the seabed. Other, more

distant volcanic activity produced what are by comparison gentle underwater humps. The broad crown of this rocky pinnacle did not quite reach the surface, but jagged extremities did. Thus exposed in water that was reliably not colder than 65° F (18° C) because of the Gulf Stream, the tips attracted tiny coral creatures whose shells over the next 70 million years were compressed with sand to form a 250-ft (76-metre) cap of limestone – in other words, Bermuda.

In due course these lumps were vegetated

by flotsam, a random process relying on incalculable odds. Migratory birds, alighting on this lonely spot 600 miles (960 km) east of Cape Hatteras, North Carolina, introduced other forms of life. By one means or another, Bermuda acquired a truly native creature, a lizard known as the skink. The more celebrated frog that contrives to make a whistling sound by rubbing its legs together is a 19th-century trespasser from the West Indies, as is the bass section of the nocturnal chorus, a giant toad brought in to combat cockroaches.

The first humans ashore were 16th-century European sailors, usually the victims of

Preceding pages: the stamp of approval; a beach beauty; black and white harmony; sailing into the future; symbols of justice; sun shields. **Left** and **right**, Life on the Rock.

shipwrecks on the huge encirclement of reefs, a reminder of the volcanic crown which remains, for the most part, about 50 ft (15 metres) beneath the surface to provide some of the world's best scuba-diving. The vivid clarity of the water and its even temperature invited (and invites) underwater exploration as naturally as snow put Norwegians on skis.

A Bermudian anticipated modern scuba-diving by descending with his head inside an upturned barrel. It was a crude contraption but it enabled him to remain submerged for 40 minutes and his services were in great demand by treasure hunters locally and in the Bahamas. The reefs around Bermuda are a

trusting or stupid that the settlers could scoop them out by hand.

In spite of their fearful reputation, the birds proved to be as innocently trusting as the native fish. The Reverend Hughes, Bermuda's first clergyman, wrote amazingly of birds strolling nonchalantly among a row of boiling pots as if volunteering to jump in with friends and relatives who already occupied them.

Closer acquaintance with conditions in Bermuda revised the Spanish view that it was the forbidding "Isle of Devils". The cedar was excellent building material, especially for boats, because it was so fine-grained. Palmetto leaves provided plenty of

museum of marine mishaps, compulsive viewing for experienced divers with tanks, snorkellers or simply spectators dry and comfortable in the many observation boats which run excursions.

English settlers shipwrecked on their way to the new colony of Jamestown, Virginia, in 1609 were the first human inhabitants of consequence. By then the ecology had developed a long way from flotsam and bird droppings. The islands – seven large ones interspersed with scores of smaller ones – were thickly covered in cedar and palmetto trees; the waters teemed with turtles, oysters and hitherto unknown types of fish, many so

thatch and furthermore this useful tree grew delicious red berries, heads that could be cooked like a cabbage and a juice that was both potable and potent. The diet of seabirds and fish was augmented by wild hogs, which had multiplied prolifically from breeding pairs left behind by Spanish sailors.

The ecology of a remote archipelago in mid-Atlantic was so delicately balanced that even the introduction of a few hogs threw it out. The hogs brought the cahow perilously close to extinction by digging up its burrowed eggs. Man's attempt to settle the islands had opened a Pandora's box. An accidental invasion of ship-borne rats stripped the islands bare like a plague of locusts. Most of the vegetation was burnt in a desperate attempt to halt the rats. The cedars recovered but were reduced over the years in the interest of profitable boat-building. The last straw for the cedar trees was a scale insect epidemic in the 1940s.

Men could not turn the clock back, but they did the next best thing by introducing a rich variety of flora which would never have reached Bermuda by natural means. The result is marvellously lush, turning the whole colony into what could quite easily pass as a botanical garden. The amount of land set aside for conservation is especially commendable in view of the pressure on

on the easy pickings of casual piracy. The discovery on a beach of a large lump of ambergris, part of a whale's stomach used in the making of scent, caused frantic excitement because it was worth at least its weight in bullion. No more appeared because, rather like oysters and pearls, only sick whales produced ambergris, and whales around Bermuda were then bursting with rude and robust health.

Tobacco cultivation started promisingly but petered out. The settlers turned unromantically to the cultivation of potatoes, but that didn't work either. Problems on the American mainland – the Revolutionary and Civil Wars, prohibition, etc – dangled tanta-

space. The fact that 95 percent of the plants were foreign, even if they now grow wild, means that Bermuda is not what it once was, but only botanical fundamentalists would doubt that it is in almost every respect very much better.

Natural Bermuda was fascinating but could not sustain an economy. The early settlers were great dreamers. While governors cajoled them into building forts and undertaking other public works, they pinned their hopes on uncovering buried treasure or

Left and **above**, history re-enacted in the town of St George's.

lising black market profits in front of these off-shore opportunists, but they did not represent the basis of long-term growth. Any prediction that Bermuda would one day be in the top division of international wealth-per-capita would have been blamed on the mind-numbing effect of palmetto juice.

Sounder economic prospects evolved around New Englanders who wanted to warm themselves during the winter but could not afford the time, long before air travel, to sail as far south as the Caribbean. They took their cue from Princess Louise, daughter of Queen Victoria and wife of the Marquess of Lorne, Governor General of

Canada. Her winter holiday in Bermuda in 1883 attracted considerable publicity, enough to get entrepreneurs busy on a hotel which was completed a few years later and duly named after her, the Princess.

One of the curious Americans who came to see what people were talking about was Mark Twain, who evidently had a rough passage. "Bermuda is Paradise," he remarked, "but you have to go through Hell to get to it." Reference to paradise helped to redress the colony's balance in literary circles after some of Anthony Trollope's unflattering comments: "There can be no place in the world as to which there can be less said than there is about this island…"

"especially to the person who is tired and nervous, run down in body and mind. Its tranquillity is soothing, and furthermore it is remarkably free from repellent blemishes."

Such enthusiastic endorsements were difficult to reconcile with *A Plaine Description of the Barmudas*, published in 1612: "nothing but gusts, storms and foul weather."

The tourist industry, then as now, was geared to the well-heeled visitor. The yachts that call throughout the summer, the standard of the hotels and golf courses with seemingly not a blade of grass out of place banish any doubt on that score. With the need to import practically everything, prices were never going to be cheap.

Travel writers were soon passing judgement on this new destination. William Brownell Hayward was satisfied; his verdict is as appropriate now as it was when he handed it down nearly a century ago. "You leave ice, snow, dirt, noise, bustle, the glitter of wealth, the sordidness of poverty, all the elements that combine to make the fascinating yet wearisome turmoil of New York, the Western metropolis, and in forty-eight hours find yourself in a pure and balmy atmosphere, a silent restful land, where modern progress has yet to remove the rust of antiquity and obliterate ideas of old-fashioned simplicity." He recommended the colony

A 19th-century English visitor complained about shortages but seemed to have the situation under control: "Preserved meats from Fortnum & Mason, however, are very useful as a reserve on days when it is impossible to procure fresh meat of a tolerable kind." He was not keen on local cuisine – "the females make wretched bad cooks" – but was impressed by a novelty, ice from America. He thought the importers, Gosling & Co. (still in business on Hamilton's Front Street), deserved the thanks of the whole community. "Applied to the forehead, it will sometimes stave off and at all times mitigate fevers; and sore eyes, occasioned by the glare of the sea, or the white buildings, are greatly relieved by the application of ice two or three times a day."

The islands were soon able to make their own ice, and visitors did not long have to concern themselves with emergency reserves from Fortnum & Mason. Few modern travellers would regret the passing of boiled palmetto heads as a staple, even if they were said to be better than the cabbages they resembled, although it is a pity that more recent local specialities like codfish with bananas, shark hash and conch stew are not as widely available, if only for experimental purposes, as they once were.

Hotels and restaurants lean towards "in-

tainable – barmen put their creative talents into rum concoctions.

Supermarkets brimming with delicacies of every description are the badges of a society with money to spend. The articles on sale reveal the extent to which Bermuda depends on the United States for its supplies. The logistics of life are concealed, however, behind a facade echoing traditional England, including the ritual of afternoon tea, dressing for dinner (which, for men, leaves open the option of Bermuda shorts) and similar police uniforms, complete with hard hats.

A jovial local character strikes the desired note of charming rusticity. He sports a sun helmet which could have been left behind by

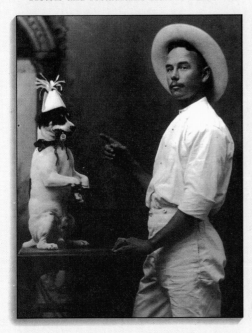

ternational" cuisine and maintain high standards at corresponding prices. *Dining Out in Bermuda* is simply a compilation of facsimile menus without editorial comment; there are humbler establishments which can't or won't advertise but should not be ruled out on those grounds. Chowder is uniformly good; especially so with a few drops of sherry pepper sauce, a local speciality. Bars carry every imaginable form of drink. Palmetto juice is unfortunately no longer ob-

Left, Mark Twain on holiday in Bermuda. **Above left**, unidentified man with dog, *circa* 1895. **Above right**, "Mark Swan", *circa* 1890.

a 19th-century British Army officer and chugs about on a tractor and trailer combination piled high with fruit and vegetables. The impression is of fresh produce cultivated with his own hands. In fact, he collects the avocado pears and most of his merchandise from the airport, almost as fresh as when it left Florida.

Mid-Atlantic mentality: Bermuda does not relish the common mistake of being lumped together with the very different Caribbean. To do so is a geographical nonsense, but in any event the islanders see themselves as something quite apart, culturally suspended between Britain and the United States, a curious blend of the 19th and 20th centuries.

As a self-governing British colony, the official position is that Bermuda could become fully independent for the asking. The issue has been raised from time to time – not excluding the possibility of incorporation into the United States – but there is evidently no pressing desire to change the *status quo*.

The colony potters along like a well-managed ducal estate, and Bermudians would probably be pleased to be thought of as neo-Victorians with powerful convictions about what is right and wrong. Women who wear hair curlers in public are wrong, as are men who would presume to ride a motor cycle shirtless. The thought of topless sun-

sometimes seems, but is not, too good to be true. All too often visitors in a foreign land may wonder whether the hospitality really runs deeper than providing a good home for their money, but the Bermudian waiter's easy laugh has the ring of truth.

Not Miami: Appearances matter greatly, to the extent that Colonel Sanders, of Kentucky and fried chicken, was *persona non grata*, along with other well-known franchises, in case their presence and especially their ubiquitous signboards made Bermuda look too much like Miami. The colonel, his goatee and chickens were eventually conceded a discreet roost away from Hamilton's genteel harbour. The only McDonald's arches are

bathing makes Bermudians shudder. Alcohol must not be consumed in a public place and there are strict laws against littering; this means that illicit drinkers sip furtively from bottles mummified in brown paper and then, as responsible citizens, carry the incriminating evidence around until they find an approved receptacle in which to deposit it.

Bermuda seems to have devised a compromise which pays at least lip service to noble ideals but leaves strategic loopholes open for fun. The net effect is not oppressive. The workers on this particular estate are neither surly nor inclined to tug their forelocks. The cheerful observation of common courtesies

hidden behind the perimeter fence of the US Navy base, a sore temptation for the younger generation who are permitted to sample its hamburgers only on Wednesdays.

Stout resistance to one American innovation, the motor car, crumbled during World War II when the war effort was acknowledged as more important than Bermuda's long-standing antipathy. The ban on cars had been made official before World War I, when one which had slipped through the net, a machine known as "The Scarlet Runner", frightened a horse into bolting and nearly caused a man's death. The ban stood throughout the first war, the military having to move their equipment around in horse-drawn carts, as they were still doing in the early days of the second.

A few years earlier the governor, Sir Reginald Hildyard, had resigned in a rage when the Legislature refused to let him have an official car. Bermudians were content with their horse buses, boats, bicycles and, from 1931, a narrow-gauge railway which ran from Somerset to St George's and is now a picturesque trail for hikers.

While the guiding principle in the design of Bermuda's roads had traditionally been to make them no wider than was necessary to roll a barrel, the military vehicles which crammed the islands during World War II

bans on drivers convicted of scorching about at all of 30 mph. As an alternative to scooters, taxis are plentiful. The pastel pink buses and the service they provide are exemplary.

Cars are limited to one per residential unit. With the decision that parts of the same house could qualify as residential units if they had self-contained cooking facilities or met other structural requirements, the islands rocked on their volcanic perch to the rhythm of hasty D-I-Y home improvements. Other rules were piled on: a moving car had to contain the registered owner or a member of the owner's family; anyone selling a car could not buy another for at least one year. When Bermuda installed its first set of traffic

needed rather more space. The improved roads weakened the case for re-imposing the ban after the war, but there was nevertheless a fierce argument before the Legislature relented in 1946.

The joys of private motoring paled as a quart of cars tried to wriggle into a pint pot. As matters stand, there are no self-drive hire cars; the most an independent traveller can aspire to is a moped or scooter. The maximum speed limit is an undebatable 20 mph (35 kph), with courts imposing six-month

Left, a "birdcage" for all seasons. **Above**, an enthusiastic spectator.

lights in 1978 there were protests about encroaching "urbanisation".

Interchangeable currency: Nevertheless, Bermuda knows what to do in order to earn the compliment that long-suffering travellers bestow like a citation when at last they come across a worthy recipient: the place "works". The telephone system certainly deserves the accolade – not surprisingly, since it is an essential part of Bermuda's expanding role as an off-shore tax haven for international companies. For the same reason, bank tellers do not stare at foreign notes as if they had dropped from Mars. The American and Bermudian dollars are on par and fully interchangeable, and Bermudians consider their dollar to be every bit as good as the mainland version.

By contrast, the supply of hot water – that other yardstick of the less intrepid tourist – is more problematical. The water does run and it is hot, but somewhere along the line Bermuda seems to have been dealing with bathroom equipment suppliers with opposing views on how the things ought to function. Some taps open anti-clockwise, others not, which would not be too bad if pairs of taps were consistent. As it is, trying to adjust the temperature of a shower with taps which rotate in opposite directions may be a challenge which visitors staying in an otherwise

which dominate the Bermuda telephone directory. Column after column is devoted not so much to "Smith" and "Jones" but to names which would be unusual anywhere else, like Lightbourne. People whose names get into the newspapers – in the social columns or through answering charges in the magistrate's court – appear to be drawn from the same small pool of families. The same names also loom large in the colony's colourful history, applied impartially to heroes and villains.

"The great difficulty in the colony," an army officer once sniffed, "is where to draw the social line. Except professional persons, all the best families, with scarcely an excep-

admirable private guest house are not ready to encounter first thing in the morning.

Nevertheless, the milk on the breakfast table of one of these private guest houses, let alone a large hotel, will always be fresh. Taxis have meters; not only do drivers scrupulously switch them on and off, they are knowledgeable and engaging guides. One does not haggle over prices in the shops along Hamilton's beautifully preserved waterfront; they sell cashmere and fine china, for example, not fake watches.

The names on some of the waterfront shops (such as Frith) and on bottles of sherry pepper sauce (Outerbridge) are among those

tion, are employed in retail trade, of a kind that, in the mother country, is considered somewhat incompatible with the social position of a gentleman. Even the lawyers and the clergy have, for the most part, relatives who keep, or are subordinates in retail stores."

In the next breath, however, he removed the sting. "Yet to confound these gentlemen with petty English traders, on account of similarity of occupation, would be both illiberal and unjust." He followed that up with an observation which anticipates the spirit which people employed in the tourist industry bring to their jobs in the present age. "The setting up of a new store was considered not merely as a profitable speculation, but also as a most praiseworthy and patriotic act."

A roll call of Bermudian names no longer carries any reliable indication, if one were sought, of race, colour or class. The impression of a population divided among a few, huge extended families is the result of slaves adopting the names of their masters when they were freed. None had surnames before then, and many had arrived in Bermuda from the Caribbean with Spanish first names which were quickly Anglicised. According to local folklore, the distinguished Trimingham family declined to allow their slaves to adopt their name as a whole, obliging them to use only one or other of the syllables. The

not make it a sinecure and there were several attempted uprisings, the most bizarre being at the instigation of Irish slaves (Cromwell's victims and, by all accounts, thoroughly unsatisfactory servants) who wanted to stamp out Protestantism.

The pressure for integrated racial equality was fuelled by the civil rights movement in the United States during the turbulent 1960s. The system enforced in Bermuda until then was in all but name apartheid: separate schools, separate seating or total segregation in hotels, restaurants, churches and cinemas, and a grave stigma was attached to the idea of mixed marriages.

The battle had been practically won when

family tolerantly tell a different story.

The numbers of whites and blacks in Bermuda were fairly evenly balanced from about 1623, 11 years after the arrival of the first settlers. The blacks make up 60 percent of the total population, the balance including not a few Portuguese immigrants and the descendants of North American Indians whose high-boned features are apparent in some persons of mixed blood. Slavery, as practised in Bermuda, was probably as relaxed as slavery could ever be, but that did

Left, heavenly images. <u>Above</u>, Vince Cann, taxi guide extraordinaire.

Governor Sir Richard Sharples and an aide were assassinated in 1973 as they strolled in the grounds of Government House. The conviction and subsequent execution of two blacks, one a convicted armed robber who had murdered before, lit a fuse which threatened to tear Bermuda apart. Two guests and an employee died after an arson attack on the Southampton Princess Hotel. The rioting ended before the arrival of British troops, but not soon enough to prevent a flood of cancelled hotel bookings.

The scars of racial confrontation have healed to the extent that they are now invisible. The process may have been accelerated by the realisation that everyone was in the same proverbial boat and that the economic consequences of public disorder would sink it. As far as visitors are concerned, there is no such thing as a no-go area. Whites need have no qualms about entering the kind of solidly black bars which in parts of New York or London might look like the jaws of death, and vice versa. If there is a problem, it is being allowed to pay for one's own drink.

No ghettos: Bermuda is affluent in a way that small oil-producing states are not. The wealth is distributed far more evenly among the population, so there are no ghettos and none of the so-called ghetto mentality. It is said to be the ninth richest country in the

world in terms of per capita Gross Domestic Product. In any case, there is full employment and even menial jobs may pay $30 an hour with no deductions for income tax unless a small "hospital tax" is so regarded.

Revenue for the usually balanced national budget is raised through indirect taxation. Percentages added to hotel bills and a departure tax at the airport are obviously aimed at visitors, but locals, like anyone else, pay the duty levied on imported goods – a category which embraces almost everything. Expectations are generally high, and it is not uncommon for ambitious people to hold down two or even three jobs.

Although the size of the population remains relatively stable, the affluent younger generation aspire to their own homes sooner or later, and meeting these expectations adds to the pressure on limited space. The price of an ordinary family house had risen by the early 1990s to about $300,000 in spite of measures to shield prices from the influence of eager foreign buyers. They may not buy property with an annual rental of less than $37,000 and, once bought, there are restrictions on what they can do with it. A foreigner may not bequeath a property to another foreigner; nor, for that matter, may a Bermudian to a non-Bermudian.

The amount of money swilling about in Bermuda has unfortunately attracted the drugs trade, not only because there are people who can afford to buy drugs but also because of Bermuda's position as a logical transhipment point for traffic originating in the Caribbean and Central America. The tragic concomitant of drug abuse has been dirty needles and a near epidemic of AIDS. When Bermuda buried its 100th AIDS victim in 1989, some of the glitter had gone from its achievement of being ninth in the table of Gross Domestic Product.

This single blemish on Bermuda's otherwise elegant gentility will not intrude on visitors, nor does it deter some of them from looking into the possibility of extending their stay – for a year or two! The rules, alas, are tight. A foreigner can only take a job which has been advertised three times locally without producing a suitable candidate. In practice, the only jobs available are either specialised or involve working at unsocial hours. Work permits are valid for only one year, after which the job must be re-advertised and the whole process gone through again. Visitors are not allowed to land in Bermuda without a return ticket and would be rash to try.

As the following history shows, the early days of Bermuda were notable for intermittent spells of mutinous laziness and drunken anarchy – a clumsy way of saying, in many cases, that a freak of nature had produced a place which was too good to be squandered on work. The modern visitor to Bermuda may be inclined to concede the point.

Left, outside Anglican Trinity church in Hamilton. **Right**, a boy and his dog.

TEMPEST.

Alfred Hitchcock could have taken the idea for his film *The Birds* from the terrifying reception given to Bermuda's first visitors, shipwreck victims clawing their way to shore. Bombardment by diabolical birds apart, the islands were notorious. "The islands of the Barmudas," a 1612 document noted, "as every man knoweth that hath heard or read of them, were never inhabited by a Christian or heathen people but were ever esteemed and reputed a most prodigious and enchanted place, affording nothing but gusts, storms and foul weather, which made every navigator and mariner to avoid them as Schylla and Charybdis or as they would shun the Devil himself." Sir Walter Raleigh was more matter of fact: "a hellish sea for thunder, lightning, and storms."

The earliest Spanish sailors to the New World were certainly well aware of the islands because their return voyage took them up the coast of Florida until they picked up the westerly trade winds. The crescent-shaped archipelago was the point at which they changed course for the Azores and home. They had no desire to go ashore nor to linger in the area because it was an obvious stalking ground for pirates hoping to intercept Spanish *cargazoone* of sugar and tobacco, the latter a novelty which had quickly become a craze throughout Europe.

King James I of England deplored the habit: "the barbarous and beastly manners of the wild, godless and slavish Indians… so vile and stinking a custom."

Horror story: One of the first Englishmen to sail past Bermuda added to the bad publicity. He saw a monster rising from the depths. "From the middle upwards," he noted, "he was proportioned like a man, of the complexion of a mulatto or tawny Indian."

The islands were first visited, as far as anyone knows, by Juan de Bermudez in 1503. The hostile birds which taunted him were described in some detail by a subsequent visitor, Captain Diego Ramirez, another Spaniard whose ship ran aground opposite what is known as Spanish Point,

where the remains of later casualties are still to be seen. From his description the birds were obviously the celebrated cahow, about the size of a pigeon but with a three-foot wingspan. They were black and white, he said, web-footed and had very strong longish beaks with white saw-like edges which curved at the tip. "When we landed," the Captain wrote, "they came to us, perched on our heads, uttering a multitudinous chorus of cries… such an outcry and varying clamour that one cannot help being afraid."

Ramirez tried to comfort his alarmed crew. "The sign of the Cross at them!" he shouted. "We are Christians." A negro who had gone ashore with a lantern let out a howl. "The devil is carrying off the negro," gasped Ramirez. "All ashore!"

"It was these nightbirds!", he wrote. "So many came to the light and dashed against the negro that he could not defend himself with his club, neither could the men who went to his help either. Finally we solved the mystery and they brought more than 500 birds to the ship. We cooked them with hot water and they were so fat and good that every night the men went hunting and we

Preceding pages: Flatts inlet by Thomas Driver. **Left** and **right**, illustrations from *The Tempest*.

dried and salted more than 1,000 for the voyage besides what the men ate… They are so plentiful that 4,000 could be killed at the same spot in a single night."

Catching fish presented no problem either: "great numbers of fish; groupers, parrot fish and especially red snappers which are so stupid that we caught them in our hands with pointed sticks and bent nails." There was evidence of earlier shipwrecks in an old mast and pieces of shaped wood, but no sign of life. Ramirez's account lay forgotten in the archives of Seville for 350 years, but news of the birds had spread. Bermuda was fixed in mariners' minds as the Isle of Devils.

By 1511 the islands were included in

Spanish charts. Bermudez returned to them in 1514 or 1515 with Gonzales Ferdinando d'Oviedo, who had been privy to discussions between Queen Isabella of Spain and Columbus about the latter's ambitions. Bermudez and d'Oviedo intended to drop off a breeding stock of hogs on Bermuda which would provide a future source of fresh meat for passing ships. The weather prevented their landing, however, and they were forced to sail on.

A few years afterwards, a Portuguese vessel on the way home from San Domingo wedged itself between two rocks on a reef. The crew were able to salvage all but the hull

and, over the next four months, built a new ship out of local cedar to return to San Domingo. One of the stranded sailors passed time carving into a rock the initials "R" and "P" – probably "Rex Portugaline" – and the date, 1543. The so-called Spanish Rock (the carving was until recently attributed wrongly to a Spaniard, and controversy still reigns on this topic) is in the Spittal Pond nature reserve and bears a bronze casting of the original inscription.

Exactly 50 years later it fell upon Henry May to become the first recorded Englishman to set foot on Bermuda. He was being given a passage home in a French ship commanded by a M. Barbotière. The crew were well aware of Bermuda's notorious reefs and, under the impression that they had safely passed them, "threw aside all care, and gave themselves up to carousing. Amid this jollity, about midnight, the ship struck with such violence as to make it evident that she must speedily sink."

It took all the next day to reach land, by which time they were "tormented" by a thirst which was relieved by the discovery of a rock filled with rainwater. The land, May noticed, was an unbroken forest of cedar.

"Now it pleased God before our ship did split that we saved our carpenters' tools, else I think we would be there till this day," he wrote. "And having recovered the aforesaid tools, we went roundly about the cutting down of trees and in the end built a small bark of some 18 tons for the most part with tronnels and very few nails… Instead of pitch we made lime and mixed it with the oil of tortoises." They had 13 live tortoises as food for the voyage and, eventually, "it pleased God to set us clear of the island, to the no little joy of us all…"

Involuntary settlers: While Spain prevaricated for a century over whether Bermuda was worth settling, the English set their sights set on North America. The first settlement in Virginia had failed, so in 1609 a more determined effort was initiated. A new Virginia Company, given a charter by King James, campaigned to raise funds and enlist volunteers for the expedition. In spite of the earlier failure, Virginia was promoted as "earth's only paradise". The response was enthusiastic and, even before the charter was sealed, its list of "Adventurers" (nowadays "financial investors") included 21 peers, 96 knights, 53 captains, 28 esquires and an assortment of 400 other citizens. Shakespeare had friends and patrons among them and took, like most of England, a keen interest in the enterprise.

A flotilla of eight ships assembled in Plymouth to convey the new settlers, 600 in all. The admiral was Sir George Somers, a shareholder in the company who had sailed with Drake and Raleigh and done a little piracy on the side before entering Parliament as the member for Lyme Regis in Dorset. He was then 60.

The master of the flagship, *Sea Venture*, was Captain Christopher Newport, a veteran of three previous crossings to Virginia. He

Thomas Gates. Like Somers, he had sailed with Drake and was on his way, accompanied by his secretary, William Strachey, to become Governor of Virginia.

On 23 June, after what had until then been a smooth voyage, "a dreadful storm and hideous began to blow from out the northeast, which swelling and roaring as it were by fits, some hours with more violence than others, at length did beat all light from the heaven, which so like a hell of darkness turned black upon us, and overmastered the senses so that the terrible cries and murmurs of the winds shook even those of our company who were best prepared to face them." This graphic account of the storm, by Stra-

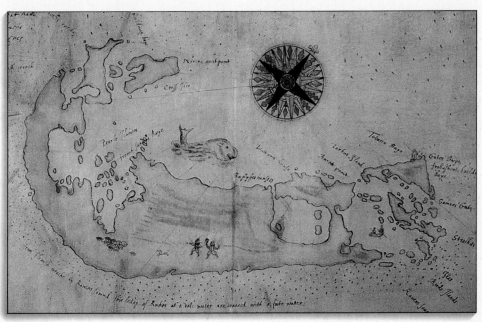

knew the storms of the Atlantic well and had confidence in his ship, a fully rigged and fairly heavily armed galleon.

Sea Venture carried 150 passengers. Among artisans and farmers heading for a new life was an ostentatious fellow who wore a cape, feathered hat and sword and travelled with a servant. Henry Paine described himself as a "Gentleman", although he was heading for a small place in Bermuda's history in a less flattering role. The most distinguished passenger was Sir

Left, statue of Sir George Somers. **Above**, map of Bermuda from 1609–15.

chey, almost certainly provided Shakespeare with material for *The Tempest*.

"Fury added to fury," Strachey continued, "one storm urging a second more outrageous than the former... It could not be said to rain, the waters like whole rivers did flood in the air." The *Sea Venture* sprang leaks which the crew attempted to stop with pieces of beef. All hands took a turn at the pumps, not least the admiral and governor-designate and "gentlemen who had never had an hour's work in their lives".

Sea Venture had a cargo of 12,000 lbs (5,500 kg) of biscuits, the prospect of finding fresh food in Virginia being poor. Mixed with the deluge of rain and sea water, the biscuits practically turned into cement and clogged the pumps. The crew thought they were doomed and began "taking their last leave… until their more joyful and happy meeting in a more blessed world." The passengers, too, were "commending our sinful souls to God" when on the fourth day of the storm Sir George Somers, "peering through the curtain of fine rain, described land".

Sea Venture was still a mile from land when it struck a reef. The women and children were put into the longboat with Sir Thomas standing at the prow. On reaching shallow water he leapt out and proclaimed: "Gates, his bay!" Luckily, *Sea Venture* was

"is very good meate, either raw or sodden, it yieldeth a head which weigheth about 20 lb, and is farre better meate than any cabbage." Another interesting discovery, albeit one with mixed blessings, was that the juice made a potent drink.

A mysterious sniffing noise heard during the night proved to be an inquisitive wild hog, indirect evidence that someone had succeeded in introducing these animals where Ramirez had failed. The only indigenous mammal on the islands was a lizard called the skink, a snake-like creature now found only on the islets in Castle Harbour. Apparently oblivious to danger, the hog allowed its back to be stroked, and did not

ORDER ACANTHOPTERYGII.
FAMILY SERRANIDÆ.

30

SERRANUS GUTTATUS
EPENEPHELUS GUTTATUS
Hind
July 1876.

wedged between two rocks and over the next few days the crew were able to salvage the cargo, including hogs and the ship's dog, and strip the vessel of useful timbers. This left only the rib-cage of the ship, which rolled over and sank.

Misgivings about being stuck on the frightful Isle of Devils were pleasantly revised. The palmetto tree not only provided leaves which could be used as shelter but the berries, said Silvester Jourdain, were "very pleasant and wholesome" and "upon which the hogs do most feed; but our men finding the sweetness of them, did willingly share with the hogs for them." The head of the tree

object when a rope was wound around its hind legs. It was the first of many such gullible meals.

The 60-year-old admiral, former pirate and sitting MP, had a small fishing boat built while the longboat was being fitted with a deck for the voyage to Virginia. Sir George's first day out in the new boat produced no fewer than 500 fish. "Fish is there so abundant," Jourdain wrote later, "that if a man steppe into the water, they will come round about him, so that men were (reluctant) to go out for feare of byting." The fish were "very fat and sweete". Mullet and pilchard were caught by the thousand, and, attracted by lights, enough crayfish could be taken in a night to feed the entire population.

Whales were frequent visitors, and the stranded settlers once watched a sword fish and thresher shark chasing a whale. "The sword fish with his sharp and needle fin pricking him into the belly when he would sink and fall into the sea, and when he started upwards from his wounds, the thresher with his large fins like flails beating his above water." The indefatigable admiral visited one of the smaller islands and returned with 32 more hogs as well as confirmation that there seemed to be no snakes, rats or mosquitoes anywhere, although there were many flies and large cockroaches. To conserve

with a human entourage dressed in baggy Elizabethan costume and feathered hats. It was partly in recognition of his detailed map-making that the company decided to call the islands after him, killing two birds with one stone by throwing in a sainthood to appease England's patron.

One of Sir George's trusted men was put in command of the converted longboat for the voyage to Virginia. Picking a route through the reefs was always going to be dangerous, so it was agreed that a watch would be kept on St David's Island by day and beacons left burning at night for their return on completion of the mission or, in an emergency, before. Gates's assiduous secretary took his

supplies, hogs were slaughtered only when the weather prevented fishing. The ship's dog, fully recovered from its ordeal, proved a cunning hunter of wild hogs, fastening its teeth into their hind legs.

Reasonably satisfied about the food supply, Sir George went off for days on end in his little boat to map the islands. He discovered an archipelago of seven main islands and many smaller ones aligned roughly in the shape of a fish hook. He embellished his map with a drawing of the dog chasing hogs

Left and above, from *Fishes of Bermuda*, painted by Lady Lefroy between 1871 and 1877.

turn at a point since known as Strachey's Watch. In the event, the precautions came to nothing: the longboat was neither seen nor heard of again.

Unwilling to stake all on the longboat reaching Virginia, Gates and Somers got to work separately on two new ships – a hint of the division that existed between the passenger-colonists and the professional seamen in the party. The construction of Gates's boat, *Deliverance*, took place close to where he had proclaimed his bay and had a monopoly, bar one small item, on the materials salvaged from the *Sea Venture*. The work was under the supervision of the ship's carpenter,

Richard Frobisher. The name of the building site, originally Frobisher's Building's Bay, is more generally referred to now around St George's merely as Building's Bay.

In the circumstances, the design and construction of *Deliverance* was an extraordinary achievement. The full-size replica on what used to be Ordnance Island in St George's is awesome. Although more modest in size (30 as opposed to 80 tons), Somers' ship, *Patience*, was perhaps an even greater feat. The only part of the stricken *Sea Venture* that went into it was a single iron bolt. The rest was built of local cedar and held together by carved, wooden dowels. The seams of the 30-ton craft were caulked

build a third ship on one of the other islands to take them back to England. Gates disingenuously seemed to agree to their demands. *Ex officio*, however, he had the right to nominate the island concerned, and the one he had in mind was a rocky outcrop. Of course, he added, the men would have to fend for themselves. They would not be supplied from the company stores. The rebellion melted; work on the building of *Deliverance* resumed. The governor was disappointed that the ship's carpenter was among the rebels. He was reduced in the governor's estimation to nothing more than "one who made much profession of Scripture, a mutinous and dissembling imposter".

with a mixture of wax, crushed coral rock and turtle oil. Unfortunately, no trace of the ship remains.

The forced pace of the work on the ships in stifling heat caused grumbling, especially among those who began to feel that they were probably better off where they were rather than pushing on to the food shortages, disagreeable climate and restless Indians in Virginia. The sailors' aspirations leant towards the luxurious life available in England on the proceeds of Spanish treasure which they were confident of finding if only they had time to look for it.

The rebels told Gates that they wanted to

Bloody murder: Over at his building site on "The Main" (island), Sir George had to deal with a murder. The murderer, Edward Waters, was bound to the body of his victim to await hanging in the morning. His shipmates freed him during the night and he fled into the woods. He was later pardoned and allowed to return to work.

While this was going on, the first baby was born in Bermuda. The father was John Rolfe, who later made history in Virginia by taking as a second wife the Indian princess Pocahontas. The baby did not survive.

The incipient mood of mutiny was revived by the doings of the questionable "gentleman", Henry Paine. He stole weapons and distributed them to conspirators. Paine then became involved in an argument with a captain of the guard, at the height of which he struck him in a flood of expletives which "would offend the modest ear too much to express it in his own phrase". The plot spilled out and the governor decided matters had gone too far: Paine was to be hanged immediately. "...And the ladder being ready, after he had made many confessions, he earnestly desired, being a Gentleman, that he might be shot to death, and towards evening he had his desire; the sun and his life setting together." Henry Paine thus earned the questionable distinction of being the first of many people

"caretakers" in the meantime. The two fugitives watched from their hiding place as the two ships picked a way through the reefs and, bound for Virginia, drew out of sight.

Jamestown, when *Deliverance* and *Patience* got there in 1610, was miserable. Some of the settlers whose ships had ridden out the hurricane which wrecked *Sea Venture* fared less well against the Indians and had already been murdered. The survivors were about to evacuate when relief arrived in the person of Lord De La Ware. It remained to persuade the truculent Indians to trade some of their corn, and Sir George Somers, spotting his opportunity, said he knew of some hogs that might appeal to the Indians.

who were to be executed in Bermuda.

Two of the conspirators, Christopher Carter, a veteran of the earlier, half-hearted mutiny, and Waters, the reprieved murderer, went into hiding and turned a deaf ear to entreaties to give themselves up. They had still not reappeared when *Deliverance* and *Patience* were ready to leave for Virginia, although it seems that Somers may have been nurturing the hope of an early return to Bermuda and had secretly appointed them

Left and **following pages**: the replica of *Deliverance*. **Above left**, Somers and the *Sea Venture*. **Above right**, Somers' grave in 1905.

The hogs in question were, of course, in Bermuda, and Sir George proposed fetching them in *Patience*.

It will never be known exactly what Somers' intentions were – did he really care, for example, whether the Indians ever saw the hogs? – but Carter and Waters were apparently expecting him. They were no longer in hiding and rowed out to meet *Patience*. The strain of the voyage was too much for the old admiral, however, and he returned only to die. His body was embalmed and put aboard *Patience* for onward passage to Lyme Regis, his parliamentary seat, but his heart was removed and placed in what is now the Somers Garden in St George's. A plaque with some dreadful doggerel by a later governor, Nathaniel Butler, marks the spot.

The hog mission forgotten, *Patience* now sailed for England, leaving Carter and Waters to resume their vigil. They had additional company in the person of one Edward Chard and the *Sea Venture's* dog, the celebrated hog-hunter – a situation which was to become the basis of Washington Irving's historical tale *Three Kings of Bermuda*.

Three kings: What Matthew Somers, who returned to England with his father's body, had to report about Bermuda persuaded the Virginia Company to establish an offshoot, the Somers Island Company. The King granted a charter which empowered the company to colonise and govern the island more or less in accordance with English law.

Back in Bermuda, the "three kings" were industrious, clearing Smith's Island to plant a variety of crops, including tobacco, and salting vast quantities of pork for the winter. They were one day scouring the beach in Somerset for pearls when they came across a prize immensely more valuable. Ambergris, the smelly contents of a sick whale's stomach, was a key ingredient in the production of scent and worth £3 an ounce in London. One of the pieces they found weighed 80 lbs (40 kg), enough to set them up for life.

The ambergris, like any treasure or pearls that might be found, legally belonged to the company. It was clearly a case, the men decided, of the company not needing to know about their discovery. Chard claimed the bulk for himself because he had actually spotted it. Carter and Waters disputed this, the beginning of a "most hot and violent contention" which was to go on for two years. It obsessed them even when fishing and on one occasion led to "a fierce combat" with oars. After toppling overboard, they continued the struggle in the water. The dog was roused into joining another of their fist-fights and in the excitement bit Waters, his nominal master. Carter emerged as the peace-maker and hid all weapons.

Instead, they resolved to build a boat which would take them to Newfoundland with their precious cargo. From there, they would not have to wait long for a passage to England. Just then, however, a ship threaded cautiously through the reefs. The first intentional settlers had arrived.

Bermuda's first official governor, Master Richard Moore, a former ship's carpenter, was full of good intentions. He was impressed by what the "three kings" had achieved when they weren't fighting over the secret ambergris, although he immediately moved the main settlement from Smith's Island to St George's. One of Moore's first tasks was to build a small, thatched church on the site of the present St Peter's, which, even in its later guise, still qualifies as "the oldest Anglican church in continuous use in the western hemisphere".

Moore's second priority was the construction of forts to ward off Spain. He asked the three kings about commercial prospects such as pearls, tobacco, whales, silk, yellow wood – and ambergris. They told him what they knew. On the specific point of ambergris, however, no – none at all.

In fact, they were already conspiring with the captain of the newly arrived ship to sneak off with "their" ambergris. The captain indiscreetly mentioned its existence to one of his passengers, Edwin Kendall, who was intrigued. The story leaked, and Carter tried to save his skin by confessing all to Moore. Chard and Kendall were promptly locked up, and, without much fuss, Chard was sentenced to death. A gallows was erected on the island where the replica of *Deliverance* now stands, but virtually as the rope went round his neck Chard's sentence was commuted to three years' imprisonment.

The first of Moore's forts – he planned to fortify all the obvious seaward approaches, especially what is known as Castle Island – was named after Gates. In Spain, the Duke of Medina Sidonia, a name forever linked to the Armada, was proposing to attack the 200 settlers "and send them off to England".

The urgency in preparing defences diverted the energy that would otherwise have gone into food production. The hogs had depleted the burrowed eggs of the cahows on the populated islands, and the men had depleted the hogs. Moore needed more help

from the company, and the best way to drum it up was to use the fabulous potential of ambergris as bait. Instalments of it were duly despatched to England at enticing intervals.

In the meantime, there were complaints about the work load because of the rush to build forts. Two men were so persistent in their moaning that Moore had them charged, mentioning in passing that the penalty on conviction would be death. "One fell dead of palsy on the spot and the other was so frightened by the event that he reformed."

Rat pack: An invasion altogether different from the Spanish threat nearly finished off the young colony. Daniel Elfrith, an English pirate, was warmly received when he turned up with a Spanish prize loaded with grain. As the grain tumbled out, so did rats – ravenous creatures which devoured anything and everything like an Old Testament plague. When they had eaten through one island, they swam to the next. Dogs killed them by the thousand, cats went wild and grew fat on them, but nothing could stop the rats. They were found in the stomachs of fish which had swallowed them whole as they swam in shoals across channels.

Settlers continued to arrive but couldn't be fed. For Bermuda this was "starving time". Moore dispersed the population to islands where there were fewer rats. The Rev. Lewis Hughes, a Welsh Puritan, was sent to Cooper's Island, which still had a good stock of cahows. He hated his companions – "ungodly, slothful and heartless men" who were "so greedy that they would not wait until their meat was cooked but more like dogs than Christians did devour it blood raw." He described the scene on the island: "Every cabin had pots and kettles full of birds boiling, and others roasting on spits while the living wild birds walked among the people in the cabins, making their strange

"with never a rag on his back but yet with a good store of fat on his belly".

The Puritan Hughes was appalled at the amount of excessive drinking. The heaviest drinkers were to be found in Somerset and St George's, and if ever the two should meet anything could and probably would happen. On just such an occasion, one of the revellers dropped dead. The inquest found him guilty of causing his own death. Hughes wrote approvingly of what happened next. The body was placed on the road with a stake through it; the survivors were made to wear placards on their backs which read: "These are the companions of him which killed himself with drinking." One was taken to the

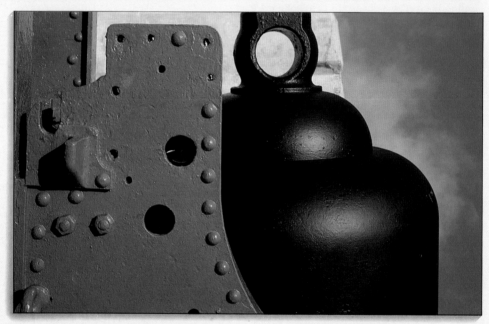

noises as though begging to be taken." The diet of undercooked cahow proved too rich for weakened stomachs and many died.

An isolation camp was established at Port Royal for sick colonists who were supposed to be cared for by healthy ones. The reluctant nurses had no great liking for their responsibilities; so, rather than bother with fishing for food, they merely slaughtered the company's few remaining cattle. Asked what had happened to the cattle, they said the beasts had gone swimming to escape the heat – and drowned. Men loath to work disappeared into the woods and lived off crabs and snails. One of them surfaced long afterwards

whipping post; another, a soldier, was saddled across a cannon. The ensuing explosion "did shake him terribly".

Hughes was equally pleased about the punishment meted out to whores. "For their comfort and to cool them a little they are now and then towed at a boat's tail up and down the harbour." The self-righteous but nevertheless plucky Puritan was later revealed as someone who enjoyed, or anyway indulged in, a fairly adventurous sex-life himself.

Eventually, on 14 March 1614, the long-anticipated Spanish "invasion" took place. Two merchantmen on their way home from San Domingo had been ordered to find out what was happening in the colony. They saw smoke rising from two forts, one made of timber, the other of masonry, about 100 metres apart. The colonists mistook the ships for English vessels bringing supplies. They went out in two launches to meet them and were "a musket shot off" when they realised their potentially fatal mistake.

The alarm sent Governor Moore hurrying to the fort on Castle Island. The fruit of two years' labour was about to be tested. In the excitement, the defenders very nearly perpetrated what would have been a spectacular own goal. One of them knocked over a keg, spilling enough gunpowder to blow the whole place sky-high. The men "tramped

was yet another pestering request for more ambergris, with the implication that Moore might be keeping some back for himself. Moore felt he had to clear his name and set off for London. He managed to vindicate his actions but decided against returning to Bermuda. He joined up with Raleigh and was later killed in action.

Drunken anarchy: The arrangements Moore made for the running of Bermuda in his absence were described as "the very worst that he ever committed during the whole of his abode, for not any one of these thus put in authority were fit for the place or capable of the employment." The plan was that the colony should be run by a council of six, each

back and forth and all over it" but no explosion occurred and it was perhaps as well that only one of the cannons worked.

Moore took over its operation personally. His initial shot sailed over the main mast of the first ship. His second hit the rigging and the Spaniards turned tail. They could not have known that only a single cannon ball was left in the arsenal.

The governor expected the company's congratulations for his repulsion of the Spaniards. Instead, the next communication

member taking turns at being governor for a term of one month.

Lots drawn, the first of them was Charles Caldicott, and at once there was an indication of what the future held. All work ceased. No further progress was made on Moore's cherished fortifications, nor on the farms. The only interruption of a leisurely existence of swimming, pleasure boating, eating palmetto berries and drinking the juice was the need to make stills which would provide a wider choice of liquor, and to repair an old Spanish ship for the purposes of piracy. Caldicott and two of his governor colleagues assembled a crew of 36 eager, would-be

Left, military hardware. **Above**, settlers enjoyed drink made from the palmetto tree.

pirates. Those who stayed behind were promised a share of the spoils. "Afterwards roving at sea," noted the surveyor Richard Norwood, who had declined to join them, "they were driven to great extremity and at last, as I have heard, taken by the Spaniards who hanged up divers of them, and what became of the rest I know not."

With Caldicott at sea in 1615, the next governor in line was a Captain Mansfield who "had only so much more wit than his fellows as to help him to be so much the more vicious." He declared a policy of "general leave to play so that now the bravest fellow was he who could drink deepest, bowl best with soccer shot in the Governor's garden

and win the most loblolly", the last being a popular gruel.

Mansfield reluctantly made way for Christopher Carter, one of the former three kings. He had been rewarded for spilling the beans about the ambergris with the title to Cooper's Island. He was convinced the island held Spanish treasure and was too busy trying to dig it up to have any time for affairs of state. With no one to egg them on, the settlers slipped happily into bone idleness.

The tempo of "perpetual night" did not change under Carter's successor, Captain Kendall, the following month. "Not a hoe, axe, pickaxe or shovel was so much as once

heard in the streets; not an oar seen or heard unless when their stout stomachs compelled them to it." Evidently resigned to not finding the elusive treasure, even Carter was content to "sit still, eat and especially drink at his ease and to the full".

With three of the governors-designate still occupied at sea, whereabouts unknown, the prospect of another month of Mansfield in command distressed those in the colony who were not part of his coterie. He affected best behaviour while there was a supply ship in port which would soon be returning to England with the latest news. As soon as it left, however, he reverted to type, confiscating for his own use all the drink the ship had delivered, a year's supply for the whole colony. The amazing drinking bout which followed had the colonists turning to the Rev. Hughes for guidance.

On getting wind of the stirrings, Mansfield and his "Bacchanalian crew" occupied Warwick fort above the town, stocked up with ammunition, raised a flag and dared anyone to challenge them. Hughes went to remonstrate with him. Mansfield dared not harm Hughes, but he arrested one of his supporters and tortured him so badly that he had to be sent to Carter on Cooper's Island to recuperate in private.

Ostensibly to give the colony a treat, but in reality because he had finished the company drink, Mansfield declared public celebrations. Led by heralds and flying the governor's flag, he traversed his domain, leaving one settlement for the next as soon as he had drunk what the inhabitants had to offer.

Having consumed every drop they could uncover throughout Bermuda, Mansfield and his entourage returned to St George's to ponder their next move. News of a Flemish ship in distress, and the possibility that it was carrying gold – not to mention the odd bottle or two – sent governor and friends rushing to the shore. The wreck yielded only a disappointing £20. Mansfield said he would look after it personally.

Mansfield had quite cleverly concealed his excesses from the officers and crew of the returning supply ship, but that could not explain to the company's satisfaction why a ship which was supposed to return brimful with local produce, especially tobacco, was completely empty. Colonies like Bermuda were founded for no other reason than profit, so clearly something had to be done. The man chosen to restore order and profits was Daniel Tucker, planter.

Stern discipline: Dan Tucker's experience as a planter in Virginia had impressed on him "the improvement... wrought by stern discipline". He demonstrated his convictions at once. A drunk heckled him while he was introducing himself to the population; the man was removed from the room and hanged. Henceforth, Tucker announced, a drummer would wake everyone up at dawn for serious work. Another protester naively raised his voice and was immediately sent to prison, "weighted with irons, and kept upon the ground night and day in grievous pain".

warning signs. "When in a morneinge his hatt stoode on one side or such a coloured sute of cloathes was worne, there was noe comeinge nere him all that whole daye." Hoping that safety lay in numbers, almost the entire work force threatened a go-slow strike. Tucker rose early the following morning to "cudgell with his owne hands not fewer than fortie of his poore workmen" before breakfast.

His methods were at least a tonic for the economy. He cleared the ground for planting and had timber squared for building purposes. Plantains, sugar cane, figs, pines, cassava and pawpaws were imported from the Bahamas, and replacement hogs from Vir-

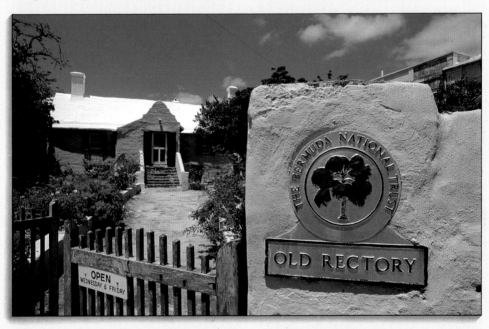

To prevent any further misunderstandings from occurring, the governor posted a proclamation: "Whosoever shall use any art or means to the disgrace of any member of this plantation, or give any backbiting, slanderous disgraceful words... shall on the first offence ask public forgiveness upon their knees in church. And for continuance... to be whipped and ask the like public forgiveness with addition of such further punishment as shall be inflicted upon them."

Tucker's subjects soon learnt to recognise

Left, Bermuda is ringed with ancient forts. **Above**, the Old Rectory dates from 1705.

ginia. Tucker did not want to be too dependent on tobacco, but it was not long before he was able to send 30,000 lb (14,000 kg) back to the company, the first significant return on its investment in Bermuda.

Whaling was less successful. The sperm whales which swam past Bermuda in early spring were too fast and powerful for conventional whaling methods. The whalers were able to strike with harpoons but after "many trialls, hazards, adventures and many rayleinges against poor Mistris Fortune, not so much as one piece of whale" was landed. When wounded, the whales were "exceedingly fierce".

Tucker tackled the rat problem with the same iron discipline he used on his men. As neither dogs, cats, traps nor poison had worked against the rats, he decided to burn the islands – not once but twice. Acre upon acre of valuable cedar went up in smoke to the distress of the owners, some of whom had powerful friends and relatives in the company. Among them were Robert Rich, who was related to the Earl of Warwick, and William Pollard, a gentleman of the household of the Earl of Pembroke.

Rich and Pollard had both made known their opposition to Tucker, the latter going so far as to say that rather than supply any more workers for Tucker's public works "he

ordinary passenger in the same boat. Lock him up while you're about it, he ordered.

Tucker was two weeks getting back. Pollard and Rich prudently acknowledged their offence as "heynous" and "submitted wholly to the Governours mercye". He "thereupon that he might shewe… that he always proceeded with mercye rather than justic, not only remitted their transgressions, but instantly restored them to their formers places of command, in as full and ample manner as ever before."

What had been occupying Tucker's mind when the boats crossed was a devious scheme which was to contribute to his ultimate downfall. A survey had just shown that

himselfe would lie in yrons for them". There were grave penalties for not reporting such talk, so witnesses put him under arrest with the intention of delivering him to Tucker.

Pollard was on his way to Tucker in a small boat when the governor passed in another boat going the other way. Tucker was "so deep in thought that they had difficulty in stopping him", but Pollard's captors were able to draw alongside and present him with their prisoner. "Fretting at being thus waylaid", Tucker told them to lock him up in St George's until he returned. "I have more serious thinges to thincke of at this time," he remarked. He then spotted Rich, who was an

the islands were larger than had been supposed when the land was distributed among the "tribes" named after the principal Adventurers of the Somers Island Company, men like Sir Edwyn Sandys and William Cavendish, Earl of Devonshire. (These "tribes" were the forerunners to today's parishes.) In addition to these private holdings, each divided into 50 "shares", there was "public land" amounting to about one-seventh of the colony which was supposed to produce sufficient revenue to pay the salaries of the governor, sheriff, clergy and others. Ordinary settlers were expected to work this public land and in certain circumstances they could even end up owning parcels of it.

The survey wàs done by Richard Norwood, who was sent to Bermuda to look for pearls. Unable to find any, he hollowed a canoe out of a tree trunk and proceeded to paddle around the islands doing a survey which stands the test of time remarkably well. Before he set off, Tucker asked him to keep an eye open for some good, unoccupied land to which he could then lay claim. He was entitled to three shares, i.e. 75 acres.

Norwood did better than that. He discovered that there were actually 200 more acres to Bermuda than had previously been realised. Tucker was determined to have the lot. An "overplus" of 200 acres was vague,

haled, by the strength of men, to the place wher he appointed." No remuneration was offered for any of this work although some of the labourers "were well payd with sound cudgellinge by the Governours owne hand". The work went "nimbly forward".

The Rev. Hughes compared Tucker's "large, hansome and well contrived house" with the "thacht hovell" of St Peter's Church, was disgusted, and said so. When Tucker next saw him he remarked: "Take you heed of and looke well to yourselfe: for if you serve me so but one more, I shall tie your neck and heeles together until your back crack, and so helpe you to repentance." Hughes was not intimidated, so Tucker

however, so Tucker ordered Norwood to rig the survey so that the unsuspected acres were specifically in the very valley which Norwood had recommended as being of "fatte and lustye soyle".

Tucker decided to erect a house. The site of the house, between Southampton and Sandys, meant that timber felled at St David's had to be "squared and framed… by the choysest workmen" at St George's before being "conveyed in flotes as near to the overplus as he could, and from thence to be

Left, Bermudian cedar tree before and after. **Above**, close-up of St Peter's cedar door.

turned on Rich, who decided it was time he returned to England to expose Tucker, especially the overplus scandal. The governor knew the repercussions would be some time coming and continued with plans to replace St George's Town with a new capital, on the opposite shore of Castle Harbour. He proposed to call it Tucker's Town.

Tucker had to be tricked into leaving Bermuda. Ensign Wood, whom Tucker had once wished to hang, made known the existence of a letter which purported to be from a friend in England saying that Tucker had better journey to England fast to defend his reputation. Tucker snatched the letter out of

DELVING INTO HISTORY

At an age when most schoolboys were reading comic books for recreation, John Adams was delving into the very government records of which he is today custodian. "I became interested in genealogy from the age of 13 because I was curious about my roots, and I began visiting the Government Archives then," he remembers.

The old records were a good introduction to Bermuda's history because they exposed him to "some of the sources which are so invaluable to research, such as church records and civil registers." The inquisitive youngster then tried to relate his findings to the British history he was learning in school. "That's when it became really fascinating," he now recalls.

After boarding school in Groton, Massachusetts, and later the University of Pennsylvania, Mr Adams transferred to Trinity College, Connecticut, where he elected to take advantage of a strong history department to major in 17th, 18th and 19th-century British and American history. "I felt it was relevant to an understanding of the way Bermuda developed."

Graduating from Trinity with an Honours degree, he returned home. It was time to earn a living and plan for the future. A brief stint in a local store convinced Adams that the retail world was not for him, so he returned to education, specialising in 19th-century history at America's Yale University.

Back in Bermuda, he began by assisting historian Vernon Tvea in his preparation of the Rich papers for publication. (Robert Rich was a major shareholder in the Bermuda Company formed in 1615 and his documents provide a fascinating insight into the early development of the island.) Later on, when the Bermuda government created a post of assistant archivist, Mr Adams was advised to obtain a degree in archive administration so that he could apply. With a young archivist already heading this government department, John Adams could see no real chance of promotion and so demurred.

However, the subsequent death of the archivist, Miss Helen Rowe, changed John Adams's prospects dramatically, and he successfully applied for the position of archivist-designate. He had found his niche. "It was a wonderful surprise to be appointed, and I was very, very happy."

Following a year's study in a Master's programme at London University, John Adams is today in control of putting Bermuda's archival house in order for the benefit of future generations. "My goal is to make the rich historical records that we have in the archives as accessible as possible to the public. That is a wonderful challenge – and a lot of work."

As a member of the Bermuda National Trust, he makes good use of his deep commitment to the urgent preservation of the island's architectural heritage. As the former chairman of the Trust's Historic Buildings Committee, he has initiated a survey of historic buildings, and helps to mastermind teams of volunteers who comb the island matching buildings to an ancient 1898 Ordnance Survey map.

"Preservation is essential for Bermuda for a variety of reasons," he says. "Economically, preservation is important as the fine old buildings we have form an integral part of the Bermuda charm which attracts visitors. These buildings are also a major feature of our heritage, one of which Bermudians can be very proud. The work of local builders in the 18th and 19th centuries showed great skill with materials, and a sensitivity of vision which has been lost by so many of their descendants."

The recent intrusion of rampant, modern development and the incursion of alien building materials used insensitively greatly alarm this committed preservationist.

"What is happening is that Bermuda is starting to look very rootless and transient," he says. "We are up against a lot of opposition, ignorance and greed here. Every time an 18th or 19th-century building is mutilated it is as if one of our roots has been pulled out.

"My job is to awaken people to the beauty and importance of our architectural heritage and the natural environment, thereby preserving a quality of life in Bermuda which is wonderful both for us and for our visitors."

Wood's hands and read it pensively. While making arrangements to leave, he was persuaded by Wood to let Miles Kendall take over as governor in his absence. The news of Tucker's impending departure came as such a relief that his broad hint about a farewell "present" produced an immediate donation of 1,500 lb of finest tobacco in case he changed his mind.

The man who deputised for Tucker was, by one of the more sympathetic assessments, a "good fellowe" and "conveniently manageable". According to his successor, however, he was "a man mainly marching downhill to all dunghill actions, senseless of reputation and utterly incapable of all noble re-

who not only challenged Butler's authority but interrupted a sermon in St Peter's to call the Rev. Hughes a fool. He was "to be conveyed manacled through the main to Southampton there to have one of his ears nailed to a post to be especially erected for him and to be named 'Harriott's Post' and so to remain for the space of one half hour." After which he was to be taken back to St George's, placed in the pillory, fined 1,000 lb of tobacco – and have his other ear cut off. When that was over, he was to remain a prisoner during the governor's pleasure.

Having made his point, however, Butler wished to show that he was not going to be another Tucker, and Harriott was allowed to

spects." The situation was a repetition of Moore's departure in similar circumstances: a local man suddenly in charge preferred to ingratiate himself by throwing open the official drinks cabinet and inviting cronies to a non-stop party.

Order and witchcraft: Captain Nathaniel Butler, brought in to rescue the situation, was the most positive of Bermuda's governors (1619–22) under the Somers Island Company. He was not a man to be trifled with, a lesson driven home to one Henry Harriott

Above, St Peter's cemetery contains graves of probable descendants of early settlers.

keep one ear. Butler was generally scornful of Tucker's methods, which he described as "dissonant from the laws of England… every petty larceny and two-penny pilfery being equally rated with the highest felonies and censured with death."

Harriott's fine in tobacco reflected the trend towards using tobacco as currency rather than Bermuda's distinctive Hog Money, which did not exist in sufficient quantity to cover everyday commerce. These coins, specially minted for Bermuda, were silver-plated copper; a hog and the value expressed in Roman numerals on one side, a sailing ship on the other. The hog motif was undoubtedly a tribute to the wild pigs which dominated the diet of the grateful early settlers. Hog Money is highly prized by collectors.

Tobacco road: The value of tobacco as currency was not based on a compulsion to smoke. Officially, the things money could buy were products delivered by the company's magazine ship, which called once or perhaps twice a year. The ship collected as much tobacco as it could for the return voyage, so transactions did not depend on cash. In any case, the export of Hog Money was forbidden.

Workers were paid in tobacco. Craftsmen received two pounds a day, labourers one.

servation measures to protect turtles, established regular Assizes and a legislative assembly (the second parliament in the New World), and replaced the old St Peter's church, about which the Reverend Hughes had never stopped complaining, with a new one made of stone which still stands, and built the State House.

As a writer, especially of letters to the company defending his policies, Butler was capable of polished vitriol, but as a poet he left room for improvement. Discovering Somer's grave in a state of neglect, Butler mounted a slab of marble over it and was personally responsible for the inscription. He moved the date of Somer's death, which

When the company shipped out boys (as labourers or apprentices) and young women (as wives), they were sold to the highest bidder in tobacco. Prices were expected to cover at least the cost of the passage. These human cargoes sometimes turned sour: one lot, drawn from English prisons, were found to be suffering from jail fever, wrongly diagnosed as plague. The men were isolated on Castle Island; the women, many of whom were pregnant when they arrived, were given to anyone willing to live with the risk.

In most respects, Butler was progressive: he organised the construction of bridges between the larger islands, introduced con-

was 1610, by a year in order to achieve a desperate rhyme:

In the year 1611
Noble Sir George Somers went home to heaven...

He had other problems. One was Kendall, who feigned sickness to avoid coming to trial and slunk away to England. He later made an unwelcome return and so, too (after Butler had left), did ex-Governor Tucker, who modestly demanded official status as one who was above the law, presumably answerable only to God. Tucker had managed to settle the overplus controversy so that he retained the controversial house. In the event, he didn't need legal immunity because he was able to behave himself until his death in 1626, when he was buried in the graveyard of Southampton church.

A local dynasty: Tucker's property was inherited by two nephews, George and Henry, and down this line a local dynasty came into being, in the early days almost as notorious as the old man (for treachery during the American Revolution) but later respectably eclectic in good works, not least Mrs Terry Tucker, who married into the family from the Isle of Wight in England and turned out scores of books and papers about her adopted land. Mr Teddy Tucker is a distinguished underwater explorer.

the best of the crop for themselves and handing over to the company the dregs. The better tobacco was especially useful for black market dealings with passing ships. With the company officers concentrated in St George's, the bays and lagoons of the other islands made furtive contacts a fairly simple matter. The black marketeers matched tighter surveillance with ruses like stuffing tobacco into barrels of fish. Reviled company "searchers" sniffed out illicit tobacco stashed in, around and under houses, often in purpose-built vaults. On discovery, the culprits were imprisoned, soundly flogged or (the fate of Captain Kendall, among others) clamped into the stocks with the placard:

Tobacco production soared under Butler, but hopes that it would underpin the economy were dashed as thoroughly as those attached to ambergris, whaling in general, and semi-official piracy. Tobacco, which was in the first place not as good as that grown in Virginia and the Caribbean, was further knocked out of commercial contention by having to carry an additional tax by which the Somers Island Company hoped to recoup its losses in Bermuda.

The tobacco growers resorted to keeping

Left, Governor Butler protected local turtles.
Above, plague victims were put on Castle Island.

"This for the concealing of tobacco."

The civil war over tobacco came to a head under one of Butler's successors, Captain Henry Woodhouse, a military man whose faith in the efficacy of stern discipline almost rivalled that of Tucker's. A Mrs Margaret Heyling, convicted of stealing a turkey, was let off a penalty of 12 lashes on her naked back but was made to sit in church for six months, in the corner as it were, with a humiliating placard. Woodhouse lost the moral high ground when she was later declared innocent – he had to compensate her with 100 lbs of tobacco – and with the disclosure that he was leasing public lands and pocketing the proceeds. Forced to resign, he remained to torment his successors.

The list of company governors after Woodhouse includes household names in Bermuda: Roger Wood, progenitor of a famous family; John Trimingham, merchant; and Sir John Heydon, commemorated in the Heydon Trust Estate. Trimingham first won attention as the leader of a demonstration protesting at the beheading of King Charles I in England.

Bermuda was predominantly royalist in so far as the troubles "at home" were played out on its shores. It was caught up in the struggle between the established church and the Puritans and suffered its own purge of alleged

Men were not exempt. John Middleton, a devout Puritan, was found to have enough blue marks on his body to justify an investigative ducking. He, too, floated and was forced by his religious convictions to acknowledge that there could be only one answer: "I am a witch," he declared. He was hanged, followed by two women whose names he mentioned in connection with strange goings-on concerning cats.

Bermuda struggled to keep up with political and religious changes in England, but with poor communications it was all too easy to be caught on the wrong foot when the Navy called, like being a Papist when a Protestant had just ascended the throne (and

witches. The 22 witch trials over a period of 40 years were held in the State House built by Butler. The first victim was Jeane Gardiner, accused of bewitching a mulatto woman. She was stripped and searched for diabolical markings – a boil or mole was sufficient. In her case, a blue mark in the mouth was the evidence which led to her arms being crossed so that thumbs could be tied to opposite big toes. Thus trussed, she was thrown into the channel where *Deliverance* now stands. That she floated could only be attributed to the assistance of the devil; so, in accordance with the practice of the times, she was dragged out and hanged.

vice versa), or a supporter of the Duke of Monmouth, not knowing that his rebellion had already been put down.

In volatile times, the way company rule worked in Bermuda could be debilitating. The fundamental weakness, from the company's point of view, was that in spite of everything Bermuda was not making money for the Adventurers. The company's interests lay in monopoly, and what was good for the company was in this instance bad for the people. The original investors lost interest and were happy to sell off parcels of land. The new owners had their own ideas about their role in Bermuda, and how loyally to serve the company's best interests was not one of them.

The inevitable impasse led to the dissolution of the Somers Island Company in 1684 and the passing of its charter to the Crown. The changes were at first barely perceptible. Colonel Richard Coney, the last company governor, stayed on in the same capacity until the appointment of the first royal governor, Sir Robert Robinson, the following year, which also marked the death of King Charles II.

The Crown was no less keen than the company had been to maximise tax and other revenues from Bermuda, but the restraints on trade were relaxed. The proviso was that

the colonists should not do business with the king's enemies, whoever they were at any particular time.

The colonists took the opportunity to abandon fruitless agriculture in favour of the sea and a ship-building industry. A ban on the construction of ships of more than five tons was rescinded. Before the end of the century, Bermuda's yards had built 76 ocean-going vessels of between 10 and 100 tons as well as hundreds of two-masted fishing boats. In the following century, they

Left and <u>above</u>, profitable ship-building replaced agriculture as a main industry.

were launched at the rate of a couple of dozen per year in sizes up to 200 tons. The local cedar was so fine-grained that it did not need seasoning. Ships made from it were relatively light and strong; they were accordingly very fast and, in light weather, could outsail most naval vessels. About two-thirds of Bermuda-built vessels were sold abroad.

Even before the dissolution of the company, Bermudians had been venturing to Turk's Island in the West Indies for salt, a valuable commodity especially in the American colonies. The salt was raked by slaves in winter, stored in Bermuda, and when the weather improved sold in American ports as far north as New England or exchanged for corn, bread, flour, meat and so forth. Trade with the West Indies produced rum, molasses and cotton.

The salt trade was so lucrative that there were attempts by both French and Spaniards to seize Turk's Island. At one point there were no fewer than 750 Bermudians engaged in the salt industry on the island, and rather naturally the thought crossed their minds formally to annex Turk's Island, which of course would have made it a colony of a colony. They had similar ambitions with regard to the Bahamas, which a few Bermudians had originally colonised on behalf of the British government. Bermuda behaved like a precocious mother-hen and in 1713 went to the lengths of sending an expedition to the Bahamas to clear out a nest of pirates who were thought to be doing the place no good. The notion of a greater Bermuda came to nothing, however, and Turk's Island was eventually made over to the Bahamas.

While Bermuda was exporting cabbages and onions profitably to the West Indies, the male colonists considered agriculture to be demeaning. Able-bodied slaves and slave-owners alike preferred to earn their living at sea, or at least in the ship-building business. Farms were left in the hands of geriatric blacks, mostly women. The lure of greater profits away from the land lulled Bermuda into an economic imbalance in that three-quarters of the supplies necessary for subsistence were being imported from the American colonies. That might have been tolerable as matters were; but 1775 was approaching and, when it arrived, Bermuda was in league with the worst conceivable trading partner, a rebel against the Crown.

Military Band on the March, Bermuda

"Our necessities in the articles of powder and lead are so great," General George Washington wrote on 4 August 1775, "as to require an immediate supply… No quantity, however small, is beneath notice… Among others, I have had one mentioned, which has some weight with me… One Harris has lately come from Bermuda, where there is a very considerable magazine in a remote part of the island; and the inhabitants well disposed not only to our cause in general, but to assist in this enterprise in particular."

Heinous crime: Washington outlined rough plans for acquiring the powder, but 10 days after the letter was written – long before his plan could have been implemented – a group of men arrived who had made a secretive night landing in whaleboats at Tobacco Bay on St George's north shore. They removed slates on the roof of Bermuda's powder magazine and dropped inside. While they were forcing a door, their look-outs were surprised by a man in uniform. He was quickly killed. With no better idea of what to do with the body, the look-outs buried it where they were, which happened to be in the garden of the sleeping governor, George James Bruere, "a man of unpleasant disposition, to characterise him mildly".

About 100 barrels of gunpowder were duly removed from the magazine and rolled down the hill to the boats. The barrels were heaved aboard, whereupon the boats dissolved into the darkness to transfer their cargo to the waiting *Lady Catherine* of Virginia, under the command of Captain Ord. The powder duly reached Philadelphia and a grateful Continental Congress lifted the sanctions which had been imposed on Bermuda as a loyal colony of the English Crown.

The discovery of the theft the following morning caused an outrage. A "most heinous and atrocious crime," Governor Bruere called the deed, and offered £100 for information. None was forthcoming. If any Bermudians had been involved, they would have been guilty of at least treason, and the

punishment for treason was unequivocal.

The story was soon embellished. One version had the keys to the magazine being stolen from beneath the governor's pillow while he slept. Another put the blame on a Captain Morgan, creating the legend of "Old Morgan", a raincloud which hangs over Bermuda at certain times of the year and is supposedly the captain's restless spirit awaiting the trial and execution of the descendants of the guilty parties.

As fellow colonials, Bermudians must

have shared some of the resentment underlying the American Revolution, but inhabitants of an isolated group of islands in the mid-Atlantic were clearly not in a position to do much about it. Many had families living in America, and not only was the economy critically dependent on American ties but they were staring starvation in the face.

The Bermudian Legislature took the extraordinary step of writing to King George explaining that it had asked the American Congress for help, without which "the people… must inevitably perish," hoping that he would understand and forgive. Congress's reply to this request for help was

Preceding pages: Military band on the march. Left, the American Revolution. Right, George Washington.

revealing: Bermuda would receive the needed supplies if it could provide arms, ammunition… and gunpowder.

In the course of time, interesting facts about the gunpowder theft were unearthed – literally so in the case of the man whom the look-outs killed and buried in the governor's garden. His bones were exhumed a century later during building excavations for the "Unfinished Cathedral". In daylight, the skeleton was seen to be wearing a French uniform, the long-postponed explanation for the disappearance of a French officer who happened to be in Bermuda on the night of the theft and had presumably gone for a stroll. The minutes of the Pennsylvania

George's post office. The Americans were in no doubt that Bermuda was enemy territory and in December 1779 despatched an invasion force in four warships. Their plans were upset by the arrival of strong British reinforcements on the very day of the intended attack. The ships withdrew. The decisive Franco-American victory at Yorktown in 1781 removed the need to try again.

An independent and belligerent United States put Bermuda (and Canada) into the front line as far as Britain was concerned, and so began a process to turn Bermuda into the "Gibraltar of the West". The need to beef up defences was given greater urgency by war with France in 1793 and, as history

Committee of Safety, dated 26 August 1775, reveal receipt of an invoice for "1,182 lb of gunpowder" in the amount of £161.14s.8d. The signatory awaiting payment was "Henry Tucker, chairman of the Deputies of the several parishes of Bermuda."

Collusion between Bermudians and American rebels over the gunpowder did not mean, however, that the islanders as a whole were bent on throwing in their lot with the Americans. Officially, which is to say in the person of Governor Bruere, Bermuda remained unambiguously loyal to the Crown and housed American prisoners (in appalling conditions) in what is now the St

shows, the troublesome Napoleon was soon to enter the equation. A pleasant cameo from the Royal Navy's thorough survey of the deep-water possibilities in and around Bermuda was the high opinion formed of a local pilot, Jemmy Darrell, who happened to be a slave. The Navy recommended his freedom as a tribute to outstanding services; Governor and Council complied.

The untested balance of power in the Atlantic created perfect conditions for privateers, and Bermudians were not slow to recognise the opportunities. Following the notable example of Hezekiah Frith, the Bermudian economy became wholly dependent on the substantial proceeds of privateering. "A rude, desultory kind of life," sniffed Governor William Brown, lately of Salem, Massachusetts. He tried to offer an alternative by lifting the restrictions on whaling, but that was not enough to divert Bermudian eyes from far bigger prizes.

Britain and America were at war again in 1812. Bermuda's unscrupulous entrepreneurs, a classification which excluded almost nobody, had recognised during the American Revolution the possibility of profiting from business with both sides during a war. What followed in 1812 enabled them to refine their methods in unknowing preparation for the bonanza presented by the Ameri-

American privateers. By the end of the war, though, the balance sheet looked better: Bermuda had acquired 43 foreign vessels, putting the strength of its merchant navy above 70 ships.

The official record of Hamilton's losses during the war coincidentally reflected the town's growing importance at the expense of St George's. Established in 1790 during Governor Henry Hamilton's term, Hamilton was both more central than the existing capital and a far more convenient place for shipping. The sea approaches were less treacherous and the off-loading facilities a greatly needed improvement. Clamours to have the capital transferred to Hamilton

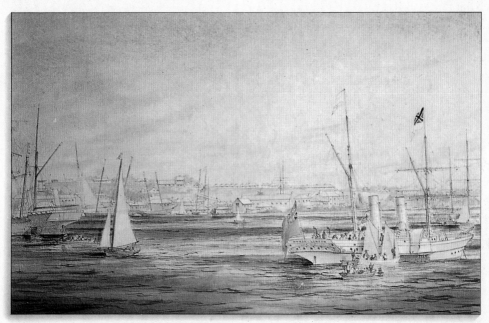

can Civil War. Bermuda was in the best possible position to benefit from the willingness of certain Americans to sell supplies to British squadrons, technically their enemy. "We hear of frequent arrivals at Bermuda of provisions from the United States," a Baltimore newspaper reported. "The traitors may yet be caught. It is a desperate game."

Bermuda's privateers had to run risks and lost many ships. The port of Hamilton alone recorded the loss of 39 registered vessels with cargoes valued at £200,000, mostly to

were first heard in 1811, and on 1 January 1815 the move became official.

American Civil War: On 19 April 1861, President Abraham Lincoln proclaimed a blockade of the Confederate states from South Carolina to Texas. This was the signal for a resumption of the cat-and-mouse game around Bermuda that had started with 16th-century pirates lying in wait for Spanish ships on their way home from the New World bulging with treasure and tobacco. The principles were unchanged, but there were naturally a few modern refinements. The Southern states had cotton, desirable in the mills of Lancashire. Britain had arms and

Left and **above**, Edward James's watercolours of Bermudian military activities.

munitions, desirable in the South. Steamships powered by coal had come into use. With finite resources, the Union was best able to enforce the blockade on the coastal approaches; there was not a great deal to be done about traffic in the North Atlantic. Confederate tactics were self-evident: big ships – no matter if they were rather slow – between English ports and Bermuda (as well as Nassau and Havana); smaller ships, with a premium on speed, for the dash in and out of Southern ports.

Lincoln had agents in Bermuda to keep him informed of what was happening. They duly reported that it was "swarming with secessionists". They might have added that Confederate activities in Bermuda. He watched, and was watched by, Mr C. M. Allen, the Union's man. Britain maintained that there was nothing wrong in transhipping cargo and therefore felt no obligation to intervene. Allen alerted the blockade fleet to the arrival of a ship from England, which meant that the runners would soon be setting off on the second leg. Walker's preoccupation was coal. In the interest of speed, the blockade runners needed high-grade coal, which would normally have been American anthracite. With those supplies cut off, Walker had to maintain adequate stocks of Welsh semi-bituminous coal.

The extra power of high-grade coal was

St George's was also swarming with sailors intoxicated by the thought of the pay on offer for blockade running. Captains could earn $5,000 per round trip, senior officers $2,500, and ordinary seamen $250. They were to be paid in gold, not Confederate currency. These astronomical sums were possible because raw cotton costing between four and six cents a pound in Southern ports was fetching 60 cents in England. The speculators did some simple arithmetic which showed that the cost of building a ship, and paying the crew, could generally be recovered by just two trips.

Major Norman Walker co-ordinated the not the only criterion. It also burnt more cleanly, a vital consideration when the ships were specially designed with the lowest possible profile. They were propelled either by screws or paddles and, in an emergency, the funnels could be telescoped out of sight. The steam was blown off through underwater exhaust pipes. As operations were usually at night, the hulls were painted a dull grey to render them almost invisible. Obviously, no lights were shown, and even the lamps on the binnacle were shrouded so that only the helmsman could see them. Cocks were excluded from the live poultry on board in case they crowed. The blockade runners, which varied between 100 and 900 tons and drew 9 or 10 ft (2 or 3 metres) of water, were capable of 14 knots – enough to outrun the fastest warships.

Excitement and, of course, the money attracted hundreds of adventurers, some of them senior Royal Navy officers on furlough. Assumed names were the order of the day: "Captain Roberts" enjoyed the admiration even of his enemies, and when his legendary steamer *Don* was eventually captured, a Union officer leapt aboard with a cry of "Well, Captain Roberts, so we have caught you at last!" To the officer's disappointment, "Roberts" had taken the mail ship home to England for a spot of leave. He moved on to

tity of Confederate gold – fuelled by an inferior type of North Carolina coal. The coal belched smoke but would not make steam. With an enemy ship closing fast, Wilkinson told his engineer to try burning cotton soaked in turpentine. The *Lee* accelerated to safety but was captured, without Wilkinson, on its next run.

Germ warfare: Dr Luke P. Blackburn was in stark contrast to the colourful characters who had turned St George's into a cosmopolitan free-for-all. He purported to be a physician of New Orleans and an expert on the yellow fever which had reached epidemic proportions in Bermuda. He refused any kind of payment for treating scores of patients. One

another romantic career after the war under his true name and a fancy title, Hobart Pasha of the Turkish Navy.

Better remembered than the *Don* was a ship bought in England for $32,000 and named *Giraffe*. It was re-fitted in Wilmington to emerge as the *Robert E. Lee*. Under the command of John Wilkinson, the *Lee* ran the blockade 26 times with cargoes of cotton to the value of $2 million in gold. Wilkinson was forced to undertake one of these runs from Wilmington – with a substantial quan-

Left and **above**, the island played a role in the American Civil War.

of Mr Allen's spies, however, exposed him: the saint-like doctor was in reality a Southern agent collecting bedclothes and handkerchiefs stained with the tell-tale "black vomit". He planned to give the infected articles as lethal presents to the poor of the North. Blackburn had already left for Halifax. The incriminating trunks were found packed, and ready to go. There are examples in ancient history of infected items being thrown over the walls of besieged cities, but Blackburn deserves an unworthy place in the more recent annals of germ warfare.

The merchants of Bermuda were making so much money out of the Civil War that the fall of Wilmington was devastating. It had not occurred to most of them that the Confederacy might lose the war, and they were left with enormous stocks for a market which vanished virtually overnight. There was no reversion to the *status ante quo*; the technological advances brought about in time of warfare had finished off the wooden boat-building industry. As small islands with nothing in the way of natural resources once the cedar had gone, the economy of Bermuda was always precariously hitched to windfalls. The cycle began with the discovery of a lump of ambergris and ended after several ups-and-downs with the American peace.

The hectic economic opportunities cre-

winters could only travel as far as a slow steamer could carry them in the time available. The Caribbean was warm but out of reach of East Coast ports; Bermuda was an obvious alternative.

Princess Louise's "discovery" of Bermuda attracted considerable publicity in the United States and Canada, and among the many who were persuaded to emulate her royal example was Mark Twain. His feelings on arrival after a turbulent voyage could not have been all that different from Sir George Somers': "Paradise, but you have to go through Hell to get to it."

Naturally, the development of tourism was disrupted by wars, even by wars from

ated by the American Civil War summarily ceased with the peace, and earning a living thereafter became a matter of cultivating potatoes, onions and arrowroot. This was altogether too humdrum an existence for some, and they were inclined to emigrate to the United States to renew more exciting business acquaintances.

Royal tourist: Princess Louise, the daughter of Queen Victoria but a resident of Canada by virtue of marriage to the Marquess of Lorne, the Governor General, alerted Bermudians to commercial possibilities which were to rescue the islands. Before air travel, North Americans seeking relief from bitter

which Bermuda could hardly have been more remote. Boers captured during the war in South Africa at the turn of the century were imprisoned on some of the smaller islands. They recognised a market for souvenirs and set about producing and selling them. World War I had a more direct bearing. Bermuda raised separate Black and White volunteer units, both of which found themselves in the thick of the trench warfare in France. They acquitted themselves with distinction and in so doing took heavy losses.

The impact of casualties in a small (albeit

Above, early visitors.

SPIES AT THE PRINCESS HOTEL

Had anyone known, there was a clue to the super-secret intelligence work going on in Bermuda during World War II. It lay in the number of young English women who arrived with one feature in common: lovely legs. They were "trappers", the nickname given to codebreakers who could read and analyse enemy communications at high speed.

"It was fairly certain that a girl with unshapely legs would make a bad trapper," a medical report noted. "Nobody has discovered what part the leg plays. There is here the basis for some fundamental research." The motives of the doctor who wrote the report were considered suspect and he was not commissioned to investigate further.

The women were involved in, among other covert activities, ULTRA, the means by which British Military Intelligence was able to decipher enemy signals. The whole purpose of the exercise would, of course, have been lost if the enemy had suspected that their codes, conceived by the supposedly infallible ENIGMA machine, had been broken. The women were necessarily tight-lipped about what they did, and that put a damper on their social lives. Among themselves, they composed and sang *The Virgin's Lament*, one of the printable verses of which ran:

I'm just a girl at MI5
and heading for a virgin's grave –
My legs it was wot got me in –
Still I wait for my bit of sin.

In addition to the electronic interception and interpretation of signals sent by, for example, German submarines operating in the Atlantic, the Bermuda station was responsible for sifting through the mail carried in ships and aircraft on their way between the US and Europe, especially Lisbon, a hotbed of spies. The targets of this surveillance were German agents in the US who were reporting on American arms shipments to Britain and other sensitive matters.

The trappers became so skilled that they could open, examine and re-seal without trace the

200,000 letters usually found in Pan American Flying Clippers on their stop-over in Bermuda.

The operations room of what was known as "Bletchley in the Tropics" (Bletchley Park, Oxfordshire, being the general headquarters) was in the basement of the Hamilton Princess Hotel. Although there is not now much to see, the hotel reception staff do allow visitors to look around.

The standard of service in these once luxurious hotels slipped. Cut off by the U-boat offensive in 1942, Bermuda ran short of practically everything. The rationing authorities decided that people would eat less bread if it was not fresh; it was therefore aged for a day before being put on sale. Unfortunately, the flour which went into the bread was very much older, and the freshest bread that could be served to the trappers and their colleagues had mould running through it.

They put up with these privations in order to score many notable successes, not all military. The Vollard Collection of 270 Impressionist paintings was on its way by sea from France to New York to be sold and the proceeds of the sale would be valuable dollars for Hitler's war-chest. The search was concentrated on the ship *Excalibur*, and when it called at Hamilton the agents were ready. Despite the furious protests of the captain, they cut open the ship's safe with oxyactylene and discovered the collection. The paintings, stored for a while in the Bank of Bermuda vaults, were sent to Canada. After the war they were returned to the owners from whom they had been forcibly removed.

After the war, Ian Fleming, who was himself in naval intelligence, put James Bond on assignment in Bermuda. At the height of Bond's popularity, there were suggestions that he actually existed and still occupied in the Hamilton Princess a penthouse belonging to Sir William Stephenson, "A Man Called Intrepid". Fans combed the hotel for signs of the private lift and the gold-plated Cadillac which their fictional hero supposedly enjoyed.

When the results proved negative, they looked around for other clues. Their eyes were drawn to a giant fish tank in one of the hotel bars. Of course, declared the *cognoscenti*, the very tank which had once contained Dr No's ghastly sharks!

still divided) community were deeply felt, although once again it was Bermuda's strategic position in the Atlantic that history dwells on. The most famous running battle in this connection was probably that involving the German Admiral von Spee. The cruisers *Scharnhorst* and *Gneisenau* under his command struck an early blow in a devastating action against the Royal Navy's Bermuda-based Fourth Cruiser Squadron under Admiral Sir Christopher Cradock.

Cradock and the entire crews of the cruisers *Monmouth* and *Good Hope* lost their lives. The defeat was avenged two months later (December 1914) at the Battle of the Falkland Islands when the battlecruisers

Inflexible and *Invincible* under Admiral Sturdee sank von Spee's squadron. Like Cradock, the German admiral went down with his ship.

World War II: A pocket battleship named after the gallant admiral, the *Graf Spee*, was the focus of one of the epic sea battles of World War II, and once again Bermuda was involved through the locally based Royal Navy squadron and its commander, Commodore Henry Harwood. The German battleships posed an enormous threat to Atlantic shipping and top priority was given to their destruction. Harwood's force, the cruisers *Exeter*, *Ajax* and *Achilles*, had no real answer

to the *Graf Spee's* 11-inch guns, but on running into the battleship off the River Plate in Uruguay they engaged in a ferocious action which virtually destroyed *Exeter* within an hour. The *Graf Spee* was damaged too, however, and was forced to limp into the neutral port of Montevideo while the battered British ships kept vigil outside. On the third day, the *Graf Spee* re-emerged but, on the orders of Captain Hans Langsdorff, was scuttled before battle could be resumed. Langsdorff later shot himself.

Bermuda again contributed troops to the Allied effort, and there were the usual cat-and-mouse (though always dangerous and frequently heroic) naval games in surrounding waters, but the colony's more important roles in the war were in new areas: as an intelligence-gathering centre and as a component in the Anglo-American lend-lease programme which provided Britain with badly needed destroyers when the US, as a neutral, was not supposed to sell them.

The US was given a 99-year lease to build a base in Bermuda. The construction of the base, and especially a large enough airport, changed the face of the islands. It encompassed most of St David's Island and all of Cooper's and other smaller islands; the channels in between were filled in to make a runway that had to take into account the prevailing, and often strong, winds. Much of the labour was recruited locally although, compared with the Americans involved, at discriminatory rates of pay which gave impetus to the trade union movement.

The number of American forces personnel in Bermuda increased sharply after Pearl Harbour. They had money to spend but very little to spend it on because of the cordon thrown around the islands by German U-boats. Bermuda was desperately short of everything, especially food and clothing.

As in the previous three centuries, the threat of direct invasion never materialised and the island defences remained untested. The Atlantic fortress became gracefully obsolete in a new age of post-war weaponry. The enduring legacies of the war were the hastily re-shaped geography of the islands and the irreversible presence of that hitherto alien object, the motor vehicle.

Left, the Cenotaph commemorates both world wars. **Right**, the military marches on.

Two Natives, Bermuda

Bermuda was uninhabited until the arrival of Europeans. There is nothing in the history of the islands to parallel the slaughter of an indigenous population as occurred in, for example, the Bahamas. The first black man known to have stepped ashore was probably not a slave but a sailor in a Spanish ship, the unfortunate fellow who was sent ashore with a lantern to look for a piece of wood and was terrified out of his wits when dive-bombed by cahows. He lost no time in leaving.

Nor were slaves, when eventually imported, necessarily black. Some of the earliest were North American and Caribbean Indians who paddled their canoes unwisely far from shore and were picked up by privateers. These chattels were later joined in Bermuda by prisoners of the Pequod and Sachem Philip wars in New England. Others were Irish, a wildly unsuccessful experiment which caused the Assizes to rule that "it shall not be lawful for any inhabitant in these islands to buy or purchase any more of the Irish nation upon any pretence whatever."

Accidental negroes: Slavery was forever controversial in Bermuda, although not always for obvious or what might be considered the right reasons. The first consignment of 14 slaves in 1619 was in reality a bribe offered to the governor, the unworthy Miles Kendall, by a passing pirate who wished to enter the harbour so that his ship "might carine herselfe and take in some necessaries". Kendall had no qualms about accepting them; his concern was how to make them his own when, strictly speaking, they were automatically the property of the Somers Island Company. The verdict on the proper ownership of these "accidental negroes" eventually went to neither Kendall nor the company but to the Earl of Warwick.

Slaves were not present in Bermuda in significant numbers until 1640, although the few who had preceded them were appearing in court records as early as 1632, usually in the grim context of being hanged, drawn and quartered for theft. Most of the negroes were

brought in from the West Indies and arrived with Spanish names. The company regretted accepting some Indians presented by a pirate named Jackson and actually freed them.

Not all Indians were so lucky. A gift of some "unruly" Mohicans from the Dutch governor of New York was accepted, as was another hapless wretch who was snatched from America while enfeebled by drink. By whatever means they got to Bermuda, there was enough Indian blood about to produce a distinctive sub-group in society which is still

evident today, especially around St David's.

The principle of slavery was sometimes examined metaphysically. According to Theodore L. Godet, a 19th-century Bermudian doctor, his compatriots two centuries earlier were squeamish about enslaving poor Englishmen kidnapped from their villages by "monsters in human shape" and sold in the colonies. Their disgust at "buying and selling our fellow-creatures" was assuaged, in the case of black people, by the thought that they were "an intermediate race between man and monkey... half human" and therefore didn't count. The English who were shipped to Bermuda in circumstances which

Preceding pages: island life around 1890. Left, *The Bermudian* by Andrew Wyeth. Right, the well-known rubber tree in Hamilton.

Godet would have deplored were technically indentured labour, although they might have been hard-pressed to notice the difference between that and outright slavery.

Godet, who seems to have regarded himself as something of a liberal in these matters, remarked in 1850 that nearly 20 years after their formal liberation, the blacks were progressing well. "They undoubtedly possess organs peculiarly adapted to the science of music" and, if they were taught and practised, "become sufficiently expert to bear an inferior part in a private concert". He was optimistic about their future development generally: "...nothing but the want of intelligence can prevent them from assuming the

If slaves belonging to different masters married, the children were born into slavery, the first going to the mother's household, the second to the father's, and so on. One piece of legislation exempted a master from prosecution if he accidentally killed a slave during the course of punishment. The deliberate killing of someone else's slave entailed compensation to the owner according to the slave's value.

The slaves did not always take this lying down. There were rumblings of discontent as early as 1623 and a revolt of free negroes and slaves in 1656 which resulted in the execution of three leaders and exile to the Bahamas for some of their supporters.

rank of the labouring classes among the white population of the islands."

The early debate about the ethics of slavery foundered on whether a slave had a soul and, if so, whether baptism would render the holder unsuitable for further servitude. As far as most of the planters were concerned, the problem was easily resolved – don't baptise them. They were supported by at least one clergyman, the Rev. Sampson Bond, who agreed that "the breeding up of children in the Christian religion makes them stubborn". Unbaptised blacks were allowed to attend church services but were expected to sit in galleries.

Slaves (and at least a couple of white men) sentenced to death were occasionally offered a reprieve if they agreed to become executioners themselves.

The rebellion of 1664 was a curious affair sparked off by the unwanted Irish slaves, who had arrived seven years earlier and been sold for £14 each – rather less than the going rate. They caused trouble from the moment they stepped ashore, and a warning was issued "that those that hath the Irish servants should take care that they straggle not night nor day as is too common with them".

The Irish seem to have got on quite well with the blacks. One John Maclarie, given the job of delivering a cask of rum, sat down and opened it in the company of the governor's negroes. The party was broken up at an advanced stage by a marshal who then sold what little of the rum he was able to rescue. The Irish managed to persuade a number of blacks to join them in an uprising for the specific purpose of exterminating non-Catholics. Just where unbaptised blacks fitted into this scheme of things is unclear.

On learning of the plot, the governor banned gatherings of more than "two or three" Irish and/or negroes. Offenders would be "whipped from Constable to Constable whilst they run home to their masters' houses". It was then that the Assizes decreed

traordinary measures against Bermuda's slave population. A 1761 enactment, for example, declared "that any negro, who met a white person during the night, and was challenged, should fall on his knees; on failure of which, such offender was to receive 100 lashes." During another crisis, an Englishman who so much as saw a slave on the roads after curfew, which was half an hour after sunset, was obliged to kill him. If the slave managed to escape, the Englishman was liable to be fined up to 100 lb of tobacco.

On the whole, though, the life of a slave in Bermuda was better than in America or the West Indies. In the absence of large plantations, there were no chain gangs nor, for the

no more buying or selling of the Irish nation "upon any pretence whatever". Owners were relieved to get rid of their Irish slaves and they seem to have been offloaded – on to whom is not recorded – before the next rebellion in 1681 which was potentially more serious: five of the ringleaders were executed and two men, who had ridden from one settlement to another calling for support, were made to ride the gibbet.

Local disturbances added to the unease caused by the atrocious slave rebellions in the French West Indies and resulted in ex-

men, much agricultural drudgery. "The most able of the male slaves were trained to the mechanical arts and to navigation, leaving only the most worthless of both sexes to be employed in the very inconsiderable tillage carried on."

The sea-faring slaves, at least, seemed to enjoy a sense of freedom. A Bermudian privateer manned by 80 blacks was once captured by an American privateer and taken to Boston where the slaves were offered their freedom. They unanimously preferred to return to their owners. As a neat counterpoint on a similar theme, an American brig carrying 78 slaves called at Hamilton in 1835, the

Left and **right**, Bermudian blacks *circa* 1890.

year after slavery had been abolished in Bermuda. The slaves were brought before the Chief Justice "in the midst of such a scene of excitement as has seldom been witnessed in the town." They were offered their freedom in Bermuda and all of the slaves accepted bar one woman named Ridgly, who chose to continue to the Carolinas with her five children.

Slavery, but not racial segregation, was abolished in 1834. Bermuda opted for total emancipation rather than an apprenticeship scheme which would have made slaves the employees of existing owners. The owners were compensated to the sum of £128,240 for 4,000 freed slaves (about 740 blacks

already being free). The Bermuda Parliament simultaneously passed an act which increased the franchise qualification from property worth £30 to £60, a condition not removed until 1965.

The kind of racial prejudice prevalent in the 19th century is reflected in a book by "A Field Officer" who, perhaps sensibly, chose to be anonymous: "Although the coloured Mudians have almost all been taught to read and write, yet their memories are so defective, and their dispositions so idle, that, with few exceptions, they forget before they are twenty everything that they have learnt." Never shy of a robust generalisation, the

field officer observed that "next to vice and dishonesty, dirt and vanity are the leading characteristics of these people. On their filthiness, it would be unpleasant to dwell, but their vanity, coupled with their hideousness, is most amusing." Etc., etc.

Although there was no overt colour discrimination in the statute books, social, political and economic realities were very much in the mould of the American South. The races attended separate schools, occupied different pews in church, didn't marry one another, and so on. Blacks adopted a form of tactical voting which circumvented the colour prejudice in the franchise property qualification and put a black carpenter, William Joell, into the colonial parliament in 1883. Others followed him, but slowly; it was not until the 1950s that blacks were a significant political force.

Using the trade union movement as a power base, Dr Edgar Fitzgerald Gordon was able to force the pace. He died in 1955, but the momentum he created led to a successful boycott of segregated cinemas in 1958. Theatres, hotels and restaurants quickly fell into line. When social proximity between the races did not bring about the end of the world, as white pessimists probably feared, black employees started appearing behind bank counters and in shops.

Bermuda had functioned all this time without any true political parties. The formation of the Progressive Labour Party in 1963 set a precedent quickly followed by the United Bermuda Party, both multi-racial. The chosen leader of the UBP was – almost inevitably in the light of Bermuda's history – a Tucker, in this case Sir Henry Tucker, banker. Under his influence, Bermuda changed what had become a quaintly anachronistic style of government into the more familiar form of a bi-cameral house.

The UBP dominated government after the 1968 election. Feeling that his job had been done, Sir Henry made way in 1971 for a black government leader, Sir Edward Richards. The UBP prospered under successive leaders at the expense of the leftish, uncohesive PLP, culminating in a convincing electoral victory in 1985 (31 seats out of 40) under Mr John Swan.

Above, harmony in the 1990s. **Right**, the Hon. C. V. "Jim" Woolridge, Minister of Tourism.

TOURISM TODAY

Tourism in Bermuda is more than just blue skies and pink beaches. An industry which is responsible for 62 percent of a country's entire revenue requires a sophisticated internal structure, not to mention a watchful eye on the marketplace.

Bermuda's tourism supplies the revenue to sustain the island's heavily imported economy, and, without the money usually generated by taxation, provides the social benefits of a large industrial nation. Education is free; so is medical and dental care up to college age. Senior citizens get 80 percent of their hospital bills paid for by the government; indigents receive medical treatment free. Scholarships and interest-free loans are commonplace.

It's not surprising, then, that the Hon. C. V. "Jim" Woolridge, Minister of Tourism, adopts a very pragmatic approach to his country's premier industry.

"Our demographics show that if we are to maintain our high standard of living here – and we have one of the highest per capita incomes in the world at $22,000 – we need to attract people with a household income of $65,000 per year, and up," says Mr Woolridge. "In fact, a recent airport survey we did showed that 62 percent of the visitors who arrived had household incomes of between $65,000 and $75,000 per year, and 22 percent had a household income of over $100,000. So I'd say we're not doing too badly."

Tourism is closely integrated into the community itself, and keeping the industry ticking over requires a delicate method of checks and balances – in other words, operating a "closed-shop" policy. In addition to the 57,000 resident population, there is a floating population of 600,000, the official visitor count.

"To go beyond 600,000 people a year, we would be outstripping our ability to maintain our image as a quality resort," says Mr Woolridge. "If you can't get adequate transportation, if the beaches become overcrowded, if the merchandise or the service in the stores goes down, then as a quality destination you're bound to suffer."

With a view to restricting numbers, there is a moratorium on the amount of accommodation provided; a hotel cannot be built unless another of equal size closes down or unless rooms become available due to the closure of smaller guesthouses. Similarly, Bermuda has reduced its quantity of cruise ships to only four a week. The ships never berth on a Sunday on a scheduled basis, in order to protect the quality of island life.

"You can't expect people to work seven days a week in a hospitality industry and then ask them to be pleasant," says Mr Woolridge. "You must have time for the family, to re-group and reflect. Plus, we know what we can afford. If we have to bring people in from outside to cope with crowds, this puts pressure on our own infrastructure, on schools, on the amount of imported food. Bermuda's natural resources are its people, and we want to protect them."

The island is particularly dependent on air transport, and although nearly one-quarter of its visitors are cruise passengers, the remaining must, of course, arrive by plane. The island maintains an excellent rapport with the airlines and in return the carriers themselves are protected: few charter flights are allowed.

"It's the airlines that service Bermuda 12 months a year that are the ones that keep the island going. In return, we make sure they have no undue competition. This kind of understanding is important; as with the hotels, our industry partners know what kind of competition they'll have, and how many players there are – or are likely to be."

The past few years have seen great changes in the marketing of holiday destinations, with many countries competing strongly for the all-important tourist dollar. Vast resorts are springing up in Mexico and the Caribbean – modern constructions built with tourists in mind. Bermuda's tiny size and complex internal structure means it can't afford to change; nor does the government really want it to.

"Bermuda is beautiful," says Mr Woolridge. "It's clean, it's traditional, and a very important factor in our favour, it's British. I think it would be fair to say that, whereas many countries are spending a lot of money in order to be different, we're spending money to stay the way we are."

Whether first seen from the air or from the sea, the feature which dominates the Bermuda landscape is not so much a vista of beaches and palm trees – but something far less glamorous and more mundane: its roofs.

Pristine clean and glaringly white, their stepped form is so unmistakably Bermudian that photographers patiently spend hours lying in wait, propped at some awkward angle against a wall, trying to capture the right shadows cast across an obscure section of rooftop, hoping for the picture which will "say it all". Painters set easels to face inland, chanelling their vision away from turquoise seas and colourful sprays of hibiscus and oleander, looking upwards, hoping that a few deft strokes on the white paper will magically capture the essence of the slopes.

The casual observer, of course, would be quite justified in wondering what this lofty obsession is all about. One may well wonder how it is that an island so generously endowed with natural beauty can be symbolised – rather accurately, as it so happens – by its roofs.

Artistically manipulated: Actually, Bermuda's rooftops are only one aspect of an entire style of architecture which is found nowhere else in the world. It is a distinctive style, a conglomeration of individual features which have been artistically manipulated into a pleasing, cohesive whole. Together, they also represent the complete embodiment of all those traits which make Bermuda so unusual. They reflect the convergence of climate and natural resources with the ingenuity of the local people.

Bermudian architecture is frequently referred to as being the country's sole truly indigenous art form; an authentic creation which only its people could have produced. Some maintain that the seeds for each feature were borrowed from distant shores and then modified to suit local needs; another school of thought argues that it is entirely homegrown, pure, without the dubious benefits of external influences. Although neither may

Preceding pages: designer beach; a Gombey dance troupe; one cycle of life. Left and right, island architecture.

be absolutely correct, there is no doubt that Bermuda does have a style which is distinctively its own.

All architecture is blatantly influenced by the peculiarities of the building materials and by the specific characteristics of the climate which they will inevitably have to withstand. The difference with Bermuda, however, is that these technical considerations have been further inhibited by two additional restrictions. In the first place, when early settlers came to erect permanent

buildings, the only suitable raw materials which could be found were corallian limestone and cedar. Imported alternatives were, and are, expensive, and awkward to acquire. Secondly, in the absence of any significant surface fresh water – there are no rivers and only a handful of small lakes – everything had to be designed around the absolute necessity for catching and storing rain water.

These early builders were well-versed in the potential severity of the weather; after all, their predecessors had been shipwrecked in Bermuda during the kind of ocean storm that Shakespeare immortalised as *The Tempest*. They were motivated less by aesthetics than by their own physical well-being, designing sturdy structures capable of withstanding the blustery torments of the Atlantic while simultaneously capitalising on any shade and breezes in the hot and humid climate. Finally, they crowned their buildings with limestone roofs, an ingenious contrivance specifically designed to catch all the fresh rainfall needed for domestic consumption. Bermudian architecture successfully met these diverse requirements of function and comfort.

Basically, the houses consisted – then, as now – of thick walls generously breeched by windows, necessary for light and air. Shutters hang decoratively at either side, or

eyed the native limestone and the cedar.

A wooden superstructure was made for the roof using hand-hewn cedar logs for the rafters. Over these they laid carefully cut "slices" of limestone. Somewhat inaccurately, these pieces of over-lapping stone are still called "slates". The lower rows were fastened first and the others added sequentially so that they ascended step-like to the crestline. To seal the roof against potential leakages, the finished surface was coated with a wash of lime.

The rain water was not gathered through conventional guttering; instead, it was corralled by a simple pattern of shallow walls which systematically directed each drop into

 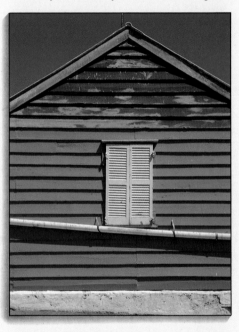

dangle from above in the traditional *jalousie* style, always at the ready to become useful should an errant storm brew. The chimneys are square, solid and firmly capped by slabs of limestone, not the more vulnerable red, kiln-fired "pots" which are so typical elsewhere. Most homes have open porches, to couple the refreshing benefits of outdoor living with the advantage of the shade.

But the challenge was always to devise a type of roof which would provide the occupants with the means to save and store the all-important rain water. Without the grey slates of Europe or the wooden shingles of North America, early Bermudians instinctively

downpipes located at strategic points along the roof edge. The water was then fed into a large storage tank dug into the solid bedrock adjacent to the main house. From this naturally cool, man-made cavern, it was carried by bucket into the house as required. This time-proven method for collecting fresh water is still practised today; the only major modifications during the past three centuries have been to excavate a water tank directly beneath each dwelling and then electrically pump water up into the house.

At first glance, casual observers may feel the exteriors of Bermudian buildings are rather flat and bland; that they are only enlivened by the practice of painting exterior walls in colours ranging from pastel pinks and blues through to the occasional outbursts of more vivid greens, tangerine and yellow. Likewise, shutter and wooden trimmings are also painted.

In truth, the fragile Bermuda limestone did indeed inhibit local architects and almost completely denied them the opportunity to embellish outside surfaces with anything sculptural. There is nothing on the island remotely flamboyant or baroque. For better or worse, there are no cherubic angels swooping downwards from corner clusters of acanthus leaves or any majestic neo-classical colonnades. Instead, Bermudians have

centuries to confirm this permanent legacy.

The designated custodian of Bermuda's architecturally rich heritage is the Bermuda National Trust, a body comprised mainly of volunteers and relying heavily on public donations and bequests. The Trust, sometimes in conjunction with the local Audubon Society, manages various properties which include buildings, open land and even some fascinating cemeteries, whose headstones record many of the less-known aspects of local history. The headquarters of this organisation are at Waterville, an architectural delight located on the edge of Hamilton harbour, just on the outskirts of the town.

Of those buildings formally designated as

opted for a more subtle decorative art form, one in which angular shadows emerge from each feature, moving continually like patterns of chiaroscuro along the walls, beneath the eaves and across the rooftops – decoration forever in motion as the sun progresses through the sky.

These houses incorporate a style of architecture which was meant to last, not something intended to survive just one lifetime before falling prey to the demolition ball. There are plenty of buildings around the island which date well beyond a couple of

Left and **right**, pastel island homes.

historic properties, several are open to the public on a regular schedule. Others are retained as museums or private residences, but the majority can be viewed by arrangement. Verdmont and Camden are referred to elsewhere in this book, but there are many others which warrant a visit. St George's, of course, is a living monument to this island's architectural heritage and it is impossible to imagine anyone being unable to enjoy a simple stroll through its winding streets, absorbing the experience of informal exposure to the past.

Among the buildings which are regularly open is the lower part of Bridge House, located within sight of Kings Square in the heart of the town. Erected at the end of the 17th century, this former mansion has been the home of two governors by the name of Popple, as well as an enterprising Virginian privateer named Bridger Goodrich. The house was therefore once a focal point for considerable plotting and planning during earlier times. In the 19th century, a family of silversmiths named Rankin worked each day in the same downstairs rooms which now, appropriately, house an art gallery. The surrounding gardens, as with most National Trust properties on the island, have been planted in a distinctive manner intended to reflect the original.

Nearby is Bermuda's oldest stone structure, the State House, which is open to the public. Built in 1620, it was originally the seat of local government. Today it is used by the Freemasons – rented for the exorbitant sum of one peppercorn, a princely due which is graciously handed over to the government during the course of the annual Peppercorn Ceremony in Kings Square.

"Buckingham", "Casino" and "Reeve Court" are all in this same general vicinity. Each is a private residence, however, and so, unless a tenant is willing to give a private guided tour, these must be viewed from the outside. Collectively, the grouping repre-

sents a characteristic neighbourhood from the 18th century, each with external water-tanks clearly visible in the back garden.

On Water Street is the Tucker House. It was built as a private home in 1712 and is currently a museum, with a small bookshop below. The museum has been laid out in a way which enables the visitor to amble through each room and perhaps recapture a true feeling for what it would have been like to live in a old Bermudian home. It is well furnished with authentic pieces and decorated with incidental mementos and family pictures so as to recreate the domestic atmosphere of a previous era.

One architectural feature worthy of particular note is the use of "tray" ceilings in the rooms. This was another ingenious Bermudian design which elevated the ceiling well up into the structural rafters, enabling warm air to rise while effectively leaving the lower section of the room cooler for the family. Evidently the Tuckers sought to enjoy the maximum in all home comforts.

At the opposite end of Bermuda, in Sandys Parish, is the magnificent estate called Springfield. Parts of the main building were constructed in the 17th century, so this property and its adjacent grounds always warrant a visit. In particular, attention should be drawn to the "buttery" which stands off the main courtyard. A buttery is a small outbuilding specifically designed during those days prior to refrigeration as a place to store the spoilables from the kitchen pantry. It was said that items kept in the buttery – a shaded and well-ventilated structure – would be safe from insects, vermin and miscellaneous bacteria for days on end. Today, the distinctive pyramidal roof of the buttery remains a popular feature on the landscape of Bermudian architecture.

Throughout the island, Bermuda's style of architecture embodies characteristics which make it quite distinctive from all others. Dominated by white roofs and sturdy walls, it survives as a permanent testimony to the ingenuity of those early settlers who exploited only two raw materials, but who successfully provided themselves with comfortable shelter in which to sit and enjoy the simple luxury of a goblet of fresh water.

Left and right, local architecture is distinguished by its roofs.

BERMUDA FESTIVAL 1990

Bermuda's theatrical scene builds to a peak in mid-winter with the annual Bermuda Festival, over 15 years old and going strong. For six or seven weeks in January and February, residents and visitors can sample a fare of music, dance and drama, plus some inspired foolery and magic, presented by international talent.

The size of visiting companies and their productions is governed by the Bermuda-sized limits of island theatres and stages. The festival's programme folder warns: "The venues of the Bermuda Festival are all small halls. There are virtually no bad seats." Bermuda Festivals Limited is an ongoing organisation; next year's programme was tentatively laid out before the curtain went up on this year's, but cannot be mentioned in public until contracts are signed.

Festival events tend to be located in the 378-seat Hamilton City Hall, the Southampton Princess Hotel (an easier venue for some visitors) or in St John's Church near the city.

Experimental theatre: The idea that tiny Bermuda might be able to mount an arts festival was first tested in 1970, when the Arts Council sponsored an experimental but ambitious Summer Festival. The play was Bertolt Brecht's historical drama *The Life of Galileo*, with UK-based Bermudian actor Earl Cameron in the title role. Laurence Olivier starred in a film version of *Othello* as a fringe event. (In some subsequent years a film series has been added to the stage events, which is always popular.) American singers gave an abridged version of Mozart's *Cosi Fan Tutte*. Ballet was provided by the First Chamber Dance Company of New York, and Arthur Mitchell brought dancers from his Dance Theater of Harlem. Also on show were exhibits of primitive Bermuda, brought by the late Richard Saunders.

After this one brave try, the festival idea lapsed until the still-continuing annual series got off the ground. This was the result of a fortuitous circumstance: the friendship of a new governor with a famous violinist. In England Governor Sir Edwin Leather had

been chairman of the Bath Festival, where he was closely associated with Sir Yehudi Menuhin. A bust of Menuhin, received as a gift, adorned the foyer at Government House. In 1974 Sir Edwin called a meeting of a dozen likely people to broach the idea of Bermuda launching its own festival. Despite the doubts of most of those consulted, ways were found to make the event a reality.

Bill Lockwood of New York's Lincoln Center was secured to act as artistic director and Stateside talent scout. After a few years,

members of the Festival Committee took on the scouting stint themselves, viewing overseas performances on their travels and screening reports from others as well as tapes and videos submitted by aspiring artists.

Successive chairmen of the festival have all been prominent and busy people. The festival's only paid functionary is manager Mrs Lee Davidson; otherwise it is some 300 volunteers who, in league with a growing number of corporate and individual financial patrons, really keep the festivals rolling.

A special feature is the local hospitality; 150 or so hosts and hostesses who make arriving artists feel at home – driving them

Left, a souvenir programme. **Right**, City Hall is a favourite festival venue.

from airport to hotels and on sightseeing excursions, giving them late suppers after performances and arranging picnics, receptions and sporting dates. Artists also enjoy free air travel and complimentary rooms at top hotels.

The performers are very complimentary towards Bermudian hospitality, occasionally interrupting their hectic schedules just to attend the festival, for this touch of home-life is light-years away from the usual routine of drab after-hours meals, cramped or inconvenient accommodation and rows of faceless crowds. The hosts and hostesses, too, relish the chance to exchange views with some of their favourite performers.

Twyla Tharpe Dance Company, the Alvin Ailey Repertory Workshop, the Boston Ballet Chamber Company (who appeared twice), the National Ballet of Canada and stars of the Royal Danish Ballet, among others. Well-known actors and actresses have recreated the personalities and works of such historical figures, authors and artists as Queen Elizabeth I, Lewis Carroll, P.G. Wodehouse, Clara Schumann, G.K. Chesterton and even Queen Victoria.

In 1984 the Bermuda Musical and Dramatic Society marked the island's 375th anniversary with a lavish production of *The Tempest*, thought to have taken shape in Shakespeare's mind after he read first-hand

Visiting troupes are impressed and grateful for the expertise and tireless work of local backstage crews, mostly from the Bermuda Musical and Dramatic Society. After their daytime jobs they may spend half the night clearing the stage of one set and erecting another for the next night's new performance. They are equal to emergencies and experienced at improvising. For example, the set plan sent from New York for *Love's Labour's Lost* was lost in the mail; the company had asked for a small forest but settled for a giant tree, for which the players brought the leaves in their luggage.

Past festivals have brought the exciting

accounts of the wreck of the storm-tossed *Sea Venture*, flagship of Admiral Sir George Somers, on Bermuda reefs in 1609.

For six years, from 1977 to 1983, Shakespeare was kept alive in Bermuda by successive acting students of New York's Juilliard Theater Company in fresh productions of *Midsummer Night's Dream, Romeo and Juliet, Othello, Much Ado about Nothing, Love's Labour's Lost* and *A Winter's Tale*. (A ballet version of *Romeo and Juliet* was staged by the Joffrey II Dancers in 1983, with Ron Reagan Junior, son of the then US president, cast as Romeo).

Classical guitarists have maintained their

popular appeal through many festivals, including Carlos Montoya in 1976, the Romeros in 1978 and 1979 and Liona Boyd in 1980. In a recent interview Miss Boyd credited Julian Bream with sparking her interest in the guitar when she heard him play as a young girl; in 1981 he succeeded her on the Bermuda Festival stage.

The Canadian Brass ensemble, who draw golden tones from their gold instruments, have been a popular attraction. In 1989 the Nashville Brass were brought from Tennessee to introduce country music to the festival repertoire. A customary feature on the programme is one or another offbeat group disporting in bouts of unpredictable mime or magic. Mummenschanz was here in 1976 and 1981, and was called in for a third time in 1986 to substitute for ailing French mime artist Marcel Marceau.

Each year festival-goers are asked to fill out a questionnaire about their tastes in entertainment. After a number expressed a wish for opera, several small operatic groups were added to the calendar.

From time to time, in response to an early feeling in some quarters that Bermudians were being left out of their own festival, local groups have been included in a variety of acts. In 1979 there was a Bermuda Night of Stars with night club singers Gene and Pinky Steede and band leader Hubert Smith. The following year brought *A Bermudian Anthology*, an imaginative depiction of the island's natural and human history. In 1982 *Joseph and the Amazing Technicolor Dreamcoat* came to life on stage. Three years later blind Bermudian pianist Lance Hayward took time off from playing a Greenwich Village club to make music at home. An unusual departure in 1981 was Benjamin Britten's opera *Noye's Fludde* presented in a church, with children costumed as assorted animals.

Award-winning programmes: Covers of festival souvenir programmes, featuring colour photographs on stage themes or island scenes, have won several awards offered annually by the International Society of Performing Arts Administrators, as well as local awards made by the Bermuda Adver-

tising and Publicity Organisation. One cover pictures exotic seashells on a swooping wave. Its finder, bank executive Jack Lightbourn, is quoted in the same programme on the science of molluscs.

Well-known local sculptor Desmond Fountain created "Samantha", a child ballerina in bronze, specially for the 1988 festival. The statue is one of a limited edition of nine, and features on that year's programme. Other articles in the programmes open doors on various facets of the Bermuda scene, like local cottage architecture, Bermuda silversmiths, old garden roses and collectable Bermuda stamps.

1990 marked the 10th anniversary of Jean

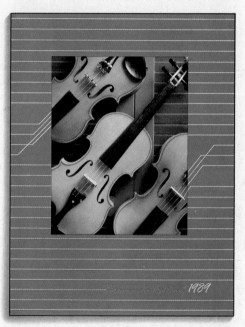

Hannant's service to the community as the festival's publications chairman. She was responsible for initiating and co-ordinating the design and production of the festival's flyers, posters, theatre and souvenir programmes. Under her care the souvenir programme has become a real benefit to the festival, generating attention abroad and stimulating advertising.

According to Jean Hannant's own account, her hectic and time-consuming stint came about in the most innocent way, by uttering the six fatal words: what can I do to help? The award-winning souvenir programmes are the answer to that question.

There is something quite magical about the thought of sailing to Bermuda. It is as if an invisible lure is dangled in front of seafarers to tempt them into a hidden lair somewhere beyond the horizon.

In a far more practical sense, sailing to Bermuda from the American mainland can take upwards of five days, and for those heading to the island from Europe, the passage will probably last at least two or three weeks. If that seems a great deal of ocean swell, bear in mind that Bermuda is three-quarters of the way across the Atlantic. The island lies roughly 600 miles (960 km) due east of the Florida-Georgia boundary and is virtually on the same latitude as Casablanca, North Africa. It does indeed sit right out there, all alone.

Bermuda Harbour Radio: However, for those with sufficient skill and enough daring to make the ocean crossing, the rewards are worth the minor inconveniences of having to wear perpetually damp clothing, and staring at little on the horizon but waves while simultaneously downing handfuls of sea-sickness pills. These discomforts are quickly forgotten as soon as the low-lying form of the Bermudas is sighted deep along the brow of the waves. Soon one of two lighthouses will appear: St David's or Gibbs Hill. But there is another bonus in store, more subtle than any of the scenic preludes previously experienced, because at this stage yachts will have floated into the welcoming, warm and static domain of "Bermuda Harbour Radio".

It is the general consensus among seasoned salts that Bermuda Harbour Radio is one of the friendliest and most helpful nautical stations anywhere in the world. The genial staff transmit quite happily for the full 24 hours of each day – dispensing navigational information to the lost and weary, clarifying clearance procedures for the uninitiated and even arranging for messages of assurance to be passed on to worried loved ones far away. This service is a fitting introduction to the courtesy and cordiality for

which Bermuda has come to be known.

The majority of sailing vessels which enter Bermudian waters tend to head for St George's, in order to clear themselves straightaway with local Immigration and Customs officials. Harbour Radio usually channels new arrivals in through The Cut and then directs them across to the other side of the harbour to the quayside at Ordnance Island, opposite Kings Square. While awaiting clearance, all vessels must fly the familiar yellow "Q" flag.

Bermuda hosts thousands of transient yachts every year and has made every effort to ensure that entry procedures are basically uncomplicated and, on the whole, quite conventional. In short, there are no peculiar stipulations and certainly nothing sufficiently abnormal to cause last-minute panics or worried scurryings below deck. Furthermore, local officials tend to be polite and helpful – mercifully unlike their typically officious and detached counterparts in so many other seaports.

Each crew member must carry personal identification and the usual travel documents; before setting sail, foreign nationals

Preceding pages: sailing from Newport to Bermuda. **Left**, *Scaramouche*. **Right**, a little something for indoor sailors.

should check for any visa requirements. The yacht itself must have a valid Certificate of Registration and is presumed still to be carrying all of the relevant paperwork with which it was issued when clearing the last port-of-call. Any crew intending to leave the boat in Bermuda should be aware that a confirmed onward ticket is required before final landing approval can be granted.

For those who may be unfamiliar with local social mores, however, a discreet word of caution: anyone arriving here for the first time would do well to note that Bermudians are diligent in their efforts to keep a miscellany of "undesirable" items away from their shores. The list includes the usual drugs and

seemingly endless miles of indented shoreline, all offering picturesque scenery.

St George's is an ideal arrival and departure point. It is quite capable of satisfying all of the conventional requirements of seafarers, from laundry facilities through to stores. Meyers have a boatyard for fixing minor and major, temporary and permanent repairs; Steve Hollis has a sailmakers' shop, Sail On, which offers an efficient service; Godet and Young can supply most basic equipment and replacement parts; Dowling's marina carries fuel and fresh water. For food supplies, any of the major grocery stores will arrange dockside deliveries. In Hamilton, all of these services can be provided through the adjoin-

all guns, but also broadens to include large hunting knives, harpoons and spear-fishing paraphernalia. Anything which is deemed to be a weapon is promptly placed in bond and is returned only when the rightful owner is about to cast off. However, those who feel defenceless without a gun will be relieved to know that Bermuda is a peaceful island; unlike parts of the Caribbean and South China Sea today, pirates have long since ceased to prowl.

Once cleared, all sailors are free to travel throughout Bermuda as, how, when and where the proverbial spirit moves. There are innumerable bays and inlets to explore and

ing waterfront properties of PW's marina and Miles supermarket.

Although Bermuda's coastline is not cluttered by cove-bound fishing villages, a variety of convenient, temporary moorings are always available. Harbour Radio or the Marine Police will be quite willing to suggest where the best anchorages can be found for overnight stays. Among the most popular spots in the East End are St George's Harbour, Ferry Reach, Shelly Bay, Castle Harbour and Great Bay, off St David's Island; off the West End, many sailors prefer to make for Ely's Harbour, the Great Sound, Riddells Bay and The Dockyard. Private berthing privileges can no doubt be secured, by prior arrangement, with the yacht clubs in either Hamilton or St George's. (They may also know of boats which require casual crew for upcoming local races.)

The Dockyard, incidentally, was developed by the British Royal Navy during that grand period when Victorian confidence seemed to acknowledge no boundaries. For decades, it served the expanding Empire as the prime North Atlantic ship-building and re-supplying depot – becoming a bustling focal point of unprecedented nautical activity. In this less flamboyant era, it houses the country's fascinating Maritime Museum and also accommodates the Marina Real del

sails, could be almost as challenging a mis-match as a grand prix engine on a roller skate. In the wrong hands, it threatens either to fly out of the water altogether or to nose-dive into the depths.

Under certain conditions, it needs as many crew as can be crammed in – the rules of dinghy racing are relaxed on this point – with the interesting corollary that, if and when these conditions change, the surplus crew may be expected to make themselves scarce and pile overboard.

Bermudians grow up in small boats much as the French do with fine wines. In the absence of motor cars until after World War II, the small boat in Bermuda was tradition-

ally the family transport and goods van rolled into one, so when it was wheeled out for fun a few sporting modifications were in order. Competitive sailing in Bermuda began in 1840 under the parallel auspices of the Royal Yacht Club (Royal Navy officers and nobs in sloops) and the Bermuda Native Yacht Club (black fishermen and boatmen in whatever was at their disposal, inevitably small open boats).

As the cost of ocean racing in sloops edged ever upwards, the attraction of thrashing around Hamilton Harbour cheaply in the family banger broke down the racial bias. The quest for speed meant more and more

Oueste, a boating facility which offers all those pampering conveniences which contemporary seafarers have come to expect of quality marinas throughout the Caribbean or Mediterranean.

The Maritime Museum also highlights the colourful history of the Bermuda dinghy, the island's premier sailing vessel and one which is unique to this small group of islands. The Bermuda dinghy, just over 14-ft (4-metres) of open boat under monstrous

Left, Bermuda fitted dinghy, *circa* 1900. **Right**, Hamilton in 1912, photographed by Walter White on his honeymoon.

sail and removable decking to reduce the amount of water taken aboard. The rules, deliberately kept minimal, permit a detachable iron fin 12 ft (3.6 metres) long as a keel and stays to support the mast. Special racing "fitted dinghies" were built from 1890s onwards, the *Victory* on display in the Maritime Museum being one of the first.

Dinghy racing, as exciting for spectators as for participants, is held on every other Sunday from late May to September in one or other of St George's Harbour, Hamilton Harbour, the Great Sound or Mangrove Bay.

Local racing is only one part of the story, however, as Bermuda becomes even more popular with foreign craft and crews. Some

leisurely sail up and down the coastline, sailing around Bermuda is not particularly hazardous. It stands to reason, however, that pleasure trips must always be tempered by a regard for the conventional rules of safety. Remarkably, many self-designated mariners continue to flout even the most elementary precautions, blatantly flirting with disaster. It is not uncommon for a freighter to become stranded on the outer reef, or to find a yacht embarrassingly perched atop some coral head in the centre of the harbour.

The number of seafarers who persist in using out-dated pre-war maps is astonishing; others chance their luck without any charts whatsoever. In recent memory, there was

of the sailing boats which call into Bermuda are on a deliberately brief visit. They may have stopped off only to collect fresh water and food or to pick up a spare crew member; others come in to effect minor changes and repairs. Some skippers use the relatively short hop to Bermuda as the "shake-down" leg of a major trip across the Atlantic or down to the West Indies – a chance for crew and boat to become accustomed to each other for the longer haul which lies ahead. Others, of course, have made Bermuda a specific objective and intend to stay.

Whether cruising among the islands of Hamilton Harbour or simply relaxing with a

even one rather expensive yacht which came to grief while using the map depicted on a souvenir placemat as its sole means for navigating the eastern channel. The simple reality is that Bermuda is encircled by a complicated network of reefs, banks and sandbars – many of which are hidden. Vessels sailing through these waters should carry a comprehensive set of up-to-date charts on board, at all times.

Another essential safety factor is the need to pay attention to local weather conditions. This is, after all, the open ocean and conditions are subject not only to the prevailing systems of high and low pressure, but also to an untiring permutation of just about every other factor which might affect the weather. Fortunately, Bermuda's strategic position in the North Atlantic has made it a key location for professional meteorologists who devote their lives to plotting the movement of the great winter storms.

In addition to this erstwhile band, the American space agency NASA has a tracking station in Bermuda, and NATO maintains an official base. There are all manner of government and quasi-government agencies which have invested millions in keeping their eyes on the ever-changing patterns of local weather. No sailor need find himself battling an unexpected squall simply because of a

reluctance to call for a report. Harbour Radio makes regular broadcasts each day and an instant update is never further away than the nearest handset.

For its part, the Bermuda government does its utmost to furnish conditions of safety and protection to all boats travelling in and through native waters. It uses various departments to ensure that marker-buoys, flashing beacons and the suchlike are effectively maintained and functioning.

Any deviations to established patterns or

Left, a joyous celebration. **Above**, a coat of paint to whiten up the day.

procedures are promptly reported to Harbour Radio which, in turn, relays them over the airwaves. Records are also kept of boat movements in and out of Bermudian territorial waters, so that an on-going log is maintained for possible use with the Coast Guard should a vessel be overdue or go missing. Harbour Radio also serves as a clearing house for information about bulky and potentially dangerous flotsam and jetsam which may be a hazard to shipping in this part of the Atlantic.

Many magnetic myths: Much has been written both in jest and in myth about the curious magnetic variations which have been reported by sailors in boats which sail the Bermudian seas. Actually, the truth is both simple and entirely devoid of anything remotely mysterious.

As a point of instant clarification, the terms "deviation" and "variation" need to be defined. "Magnetic deviation" is the extent to which any individual compass deviates from the global norm or how inaccurate the manufacturers have made it. This should have been determined already, as automatically as adjusting the hands on a watch.

On the other hand, "magnetic variation" is that amount by which all compasses vary, according to where in the world they are being used. In and around Bermuda, the recognised variation between True North and Magnetic North is approximately 15 degrees to the west. All pertinent calculations on bearings should, therefore, incorporate this adjustment.

Anyone planning to charter a boat once they have arrived should contact the nearest Visitors' Service Bureau for up-to-date prices and information. Small craft such as sunfish, up to catamarans and yachts, are available and Hal White has a splendid 54-ft (16-metre) ketch for hire which features all the conveniences of true luxury. Detailed charts can be acquired overseas or through the Department of Marine & Ports, on Front Street in Hamilton and the local Marine Police are always close at hand, eager to give assistance and advice to anyone afloat. Finally, there is the comprehensive service of Harbour Radio.

The vastness and variety of Bermudian waters provides a unique opportunity for all types of sailor to experience enjoyment. In exchange, the seas ask only for respect.

Athletic pursuits are an integral part of island life. Not only do Bermudians play a great deal – there are more than 30 organised sports on the island – but sports also play a key role in Bermuda's tourism industry. Spectacular golf courses, natural sailing facilities and excellent fishing are among Bermuda's major tourist attractions while the international events attract some of the world's top athletes in sailing, road running, triathlon and rugby.

The sports pages of the *The Royal Gazette* reflect this cosmopolitan interest in world sports and Bermudians themselves often compete at an international standard that belies the island's size and relative isolation.

Holiday Match: Nothing illustrates the Bermudian passion for sport quite like Cup Match, an annual two-day cricket game. Played between the St George's and Somerset clubs on the Thursday and Friday before the first Monday of August, it may be one of the only sporting events in the world for which a public holiday was specifically created. First played in 1902, the game attracted such crowds that by 1947 the government gave in to rife absenteeism at work and declared both days public holidays. Officially, the Thursday is the Cup Match holiday while Friday is Somers Day, to commemorate the landing of Sir George Somers in 1609.

Some historians believe the match grew out of black celebrations to mark Emancipation Day (1 August 1834) but to Bermudians the holiday is simply "Cup Match". It is not only the island's premier sporting event, it is also the holiday of the year and a major social gathering that attracts some 12,000 people from the governor and premier down. It is a carnival at which the cricket often seems incidental to chancing your luck at the Crown and Anchor tables or indulging in local delicacies such as curried mussel pie, shark hash or conch stew.

Cricket and soccer are Bermuda's national sports in terms of players and spectators.

Preceding pages: Bermuda has more golf courses per square mile than any other nation. Left and right, two island pastimes.

Cricket, played between April and September, has around 1,200 junior and senior players and 27 clubs while soccer has almost 2,000 players and 30 clubs. Like most sports on the island, they were segregated until the early 1960s, although both are now predominantly black and the leading teams remain those with origins as black working-men's or community clubs.

Internationally, Bermuda ranks among the best of the non-Test playing cricket nations, having reached the final of the International

Cricket Conference Trophy, the qualifier for the World Cup, in 1982 and the semi-finals in 1979 and 1986. Several Bermudian cricketers have played professionally, most notably all-rounder Alma (Champ) Hunt in the 1930s and bowler Clarence (Tuppence) Parfitt in the 1980s, both of whom played in Scotland. Bermuda also regularly hosts first-class tours from England and the Caribbean.

The Somers Isles Cricket League runs games every Sunday but next to Cup Match the premier games are the Eastern, Central and Western Counties Cup competitions, which are not county cricket in the English sense but area club tournaments. Soccer is the national winter sport and the Bermuda Football Association runs league and cup matches on most Sundays from October to April. Bermuda has a creditable international reputation, winning a bronze medal at the 1978 Central American and Caribbean Games. The island plays at all levels of international competition from the World Cup and the Olympics to regional youth tournaments; it is also a popular touring destination for English and European clubs.

Several Bermudian players have played professionally in England and the United States, most notably Clyde Best, who starred for English First Division club West Ham United in the late 1960s and early 1970s, and

tional yachting regattas. Its position in the mid-Atlantic also makes it an ideal destination for long-distance races from the United States such as the famous Newport-Bermuda Race, first sailed in 1906, and the more recent Marion-Bermuda Cruising Race, first held in 1975. Both are sailed in June of alternating years and the arrival of the boats at the Royal Bermuda Yacht Club and the Royal Hamilton Amateur Dinghy Club in Hamilton Harbour is one of the colourful highlights of a Bermudian summer.

Bermudians have been yacht racing since the early 1800s when working dinghies were "fitted" for racing. Fitted dinghy racing in traditional 14-ft (4-metre) craft with vastly

Randy Horton, who played for the New York Cosmos in their 1970s heydays.

The top club competitions are the Dudley Eve Trophy, played over Christmas and New Year between the top four league teams at the halfway stage of the First Division season, and the FA Challenge Cup which draws big crowds to its final each April.

In other athletic pursuits, Bermuda's natural beauty and sub-tropical climate lend themselves to three sports more than any others: sailing, fishing and golf.

The protected waters of the Great Sound, Hamilton Harbour and Harrington Sound make Bermuda a natural venue for interna-

over-canvassed rigs remains the island's only indigenous sport. International Race Week, an invitational regatta which attracts sailors from North America and Europe each April, has been an annual event since the late 1920s. The 82-year-old King Edward VII Gold Cup is the world's oldest match-racing trophy and is now contested each November by some of the world's leading skippers as part of the World Match Racing Conference "grand prix" series.

The Bermuda Yachting Association includes more than a dozen racing classes and Bermudian sailors compete regularly at regional, world and Olympic level. Sailing remains a predominantly white sport, though less so in the smaller dinghy classes.

Scuba-diving, water-skiing and para-sailing are among the other water sports enjoyed on the island. Powerboat racing is a popular summer spectator sport with races held on alternate Sundays from April to November at Ferry Reach, near the airport, and the highlight being the annual Around the Island Race in July or August.

Fishing is virtually a year-round sport in Bermuda, although the best time for deep sea quarry such as blue marlin is May to November. Offshore fishing also includes world-class blackfin and yellowfin tuna as well as wahoo, barracuda, dolphin, amberjack and almaco jack. Commercial over-fishing, however, has greatly reduced reef and shore fish stocks in recent years.

Golf is another year-round sport but better in the cooler winter months. The island has more golf courses per square mile than any other nation in the world: eight in just 22 sq. miles (57 sq. km). The limited size of the island means courses can be relatively short with little room for error on the fairways but the hilly terrain makes each of them a unique test and the sweeping ocean views ensure that Bermuda's courses are among the most spectacular in the world.

Bermuda's oldest and most famous course is at the Mid Ocean Club, a 6,547-yard (5,986-metre) course in the exclusive Tucker's Town area at the east end of the island. Designed by former American amateur champion Charles Blair MacDonald in 1921, it was redesigned by Robert Trent Jones in 1953. Eisenhower and Churchill once met here and the fifth hole over Mangrove Lake has been called one of the best par fours in the world. The Bermuda Amateur Match Play Championship is staged here each March. Mid Ocean and Riddell's Bay, in Warwick Parish, are both private clubs and require an introduction from a member or hotel; but there is easy access to the other six clubs.

Port Royal, a 6,425-yard (5,875-metre) government-owned course overlooking Southampton's South Shore and designed by Trent Jones in 1972, is regarded as being among the best public courses anywhere in

golf and is the site of the Bermuda Open Championship each October, which regularly attracts satellite tour players from the United States and Canada. St George's Golf Club, a tight, unforgiving course, and nine-hole Ocean View in Devonshire are other excellent government-run courses.

Undulating Castle Harbour in Tucker's Town, where Gary Player was once the pro, is another championship-class course, as is the Belmont Golf and Country Club in Warwick while the Princess Golf Club is a tricky par-54 course in the grounds of the Southampton Princess Hotel.

Bermuda is also a tennis player's paradise with more than 80 courts on the island, most

of them either clay or cement surfaces. Play is possible year-round with the tournament season running from March to December. Some courts, such as those at the Pomander Gate Tennis Club and the exclusive Coral Beach and Tennis Club, require a member's introduction but most hotel courts are available to non-guests (at up to double the rate). There are public facilities at the Government Tennis stadium in Pembroke Parish and at Port Royal Golf Club in Southampton.

Interestingly, Bermuda helped introduce lawn tennis to the United States. The first tennis equipment was brought to Bermuda by a local businessman, Thomas Middleton,

Left, equestrian event at Government House. **Right,** colourful sports fans.

in 1873. He passed the equipment on to the Chief Justice, Sir Brownlow Gray, who erected a court at his home in Paget where the game was played by an American visitor, Mary Outerbridge. The following year she laid out the first American courts at the Staten Island Cricket Club in New York. Sir Brownlow's original grass court still stands at Clermont on Harbour Road.

Running has a strong following in Bermuda. Road and cross-country races occur in June, usually on Sunday mornings, over distances ranging from 3 miles (5 km) to a full marathon. The biggest event is International Race Weekend in mid-January which consists of races under floodlights on Front

excellence, competing regularly in Olympic, Commonwealth, Pan-American and other regional festivals. As in soccer and other sports, many young Bermudian athletes win scholarships to American or Canadian schools and colleges, which further improves the overall standard.

The island's most successful modern athlete in any sport is high jumper Nicky Saunders. A bronze medallist at the 1982 Commonwealth Games, he has held the Commonwealth record on several occasions and placed fifth at both the 1987 World Athletics Championships in Rome and the 1988 Olympic Games in Seoul. In 1990 he won the gold medal in the Commonwealth Games

Street, Hamilton, on Friday night, a 6-mile (10-km) event on Saturday and a marathon on the Sunday. Grete Waitz, Joan Benoit Samuelson, Orlando Pizzolato and Rob de Castella are among the many international stars who have run in the events.

The most popular local race, however, is the Marathon Derby held on 24 May, a gruelling 13-miler (20-km) first run in 1910. Open to residents only, it is the unofficial road race championship of the island and attracts up to 500 runners, cheered on by huge crowds along the Somerset-to-Hamilton route as part of Bermuda Day.

Bermuda has a tradition of track and field

which were held in Auckland, New Zealand.

A new National Stadium with a world-class all-weather track is due to be completed at Prospect, on the outskirts of Hamilton, in the early 1990s. Triathlon has been one of Bermuda's fastest-growing sports in recent years. Annual individual and team championships have been held each September since 1979, and in 1987 the island staged the first Bermuda International Triathlon in which the world's top professional triathletes competed for $100,000 in prize money.

Swimming and cycling, two of the triathlon disciplines, have long been popular sports in their own right in Bermuda. The

Bermuda Amateur Swimming Association runs a strong national programme and competes at Olympic, Commonwealth and regional level, while the Bermuda Bicycling Association stages regular road races, time trials and criteriums – all supposedly within the island's 20 mph (35 kph) speed limit! – as well as the international Grand Prix Aux Bermudes each April.

Rugby Union maintains a popular following, particularly among British expatriates, with four clubs fielding eight teams most weekends from October to April at the National Sports Club in Devonshire. Bermuda has traditionally been one of the rugby powers in the region having won three Carib-

ally in the Bermuda Hockey Festival each September and the Bermuda Squash Open attracts world-ranked players in November. The island also has a thriving horse-riding community and three-day eventer Peter Gray, who won a bronze medal at the 1987 Pan-American Games, is one of Bermuda's best-known international sportsmen.

There are shows throughout the year featuring jumping, show classes, gymkhanas and driving. The major shows are at the Agricultural Show at the Botanical Gardens, Paget, in April and the Mini Grand Prix, at Government House, Pembroke, in November, which features world-class riders. In 1989, the Bermuda Equestrian Federation

bean Championships up to 1981.

The Easter Classic, an annual Easter Sunday game involving star guest players from Britain, and November's World Rugby Classic, which attracts leading ex-internationals from the world's major rugby nations, are two of the international highlights on the island's sporting calendar. National Sports Club is also the centre for field hockey and squash, two other sports with strong expatriate followings. Teams from North America and Europe compete annu-

Left, local games. **Above**, tennis arrived in the United States from Bermuda.

opened a new National Equestrian Centre in Devonshire which will be the venue for future international events.

Outside of cricket and soccer, the two most popular "working-class" sports are softball and bowling. Bernard Park in Pembroke hosts ball games in various leagues six nights a week virtually year-round, while Warwick Lanes in Warwick Parish has 16 lanes open seven nights a week.

Other sports in Bermuda range from boxing, netball, basketball and table tennis to karate, karting, gymnastics, darts, snooker and, on the manicured lawns of the Lantana Colony Club in Sandys, even croquet.

Bermuda's semi-tropical beauty and distinctive architecture have inspired artists for at least 150 years – ever since the pressures of turning an empty island into a homeland eased sufficiently to allow the leisure to do so. In a romantic sense, the isolated island lay like an empty canvas awaiting the touch of paint and brush. No prehistoric paintings decorate Bermuda's caves as in so many civilisations, nor are there Old Masters or masterpieces.

The earliest surviving art took the form of portraits, as visiting painters were called on to preserve the images of leading citizens rather than the beauty of their natural surroundings. Portraits by English artist Joseph Blackburn, who was in Bermuda from 1752 to 1753, hang in the Tucker House museum in St George's. Others by American John Green, painted from 1765, are displayed in his one-time residence, Verdmont. Prizes for collectors are ship paintings by "Edward James" – suspected of being an alias for a remittance man who painted, among other subjects, Civil War blockade runners en route to southern Confederate ports.

Historic illustrations: Women watercolourists recorded local flora and fauna in attentive detail. Flower paintings by Lady Lefroy, whose husband was governor from 1871 to 1877, are preserved in the Bermuda Archives, and her fish paintings in the main library. Both Edward James's and Lady Lefroy's works have been used to illustrate the history section of this book.

It wasn't until the early 20th century that more than a few Bermudians looked around them and transferred pictorial impressions to paper. The past 50 to 60 years have seen a burgeoning of visual art as local amateurs, and a few professionals, embrace the newer styles and subject-matter of the rapidly changing world art scene. There are now three flourishing volunteer art groups, augmented by several private studios and commercial galleries.

In the forefront is the 500-member Bermuda Society of Artists, with its predecessor, the Bermuda Art Association. The Association held exhibitions from 1928 onwards in the former Hamilton Hotel, where a number of paintings went up in flames when the building burned to the ground just before Christmas in 1955. The Society, in its gallery in City Hall, holds frequent exhibitions: seasonal members' shows, annual shows of work from schools, yearly photographic exhibitions and special events to coincide with the winter Bermuda Festival.

In 1984 the West End got its own artistic showcase with the formation of the Bermuda Arts Centre at Dockyard. This small gallery, housed in a building across from the Maritime Museum on the site of the former Royal Naval Dockyard, has adjoining studio facilities where two or three artists may be working at the same time in different media. Around 30 people have taken advantage of this convenient arrangement in the past few years, with pleasing results.

Newcomer to the fold of art-minded organisations is the Masterworks Foundation, which takes a different approach. Instead of promoting exposure for contemporary local

Preceding pages: *Shinbone Alley, St George's* by Ogden Minton Pleissner. <u>Left</u>, *St George's 1934* by Jack Bush. <u>Right</u>, Sharon Wilson at work.

art, it is busily engaged in "bringing home" works painted in Bermuda by visiting artists in past decades. This body, formed in 1987, took off from a loan exhibition of "Masterworks Inspired by Bermuda".

Volunteers, seeing a more lasting future for the concept, went on to organise and hunt for more pictures to bring home for display. This means a continuing drive for funds to purchase works from owners and overseas museums. One of the organisers, Tom Butterfield, had the original idea of competing in a London marathon and getting his running sponsors to pledge their donations to the Masterworks Foundation. This scheme paid off to the tune of $17,000.

muda Settlers, it is a playful depiction of the wild hogs found by English settlers supposedly left behind by 16th-century Spanish expeditions. Among postcard reproductions at the gallery is Andrew Wyeth's poignant study of a black woman, *The Bermudian*, seated by a worn wall. A Wyeth original was on show in the 1986 loan exhibition. Another wry view of a rundown area is American George Ault's 1922 watercolour *Behind the Bakery Shop*. An oil by Canadian Jack Bush incorporates the figure of a black woman carrying a bowl of fruit on her head.

Most of the retrieved paintings celebrate the glories of island seas and greenery accented by pastel houses whose snow-white

In 1989, two large local firms contributed substantial sums towards the purchase of particular works. One is a small painting of Government House or *Le Maison du Gouverneur* by French artist Albert Gleizes, who moved from Impressionism through Cubism to a simplified linear style. The other firm helped with the purchase of American Ogden Minton Pleissner's oil of *Shinbone Alley, St George's* – the fourth Pleissner work acquired by the foundation.

American Winslow Homer, who painted in both Bermuda and the Bahamas, is represented by a poster printed by arrangement with a Massachusetts museum. Titled *Ber-*

limestone roofs reminded Mark Twain of the icing on a cake.

A rich gift to "the people of Bermuda" is a small collection of paintings by British and European masters from the 15th to the 19th centuries, bequeathed by painter and parliamentarian the Hon. Hereward Watlington. The bequest carried provisos, one being that it should be housed in climatically controlled environs. The government has accepted this offer in principle.

Fortunately, the long-standing dream of a National Gallery equipped to protect valued work is nearing realisation. Plans are well in hand for this gallery and its opening by the

Bermuda Fine Art Trust, established by an Act of Parliament in 1982 for this very purpose. The two-storey gallery, in Hamilton City Hall, is backed by many local bodies and will provide a permanent home for the repatriated paintings owned by the Masterworks Foundation and, it is hoped, for those in the Watlington collection. It will also host travelling exhibitions from abroad.

Climate-control is a key factor in preserving Bermuda's paintings. Mrs Christina Wineinger, administrator for the new gallery, is quoted in an article in *The Royal Gazette* as saying Bermuda's climate is "unquestionably" the worst in the world for the toll it takes on works of art, with three

On the effects of light, Mrs Wineinger said: "Have you ever noticed how the top of a red car fades in Bermuda? That is because the ultra-violet light is so strong. It is unbelievable that it will fade acrylic paint and what it does to works of art is more tragic." The National Gallery should restore Bermuda art to its proper place and position.

Contemporary painters and sculptors now at work on the island form an ever-changing line-up. Some artists show their work only sporadically, while some leave the island and others arrive to see Bermuda with fresh eyes. Nevertheless, there are certain undisputed leaders.

Painting with light: For decades, the under-

elements – humidity, salt and ultra-violet light – all playing their part.

"The US Navy uses Bermuda to test the durability of paint," Mrs Wineinger said. "If paint can stand up here in Bermuda it can stand up anywhere – and I am talking about the Arctic… What Bermuda's humidity does to a painting is tragic. It can be absorbed by the canvas and you will see it later as mildew coming through the oils. Some very valuable prints have been totally destroyed."

Left, Bermuda inspires both painters and paintings. Above, *St George's Bermuda* **by Ogden Minton Pleissner.**

stated watercolours of Alfred Birdsey have spelled the spirit of Bermuda to visitors who seek him out at his Paget studio. He is willing to be described as an impressionist, though not in the sense of the French pioneers whose aim, he says, was "painting with light". His scenic watercolours, deliberately lacking in depth, look as if they have been tossed off at breathless speed – as indeed they are.

Background areas are indicated by a swatch of colour rather than a solid ground; stick figures of people are sketched in quick dark outlines. The effect is as if a butterfly had brushed the paper on the wing, and a spider had tracked it after wading through an inkwell. "Once over lightly" comes closest to describing this delicate technique.

Occasionally Birdsey has gone to the other extreme and produced some memorable murals. One adorns the Bermuda Tourist Bureau in Boston; another stays at home on the ground floor of the Bermuda Commercial Bank on Church Street. The artist executed this one with the help of his daughter Joanne, who sculpted the animal figures outside his studio. Daughter Antoinette goes in for flower painting. All three were featured in a Birdsey family show at the Dockyard Centre.

Bermuda has produced two distinguished sculptors: Desmond Hale Fountain for bronze statues and Chesley Trott for streamlined cedar carvings. Both have taught in schools, and Trott still does so at a secondary school and the Bermuda College.

Fountain of youth: Fountain is a full-time artist with a studio in Flatts and occasional exhibitions at the Windjammer Gallery. He admits to being a "Fountain of Youth", as he specialises in life-size figures of children caught in spontaneous poses: a boy sitting on a soccer ball, a girl reading on a bench, another spinning a hula hoop. Adult nudes also strike casual positions: the seated girl in *News Flash* scans an unfolded newspaper. On a festive note, the nude lounging on a bench in the courtyard of the Bank of Bermuda's Par-la-Ville branch wore a red hat at Christmas time, contributed by a solicitous bank executive.

A recent exhibition at the Windjammer had an amphibian air; the gallery had built a pool in the garden to display his new technique of wedding bronze and water. By piping and recycling water through the figures, he has a boy dangling a dripping fish, a girl squeezing streams from a sponge. The only monumental statue in Bermuda is his figure of Sir George Somers in St George's, unveiled by Princess Margaret in 1984.

The sculptor travels to foundries in America and Britain to oversee the casting of his wax originals which are then transported to Bermuda by boat. He exhibits in both countries, and in 1989 opened a Sculpture Gallery in the Southampton Princess Hotel, shared with other sculptors. Fountain is a Fellow of the Royal Society of British Sculptors.

Desmond Hale Fountain's *News Flash*.

Drums roll. The curtain rises on a handsome black man basked in spotlights, strumming a guitar and romancing his audience with an island ballad. He interrupts the song to make a few self-deprecating remarks about his "tan" and, before the audience stops laughing, the melodious voice slips back into another verse. Glistening grey at both temples and adorned in a brightly hued calypso shirt held firm by a red silk cummerbund, Hubert Smith Snr holds forth in the Empire Room at Bermuda's Southampton Princess Hotel.

Now in his seventies (but looking 20 years younger), the island's foremost entertainer is akin to a Bermudian icon. Hubert Smith has composed more than 100 songs, themes for movies and television and countless commercial jingles, and his voice has serenaded many luminaries. There were countless overseas tours as an ambassador to the local tourism industry, which inspired the musician to compose "Bermuda is Another World", a tribute to the island and the pride of its people.

But despite this commendable track record, Hubert Smith, like a number of island musicians, is experiencing a lessening in demand for this kind of "calypso" music.

Disco disease: "There is no question that the future of this island's music is in the hands of the younger musicians, but not enough of them are coming forward to fill the void," says Smith. The void he speaks of is one created by attrition, rising costs for hiring bands and a major culprit: the disco.

"When discos came into vogue, band music everywhere went into death throes," he laments. "Management saw dollar signs. After all, you pay one person to spin records and then don't have the cost of hiring a band. With odds like that, what's an entrepreneurial club owner to do?"

Although disco is rendering the live musician obsolete, Smith feels there is still hope. "It is a proven fact that our guests want to hear local entertainment when they come to Bermuda. All we have to do is encourage younger musicians to provide it. Visitors come for local music, and local music is exactly what they should get." If he sounds a

trifle strident, Hubert means to be just that. "I did not spend my entire life in the entertainment business to see it go down the tubes, just because mankind has discovered the synthesizer."

Musical roots: Hubert Smith can trace his musical roots back to the age of 15 when he began by pulling curtains and changing sets in a local music hall. Someone discovered his voice and gave him a small part in a show. He hasn't looked back since.

He got on to the local entertainment circuit purely by chance. The island's well-known Talbot Brothers were on a United States tour and needed a group to do a gig in their absence. Up stepped Hubert and his trio to play the Coral Island Hotel. As Hubert tells it, "the manager felt that we needed a name so he gave us the name of his hotel. That night we were born 'Hubert Smith and his Coral Islanders'."

Proud moments followed: a private audience with Queen Elizabeth II, for whose first official visit to the island he was asked to compose a song. When Prince Charles came calling he was again given the honour of composing an official welcoming tune. Smith took up his pen again for Princess Margaret's visit and over the years serenaded Churchill, Eisenhower, Kennedy, Johnson and French Premier Laniel – not to mention a host of celebrities. The Queen awarded him an honour and a private tour of the royal yacht *Britannia*. But prominent in his thoughts is the future of local music – especially since the demise of his own Coral Islanders – as hotels choose small combos and soloists over the big band.

"I'm afraid calypso in Bermuda is going the way of the dinosaur unless the young musicians make it a part of their repertoire and demand to be heard," he says, sadly. When the entertainment was mixed – a combination of popular music and calypso – he recalled packed houses. "There was even calypso for dancing."

He reminisced about some of the local entertainment giants like Kingsley Swan, Celeste Robinson, Al Harris – entertainers who achieved success on the hotel circuit, who would then go into the small clubs to play jazz when the hotels closed for the night. "All we have left now are Gene Steede, the Strollers, the All-Star Steel Band and a few reggae groups, but they don't play the nightly gigs we used to."

The death knell for local entertainment is embodied in the sophisticated tastes of Bermudian audiences, Smith feels, and as a consequence local musicians tend to shy away from calypso music. "Oh, they'll play it all right," he says, "but the trend is to resist the classification of being labelled 'native'

dance of talent to be found in even such a small island as Bermuda. He sees this talent manifesting itself after concerted nurturing and exposure to both local and foreign audiences. "What we need here is a cultural centre where younger Bermudians can perform alongside their peers. This would have the effect of improving their talents as they benefit from the experience of others."

Synthesized music: He bemoans the fact that in the studios synthesizers have usurped the role of musicians. "You want a big band

as this is indicative of a musical type-cast."

The sounds of reggae can be heard in small back-of-town clubs, but even this music is not widely available. Visiting reggae bands can still pack a hall in Bermuda and Son Rise, a local band that mixes jazz with reggae and rhythm and blues, performs, but not on a regular circuit. A product of the local Hebrew Israelite community, Son Rise pride themselves on playing "wholesome music without suggestive lyrics or movements".

In Hubert Smith's view there is an abun-

Entertainer Hubert Smith: "What we need here is a cultural centre."

sound or a set of strings and a guy turns a set of dials to reproduce that sound. This even applies to drums or trumpets. The end result is great, but is this music?"

When most working men his age have already retired, Hubert Smith demonstrates no such inclination. He spends a few days a week working to get local musicians on a better footing in the island's entertainment business, and constantly lobbies hoteliers to showcase island talent. If he could leave a legacy it would be simply this: "I would want to see more Bermudian musicians playing good music for locals and visitors alike – even if they only have half the fun I had."

Bermuda was settled by the early colonialists with the expectation of making money, preferably easy money. But as one bright scheme after another came to nothing and ruin stared everyone in the face, there were always two straws to cling to: the possibility of unearthing treasure or of slipping away for a spot of profitable piracy.

Hopes of finding treasure were not unreasonable. Spanish treasure ships returning from the New World passed right by Bermuda and, as the settlers knew only too well, ships regularly fell victim to the reefs. Treasure might even have been buried on the islands by pirates who were forever lurking around Bermuda with a view to seizing Spanish prizes. Behind the romance of buried treasure was the simple expedient that pirates taking up offers of amnesty to fight a war for King and Country, a potentially lucrative activity in its own right, needed a safe place to deposit their booty for the duration. Pirates who went down with their ships took with them the vital secret, the proverbial "X marks the spot".

The search for treasure began almost from the moment passengers and crew from the shipwrecked *Sea Venture* stepped ashore. One who chose to spend the rest of his life on the islands, Christopher Carter, turned down the offer of St David's Island in favour of the much smaller Cooper's Island because he believed it concealed a hoard. He spent years fruitlessly looking for it.

Bermuda's treasure, as it turned out, generally got no closer to shore than the reefs. Modern diving equipment has greatly facilitated the search. A local diver, Teddy Tucker, has produced a chart (on display in the Maritime Museum, with reproductions on sale locally) which pinpoints an astounding number of wrecks in local waters. Tucker himself hit the jackpot in 1955, bringing up a collection of Spanish gold bars and ornaments subsequently bought by the Bermuda government and displayed in the museum.

The prize piece in the Tucker Treasure was

a gold cross mounted with seven emeralds. As the collection was being laid out for Queen Elizabeth's royal opening of the museum in 1975, it was found that the cross had been stolen. What was supposed to be the cross was a plastic replica. The real one has never been recovered.

Scenting success: The "Adventurers" of the Somers Island Company who financed the settlement of Bermuda were as optimistic as the settlers themselves about a windfall from the sea. Their hopes soared with the finding

of a washed-up lump of ambergris, an evil-smelling substance produced in the stomach of a sick whale but nevertheless a priceless ingredient in the manufacture of scent. The discovery was not to be repeated, however, and their hopes turned to pearls. Richard Norwood, who had made a name for himself in England with the construction of a crude diving bell made out of a hogshead, was sent out in 1613 to look for them but drew a blank.

The clarity and relatively even temperature of the water around Bermuda – its incomparable cleanliness in the Atlantic is a scientific fact – was always a powerful inducement for underwater experimentation.

Preceding pages: sunken treasure? **Left**, a permanent shipwreck lies off Spanish Point. **Right**, Teddy Tucker, treasure retriever.

A Bermudian invented a "diving bell" at the beginning of the 17th century. It was little more than an ordinary barrel but it contained enough air to enable him to remain underwater for three-quarters of an hour.

Less intrepid Bermudians resorted to plucking their treasure off the reefs while it was still warm, so to speak. A Dutch ship which ran aground off Somerset in 1618 without sustaining serious damage was typical of how the system worked. Sympathetic islanders comforted the captain by saying that the ship could easily be freed in a day or two. The captain accepted their assurance and repaired to the village to relax after the ordeal. When he returned to his ship after the

rang hollow because some of the big names behind the Somers Island Company were themselves deeply, and not always discreetly, involved. In practice, a hair's breadth separated privateering, which was legal, and piracy, which wasn't. Privateers were licensed to seize ships belonging to the King's enemies (and it was virtually guaranteed that England would always be at war with someone or other) but were required to deliver their prizes intact so that the proceeds of ship and cargo could be split between the privateers and the tax collector.

Pirates were pirates because they skipped that particular formality and kept the lot for themselves. In Bermuda, there were always

agreed interval, it existed as nothing but a bare shell. He could hardly have been consoled by the suggestion that a second storm must have been responsible, nor by the fact that he was then stuck in Bermuda for a year before he could arrange a passage home.

The parishioners of St Ann's church, still standing near Gibbs Hill lighthouse, were by all accounts keen "wreckers". They are said to have interrupted a service with the news that a ship was in trouble. Tearing off his surplice, the priest led the charge down the hill.

Official policy with regard to islanders doing business with pirates or going into the business themselves was negative, but it

eager hands waiting in small bays to off-load interesting items of cargo at night before the ship put in an appearance at the customs shed in St George's the following morning.

Trading with pirates was forbidden because the company had a monopoly both on buying Bermuda's produce, especially tobacco, and in supplying the colony with goods from a company ship which called once or twice a year. Pirates might offer better prices both ways, but trading with them was a mixed blessing. Dealings with one pirate, Daniel Elfrith, master of *Treasurer*, invariably turned sour. A shipload of grain Elfrith delivered was infested with rats which in time were virtually to devastate the islands.

On another occasion, he persuaded the governor to give him 100,000 ears of corn, almost as much as the colony had been able to save, in exchange for "windie promises" and eight negroes. The promises in question were a slice of the profits of some piratical enterprise he had concocted. The corn was lost forever; the scheme flopped. "Probably nothing," a historian sighed, "during the first 20 years of the Colony stirred as much trouble as the *Treasurer*."

Bermuda was never a nest of pirates like the Bahamas, but it produced two pirates who were rated "first class" by their peers. John Bowen, "an educated fellow" who was

soon afterwards and he was left with no escape but to swim back to Madagascar, a distance of 12 miles (20 km). The locals seem to have received him with good grace, and he devoted the rest of his life to "presiding over his colony, settling disputes among native tribes, and directing a little traffic in slaves or an occasional trading voyage to Mauritius… until at last he fell a victim in a native squabble."

Falling victim in a native squabble was not the only danger. A Bermudian privateer crew captured by an American pirate were hoisted to the top of the mast and bounced on the deck; another luckless captive was "made to talk" by being tied to the bowspit

'MARK ANTONIE'
Wrecked 1777

BERMUDA

E II R

50c

probably a grandson of Richard Norwood, took 20 men ashore in Mauritius for a "hilarious" party that lasted six months. It killed him in the end – no disgrace here, although the priests would not allow him on holy ground ("a heretic", they said), and he was buried in the highway.

Nathaniel North, regarded as Bowen's equal, might seem to have blotted his copybook in Madagascar by capturing a local chief and ransoming him for $1,000. As bad luck would have it, his boat capsized

Left and <u>above</u>, treasure hunting is part of the island's history.

"with burning matches to his eyes and a loaded pistol at his mouth".

Such misfortunes apart, there were sufficient strokes of good fortune to keep Bermudians' faith in treasure and piracy alive. Thomas Tew set sail from Bermuda in 1691 and set a course for the Red Sea where he bagged an Arab vessel which netted the crew £3,000 each. He operated out of Madagascar until he had accumulated booty worth £100,000. Bermudians who had financed his expedition got their money back 14 times over and "Arabian gold showed its face on the island for a while, notwithstanding the efforts of its first recipients to be discreet."

One of the great dining mysteries of the island is that there is not a single restaurant that could rest on its laurels as serving an entirely Bermudian menu. Bermuda offers a pot-pourri of eating places, including Italian, Danish, Japanese and even Yugoslav. But to find those honest-to-goodness, rib-cleaving dishes such as peas 'n' rice, johnny cakes and paw-paw casserole the visitor is entering the realm of the endangered species, for these uniquely delicious dishes adopted by Bermudian cooks from West Indian influences are not readily available.

All-island spread: Dennis's Hideaway and the Black Horse Tavern on St David's Island serve up generous portions of turtle steak, mussel pie, fish and conch chowder and myriad seafood delicacies. But receiving a good recommendation for an all-island spread is as unlikely as being asked to take tea at Government House.

There are a few restaurants, however, which approximate this experience: the Green Lantern on Serpentine Road, Woody's in Somerset and the Checkmate Diner on Dundonald Street, Hamilton. These establishments are considered more of a saving than a source of the elusive local cuisine. For dining *sans* frills, meander through the back of town to the Ex-Artillerymen's Club (a haunt for Bermudians who served during the war years) on Victoria Street and discover Momma Stella's Kitchen.

Stella Smith, the proprietor, serves up goodly portions of local dishes, all of which can be washed down with some of her home-made rootbeer. If something stronger is required Stella suggests the club bar, where veterans regale anyone willing to listen with old war stories. Lunches are very inexpensive and be warned that one may well be enough for two people.

Another dining secret in the back-of-town area is the Angle Street Deli (on Angle Street, of course). Ed and Cora put out a varied Bermudian menu and take great pride

in their desserts which, along with the bread, are prepared daily on the premises. Everything tastes "like home cooking", the couple echo, almost in unison. Take-outs are available, or it's possible to sit down and eat with telephone repairmen and other members of the blue-collar brigade. A doggie bag may be required when finished.

On the corner of Reid and King Streets is Show Biz, a small restaurant with a musical motif and a menu of crab cakes, fish and curries. Its sister restaurant is the Conch

Shell, located in the Emporium Building on Front Street, where a striking, ebony-hued hostess greets, seats and treats each guest like a regular.

Many hotels and restaurants carry a selection of local dishes – usually fish. Succulent Bermuda lobster (when in season), garden-fresh vegetables, tangy citrus and fresh fruits are all part of the Bermudian fare. Their enemy is supply-and-demand, with local fishermen hard-pressed to provide for all hotel, restaurant and local tables. As a result, these foods are imported from the mainland when supplies diminish.

When ordering fish do specify the local

Preceding pages: island eating. <u>Left</u>, elegant service at the Lantana Colony Club. <u>Right</u>, home cooking from Ed at the Angle Street Deli.

catch of the day, which may be red snapper, red hind, yellowtail, wahoo, rockfish – the choices are endless. Don't, for goodness sake, pass up the fish chowder and don't be put off by the knowledge that this dish actually uses as its base rejected fish heads. When the post-filleted fish is thrown into a pot with spices and slow-boiled for at least two days (for that authentic Bermuda taste), the result is a very tangy blend. Add black rum and local sherry peppers and your taste buds will thank you for the experience.

Sunday breakfast: Any native cook will readily attest to the fact that the traditional Bermuda Sunday morning breakfast of cod fish and potatoes is well worth whatever it

dous, potentially alcoholic, thirst. It might be wise to call a taxi for the trip back to the hotel.

For a really exotic recipe, try the cod (soaked overnight in cold water) sautéed in onions, garlic, green and red peppers, fresh tomatoes and thyme. Let this languish for a while in heated olive oil until it becomes rather like a loose casserole, then serve with buttered new potatoes (the local variety, if in season), hard-boiled eggs, sliced avocado pear and ripe bananas and washed down with strident belts of "dark and stormies" – black rum and ginger beer. This is a native feast.

Bermudians favour fish which is simply prepared and tend to avoid any that is smothered in sauce, as sauce can often hide a

takes to get the real thing. Restaurants such as MacWilliams on Pitts Bay Road and the Paraquet in Paget, to name a few, serve this speciality every Sunday morning. But, if possible, wangle an invitation to have breakfast in a Bermudian home.

Be aware that there is a different recipe for almost every adult Bermudian, but the one favoured by those who can trace their ancestry back to the English colonists tends to be boiled cod served with olive oil and egg sauce and garnished with tomato and onion sauce. This calls for a different treatment of the cod, hence the result is chewy with a residual salt content that creates a tremen-

multitude of sins of the grill. Fresh fish with squeezed locally grown lime or lemon and a touch of butter is delicious. Imported fish need not be frowned upon, since the secret is in the preparation, not necessarily the length of time since it was caught. With imported vegetables, keep in mind that asparagus grown in up-state New York may reach local tables in less time by jet aircraft than by a lumbering lorry making stops en route to a Manhattan restaurant.

One native dish which stands out from many is cassava pie, which Bermudians include in Christmas dinners. Made from the root of a cassava, it is grated, ground, squeezed, dried and then baked (with chicken or port) to a golden brown. Its cousin, the farine pie, is another Christmas delicacy, and can be found in speciality stores throughout the year. Bermudians eat heartily at Christmas. A typical Yuletide dinner would consist of turkey, ham, mashed potatoes, pumpkin, sweet potatoes, peas 'n' rice, cassava pie, Christmas pudding for dessert – and lots to drink.

As for dining out at night, Bermudians take the view that there is a restaurant for most tastes and pockets. Tom Moore's Tavern has a lineage dating back to the 1600s and, together with the Waterlot Inn (300 years old) and Fourways (*circa* 1727), repre-

seafood house. For white-gloved service, try the nautical, hushed atmosphere of the Newport Room located in the Southampton Princess Hotel. There are no windows and the theme highlights famous vessels that took part in the historic Newport to Bermuda yacht races.

Variety of venues: Fancy going Italian? There are several Italian restaurants in Bermuda. The Little Venice on Bermudiana Road, the Tavern on the Green in the Botanical Gardens and Il Palio in Somerset are favourites. For charm and elegance, locate the Margaret Rose in the St George's Club in the old town and Once Upon A Table, a former Bermudian home decorated in Victoriana –

sents a formidable challenge in the realm of *haute cuisine*. For informal lunch or dinner try the Lobster Pot, with a nautical decor and great fish chowder. The Swizzle Inn, a stone's throw from the airport, is very casual. In the old days clientele were coaxed to "fly on a swizzle", the house concoction consisting of a variety of rums and fruit juices.

For an English pub atmosphere, try the Hog Penny on Burnaby Hill, featuring typical pub fare and the occasional curried lamb. Upstairs is the Fishermen's Reef, another

both worth exploring. For small dinner parties to impress guests, it's possible to call the proprietor Lew Harvey, and tell him 36 hours in advance that you want all-Bermudian fare. He may surprise with fresh baked Bermuda fish, fresh vegetables (the hot, spicy peppers in the fish chowder will come straight from his garden) and a wonderful dessert, syllabub. Made of guava and sherry and served in small wine glasses because it is quite sweet, syllabub is the perfect way to end a meal in Bermuda.

With this variety in dining, Bermudians – and their guests – need never go back to romancing the stove.

<u>Left</u>, casual dining often involves fish chowder. <u>Above</u>, Fourways dates from around 1727.

Front Street — Hamilton — Bermud

On a certain Sunday in January, in the first grey morning light, two container ships lie in wait at Five Fathom Hole: the 320-ft (98-metre) *Oleander* just arrived from her base at Port Elizabeth, New Jersey, and the *Somers Isle*, a container ship out of Fernandina Beach, Florida. On the horizon is the box-like shape of the Japanese car ship *Australian Highway*, just in from the Bahamas.

The two container ships are riding a little higher in the water than usual. January is a slow business month. Local businesses are not ordering the heavy volumes of consumer goods they did in the pre-Christmas period. *Oleander*, with a capacity to carry 189 containers, has just 138, while *Somers Isle* carries 44 with room for another 76. Business will pick up in mid-February when Bermuda's hotels and merchants begin building stocks for the start of the busy tourist season.

At 4.30 a.m. senior pilot Brian Richardson gets out of bed in his St George's home. Half an hour later, he and two other pilots board the pilot-rescue boat *St David* in preparation for the trip to board the ships at about 6.30 a.m. There is a steady light breeze out of the north and a light chop on the water.

The skippers of *Oleander* and *Somers Isle* are weekly callers to the island and know its channel system as well as anybody. For Mr Richardson, who boards the *Oleander*, his presence is simply to keep an eye on things and to satisfy requirements beyond navigational assistance.

Insurance scheme: "I'm there for insurance," he says with a chuckle. "If the captain (of the ship) comes in and strikes the docks and puts a hole in the ship and I'm not aboard, then that boy's going to fly home on his own. If he doesn't have a pilot, the insurance company wouldn't even consider the case. That goes for any ship."

Mr Richardson, however, knows his assistance can be essential to the safe berthing of ships. "There are lots of problems in these seas: heavy rain, poor visibility, heavy wind,

narrow channels. I'm here to help out."

The harbourmaster, Ian Clarke, says the inshore waters can be a difficult passage for ships. "I think these are among the most fascinating passages and channels in the world. These are treacherous waters. There is not much room between the reefs, and little room for mistakes. If there is engine break-down in the channels, you can be in big trouble. There is also no mud bottom around here. If you go aground you won't be able to wait for high tide and lift off scot-free. The bottom here will tear the bottom off a ship. But we've been fortunate. We don't have very many accidents here: touch wood."

With the pilots aboard, the ships move out of Five Fathom Hole in single file. The trip to Hamilton Harbour will take about 90 minutes. The ships immediately turn right along The Narrows, a 38-ft (12-metre) channel cut through coral beds. On the left is St Catherine's beach where *Sea Venture's* exhausted crew stumbled ashore so long ago. Beside it are the massive stone walls of St Catherine's fort which at one time welcomed cruise ship visitors with a shot from its formidable cannons. Just beyond the fort, the ships turn left and head down the long South Channel running the length of Bermuda's north shore. They make a rather stately procession, steaming along one after another in the early morning light.

About 10 miles down, the north shore ends, giving way to a large inland body of water, the Great Sound. It is here that the full spread of Bermuda can best be seen. The Dockyard is over the right shoulder of each skipper as he turns his ship into the Sound. At the far end of the Sound lies Gibbs Hill lighthouse. Skippers say the night-time glow from its rotating lamp can be seen on the horizon 50 miles (80 km) away.

Oleander leads the way along Dundonald Channel and then bears left into an area of small islands. The ships pass through narrow Two Rock Passage and continue on into the enclosed Hamilton Harbour in the geographical heart of the island. It's a clean, quaint-looking harbour.

The three ships steam quietly to the docks at the far end. There, as they berth one after the other – a process that will take up to an hour – they are each met by a gang of dockworkers or stevedores to unload them.

When the stevedores swing into action, it's easy to see the docks as the hub of Bermuda life. Cranes huff and lift containers from the hull of ships on to the docks. Strange-looking trucks called toploaders snort, then pick them up and lug them to storage areas. Trucks arrive. Toploaders load the trucks up solidly and the containers are on their way to the importers. "It all starts here," says docks manager Jack Robinson, looking out of his office window at the activity. "93 percent of anything you use on the island comes over the docks of Hamilton."

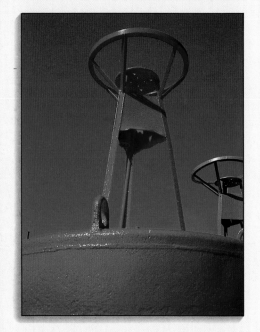

Bermuda, it should be noted, is an import society, and there is no better place to observe that fact than at the docks. There is no local manufacturing and only 600 acres (245 hectares) on the island is under cultivation. Almost everything, apart from locally produced milk, eggs and vegetables, is brought in from abroad. The container ships are the island's lifelines and the docks its great clearing house.

In a recent year, the docks handled 137,290 tons of general cargo. That compares with just 7,628 tons of air freight – excluding mail – handled at the Civil Air Terminal. Recent import statistics show

heavy reliance on the United States: 95.6 percent of all goods passing through the docks came from America. The remainder arrived from Europe, Canada and Japan.

With all that business, one might think the docks messy and disorganised. But it is striking how clean and efficient they look. It's a result, said Jack Robinson, of the containerisation of the cargo business. "Containers revolutionised the port function. Containers changed it from a labour-intensive business to a machine industry. In 1947, when I first came here, we were still using rope slings and men pushing trucks to get cargo into ships. Now it's all done by machine.

"Containers also prompted a complete upgrade of the docks labour scene. It used to be demeaning labour. Men were hired on a casual basis. They only worked when the ships were in. Bermuda was one of the first ports in the world to regularly employ dock workers – "decasualisation", they called it. Before it, a gang of men was 21 to 22 strong. When the old *Oleander* came in, the gang could move about 7 tons of cargo an hour. Now, with containers, more than 35 tons can be moved each gang hour."

In the old days, the docks were congested with traffic. There were no warehouses. Importers used transit sheds to sort their goods. People would come to the sheds to take advantage of goods sold at "ex-dock" prices. "It was a problem," Mr Robinson said. "Today, it's satisfying to walk along the docks and see that at least the confusion that I found when I first came ashore has been turned into organised confusion."

One of the big reasons for less chaos is that few containers are stripped of their cargo on the docks. Of the 15,034 containers disembarked in the past year, 11,811 were put directly on to the backs of trucks for delivery to grocery stores or general importers who personally strip them for delivery to their customers. Containers remaining on the docks are stripped and their cargo is stored in one of two sheds for pick-up.

"We have to be careful the right person gets the right item," said shed manager Robert Howse, standing in Number 7 Shed amid boxes of detergents, liquor and computers. We have to make sure everyone gets what they want and is satisfied. Sometimes, when the shed is busy and shipping is on schedule, I feel like the ball in a ping-pong game. You can have a lot of big orders sitting around and the prospect of more coming in. You've got to get on the telephone to get things out. Importers have only five days to pick up their stuff. Otherwise, we impose de-moorage charges. The whole shed is in demand when shipping is on schedule."

Outside, the three ships are tied up. There is a lot of movement about each one. The first 11 cars are driving off the ramp of the *Australian Highway*. Two big cranes alongside the *Oleander* and *Somers Isle* are swinging their loads on to the docks. Stevedores are atop both ships gesturing the crane operators to swing over for the next pick-up.

Just in front of the *Somers Isle* are two

the masts back on them and then the owners will take them from there." He is pleased.

Jack Robinson leans over a large desk with a scale model of the waterfront. He is using this Sunday morning to determine where the cruise ships will berth when they begin arriving in mid-April. He's made cardboard scale models of each ship.

"This is probably the only business where you get to play with paper dolls," he laughs. "The ships that they say are specially built for Bermuda never are. I make the models to determine where the ships can be serviced best. We have to figure out things like how to best position the ship to get crews and passengers off, how we can collect the sewage.

small yachts: a 30-ft (9-metre) boat called *Sleepwalker* and a sailboat called *Special Shoes*. Importer Skipper Tatum is standing beside them. He owns Darrell's Marine Ltd, on Harbour Road just across the water. "This is a pocket sailboat," he says of *Special Shoes*. "It was custom-built. I think there are just three of them with such beautiful lines. I found this one in Florida. Its design was taken from a small boat that sailed the oceans for eight years. The two boats will go to our boatyard at Mills Creek tomorrow. We'll put

Once they've been here, we'll iron out all the problems. It takes just one visit."

Mr Robinson looks out of his window at the docks buzzing with activity. *Australian Highway* has finished disembarking its order of cars. The cranes and toploaders are busy. Things are going smoothly. "In our business, we proceed from crisis to crisis with as much good humour as possible. That's typical of dock work. We try to avoid being overtaken by events. The good thing about our industry here is that most of us have grown up together. We know each other. It's one of the few industries left where people's words are as good as their bond."

Left, colourful buoys. **Above**, a young man fishes for a cruise ship.

Bermuda had enjoyed at least 70 million years of intensely private evolution when its tiny world was turned upside down. The harbingers were a boatload of 16th-century pigs deposited on the islands by Spanish sailors with the idea that they would multiply as a source of fresh meat on future voyages to and from the newly discovered Americas. The pigs, or hogs, multiplied so efficiently that in no time their paths were as wide as roads, the palmetto palms on either side deeply scarred by the pleasure derived from scratching their backs.

Privacy lost, an ecology which had so patiently developed its own checks and balances was defenceless. One of the notable victims was the cahow, a sea bird no larger than a pigeon but with a three-foot wingspan and a large, curved beak with saw teeth. The cahow might have survived the pigs, which dug up its burrowed eggs, but its fate was compounded by men, who ate the birds in prodigious quantities, and sealed by voracious rats. Within 30 years of the arrival of the rats, the cahow was presumed to be extinct and was forgotten, an immense evolutionary process terminated as abruptly and ingloriously as that of the dodo on Mauritius.

Environmental triumph: The rest of endemic Bermudian wildlife fared no better, and in the bat of an evolutionary eyelid, the face of the islands changed beyond recognition. The manner in which the cahow somehow clung on unseen to emerge as recently as 1951 – an absence of more than three centuries – as a defiant symbol of pristine Bermuda would not be out of place as the climax of some rousing environmental anthem.

The background to this drama (to summarise other parts of this book) was a volcanic rumbling on the floor of the Atlantic Ocean where it is at its deepest, about 3 miles (5 km). The eruption propelled a finger of rock to the surface at a point where the water was just warm enough to sustain the growth of coral. Life, such as it was, depended on the flotsam of the Gulf Stream.

Migratory land birds blown off course

during what would normally have been non-stop flight landed gratefully on this unexpected refuge off the American coast. These intruders left their mark with parasites and droppings, but in every other respect Bermuda was left to its own devices. It somehow acquired a resident lizard, the skink, which shared its domain only with nomadic sea birds when they were on the nest. Bermuda was never touched by the inter-continental migrations of men; none spilled over as they did to the Caribbean islands in the south.

It was an early, volunteer settler who was inspired to establish a pig colony in mid-Atlantic. The pigs were prospering when Captain Diego Ramirez landed in 1603 and noticed the roads they had made. The islands were covered with cedar, palmetto palms and other evergreens, he wrote. There was underbrush but very little grass. If there were any flowers, he did not mention them. He applauded the absence of mosquitoes but complained about flies. Ramirez noted a number of sparrow hawks and herons but was impressed most of all by wild birds reminiscent of the crows he had recently seen in Havana.

Preceding pages: harvesting Easter lilies. Left, palms. Right, the elusive cahow.

"When we landed," he wrote, "they came to us, perched on our heads, uttering a multitudinous chorus of cries." They burrowed in the headlands at water level, he said, emerging at night to feed in a tremendous cacophony which terrified his crew. He described the birds in detail, so there is no doubt they were cahows.

His crew gathered their wits to discover that the birds were really harmless, not the diabolical creatures which had persuaded their predecessors to call Bermuda the Isle of Devils. "The birds were so plentiful that 4,000 could be taken in a single bag. The men relished them enough to eat them all the time, and when we left we brought away more than

"faster than they could be killed". Henry C. Wilkinson, Bermuda's outstanding historian, notes drily that "these silly birds were unable to learn the ways of man and soon succumbed".

The last straw was the invasion of rats contained in a shipload of maize supplied by a pirate. As soon as they had devastated one island, they swam en masse to the next. The cahow, we now know, retreated to the safety of rocky islets, but there was insufficient soil in which to burrow. They tried nesting in natural crevices, but that put them in unequal competition with the long-tail, another sea bird, which drove them out to rule the roost.

The settlers were not as thoughtlessly

1,000 well dried and salted for the voyage."

The cahow startled other visitors until they, too, realised that the birds were just being friendly and curious. "Our men found a prettie way to take them," wrote William Strachey, chronicler of the Jamestown settlers shipwrecked on Bermuda five years after Ramirez's visit, "which was by hollowing and laughing. With the noyse thereof, the birds would come flocking and settle upon the very arms of him that so cryed: by which our men would weigh them and which weighest heaviest they tooke, twentie dozen in two hours." Bermuda's first settlers dined happily on cahows which they could catch

destructive as might be imagined. Setting fire to the vegetation, twice, was a desperate measure to contain the rats; the sacrifice of so much valuable cedar was not an easy decision. Daniel Tucker, the governor who ordered the burning, actually tried to safeguard the cahow by decree, and one of his successors introduced formal protection for the island's many turtles. Men were as often as not struggling for survival themselves in the early days, and their needs in the form of edible and cash crops took precedence over any other consideration.

Bermuda's outstandingly varied and lush vegetation as it exists today is a tribute to the settlers' attempts to make amends. Driving along any road is to unravel a chain of bright flowers and berries in hedgerows, tropical hibiscus and dusty pink oleander, virtually all imports which subsequently went wild. The fragrance in the air in spring is from citrus blossom and freesias, the latter a member of the lily family with white, purple and yellow blossoms.

The Bermuda Easter lily has a large white flower much like a trumpet and was until recently Bermuda's major, and at times only, export. Although the Easter lily enjoyed the fame, the island's national flower is actually the tiny, lavender-blue Bermudiana, which grows wild among the freesias.

and rare. They ought to be treated with the greatest consideration.

The whole of Bermuda has now taken on the appearance of a botanical garden. The official Botanical Gardens in Paget are the logical starting point for interested visitors, who would also enjoy the flora of Par-la-Ville Park in the centre of Hamilton, Fort Hamilton on the outskirts, the premier's official residence, Camden House, and Walsingham in Hamilton Parish. Bermudians have created many superb private gardens; these are not readily accessible but some may be glimpsed from the pleasant Railway Trail.

Cedars which survived Governor

The flora on a wild hillside include fiddlewood, allspice, Brazil pepper and Surinam cherry. The sage bush, also known as *lantana*, adds its pretty, multi-coloured flower; the morning glory its blue, bell-shaped flower. Examples of coastal flora are to be found among the dunes above Warwick Long Bay and Horseshoe Bay: the bay bean, fennel, a seaside morning glory with a distinctive heart-shaped leaf, golden rod, sea ox-eye, bay lavender, buttonwood and seaside evening primrose. The inland area has caves filled with ferns which are endemic

Tucker's torch and the demands of Bermuda's later ship-building industry were blighted once more by a scale insect epidemic in the 1940s. While the cedar struggles to regain its regal position among Bermuda's flora, the little skink lizard hangs on tenaciously to its illustrious status as the only native creature. It leads a reclusive existence in quarries and cliff faces, reluctant to show its face unless tempted by a pungent bait, preferably tinned tuna fish.

The skink lost its monopoly to the pigs and later domestic animals, the most celebrated being a dog which was travelling with the ill-fated Jamestown settlers of 1609. This dog

Left and **above**, not-so-wild life.

has a documented place in history: as an expert hog-catcher (it is depicted in full cry on Sir George Somers' map), as a companion to the "three kings", and as a participant in a brawl over the fabulous ambergris. In the ensuing confusion, the dog bit the wrong party, its master.

Less has been written about later dogs than Bermuda's frogs, in particular the whistling frog imported from the West Indies in the 19th century and its deep-throated cousin, the giant toad (*Bufo marinas*), a native of the same islands which was brought in to deal with cockroaches. The little frog, no bigger than a thumb-nail, "whistles" mightily by rubbing its legs together and is often mis-

however, is on the visitors, as many as 200 unpredictable species every year.

"We lie under a major fly way," says Dr Wingate. Bermuda is on the regular migration route of about 60 species. They would not normally stop in Bermuda but will seek temporary refuge if the weather is bad. Other species will have drifted off course. "An exciting place," he says, "because you never know what will turn up next. Every year we get vagrants from Europe and Asia." Some arrivals are hard to believe – the Siberian fly catcher, for example, "from the opposite side of the planet". The comings and goings take place all year long bar the summer.

Dr Wingate was made a Member of the

taken for a bird. The toads greet heavy rainfall with a lusty chorus and often exercise on roads on cool nights.

Dominant wildlife: The dominant aspect of Bermuda's wildlife throughout, however, has been the birds. With the demise of the cahow and the exception of the longtail, Bermuda's resident bird population is, even to its great champion, the distinguished ornithologist Dr David Wingate, "poor and undramatic". He makes certain allowances for the European goldfinch and kiskadee fly catcher, a small blue bird which seems to have formed an interest in golf, or at least golf courses. The focus of birdwatchers,

British Empire in 1975 and soon afterwards was awarded the Order of the Golden Ark, the equivalent of a knighthood, by Prince Bernhard of the Netherlands. These honours were the culmination of dramatic developments, the first hint of which occurred on 22 February 1906 when Louis Mowbray, a Bermudian naturalist, found an unusual bird in a nest in rocks in Castle Harbour. He thought it was some kind of petrel but sent it off, preserved, to the American Museum of Natural History for identification. Comparison with bones found in caves opened up the possibility that it was a cahow.

In 1935 a young bird collided with St

David's lighthouse; 10 years later, a similar bird was washed up on Cooper's Island. They fitted the description of cahows but were dead. The prospects of finding one alive looked unpromising because of the upheaval caused by the construction of the wartime US Navy base and airport where the cahow, according to historical references, had traditionally nested.

Although still a schoolboy, Dr Wingate was invited to join a search by Mowbray's son, "Louis S.", and Dr Robert Cushman Murphy. He describes a moment after painstaking work, usually at night, among islets and rocks. Dr Murphy had spotted something deep in a nesting crevice. He lowered

island for the cahow and build artificial nest sites with baffles which would keep out the longtails. The government declared Nonsuch Island a cahow sanctuary.

The process was nevertheless agonisingly slow: cahows take 8 to 10 years to reach breeding age and then produce just one egg a year, only half of which hatch. In 1965, Wingate became aware of another threat. "There were new and ominous signs that the breeding success was declining even further. After long and tedious research the problem was identified as DDT poison." The cahow was getting enough in its food chain to weaken the egg shells and make them prone to breakages in the nest.

a noose and gingerly lifted the bird out. He held it up to the light and drew in his breath: "By Gad, the cahow!"

Wingate completed his studies and returned to lead a full-scale conservation programme. It took 10 years to determine that there were 18 pairs alive. The survivors were living precariously on rocks in the natural crevices from which they might be driven at any time by the more numerous longtails. The urgent remedy was to secure a larger

Left and above, although the national flower is the lavender-blue Bermudiana, the entire island looks like a garden.

The ban on DDT in the United States pulled the cahow yet again back from the brink, only for danger to reappear in 1987 in the wholly unpredictable form of a snow owl which had wandered from its normal Arctic home. The owl killed five young birds, but by then the population was large and resilient enough to absorb the loss.

By 1990 the population had reached an encouraging 48 pairs. It is, sadly, not yet possible to arrange visits to the nesting sites. The cahow's survival will depend for some time yet on protecting the privacy which was disrupted, in the first instance, by the snout of a peckish pig.

THE BERMUDA TRIANGLE

The Bermuda Triangle is remarkably in-grained in the popular imagination for some-thing which became common currency only in 1964. In February of that year, *Argosy* magazine carried an article by a Vincent Gaddis about the inexplicable disappear-ance of a sinister number of ships and aircraft in a triangle of the Atlantic between Ber-muda, Florida and Puerto Rico. The phe-nomenon of fully manned ships vanishing in perfectly calm weather had been well known to mariners since Christopher Columbus, he said, but it was kept a dark secret among themselves.

Paranormal pantheon: Gaddis's revelations were taken up by other writers, and the rapidly growing snowball tossed off more magazine articles, books and films. In no time the Bermuda Triangle had joined the Loch Ness monster, the *Marie Celeste* and UFOs in the pantheon of the paranormal. The follow-ups borrowed freely from Gaddis's original article without looking too critically at his factual sources; the cult of the Triangle gaining credibility from reports that the US Navy, Coast Guard, Lloyd's of London and "top scientists" had investigated the matter and confessed to being com-pletely baffled. Several sleuths latched on to the discovery that an area around Bermuda had long been noted in Royal Navy charts as one of magnetic aberration.

One of the staple stories in the dossier was the case of the *Ellen Austin*. Gaddis had mentioned the ship, possibly as the result of coming across it in *The Stargazer Talks*, a book by Rupert Gould, which had been published in 1914 without attracting the same sort of attention as the more recent *Argosy* magazine article.

According to Gould, *Ellen Austin* was a British ship which in 1881 encountered an abandoned but still seaworthy ship "in mid-Atlantic". Some of the crew, he wrote, boarded the ship with orders to make for St John's, Newfoundland. The two ships parted "in foggy weather" but met up again a few days later. To the consternation of the

Preceding pages: a spooky view. **Right**, a ship in distress.

British crew, the shipmates who had transferred to the *Ellen Austin* had also vanished.

Gould did not say how or where he learned of this strange episode, nor did other writers who incorporated it in their work. The story was modified and embellished with almost every re-telling. The location was apt to wander from "mid-Atlantic" to "West of the Azores"; some versions had signs of a struggle on the mystery ship, others had a second rescue crew put on board – only to vanish as well.

By the time a certain Richard Winer got round to writing *The Devil's Triangle* in 1974, the captain of the *Ellen Austin* had acquired a name, "Captain Baker", and the

into a greenish tunnel in the middle of a cloud. All his instruments malfunctioned as he went "weightless". The startled pilot managed to land safely at Palm Beach and did some calculations based on elapsed flying time, distance covered and so forth. His figures indicated that his aircraft, with a normal top speed of 195 mph (250 kph), must have been travelling at an astounding 1,180 mph (1,900 kph). The crew and passengers of an Eastern Airlines flight felt a powerful jolt which caused all their watches to stop, someone else noted.

Perhaps the most famous mystery concerning aircraft is said to have occurred on 5 December 1945. Five US Navy Avenger

author a considerable amount of closely observed detail. Baker "looked back over his right shoulder" and waved a Colt revolver while urging his men aboard the derelict ship. At the height of the action, Captain Baker accidentally steps on a thumb-sized cockroach, not that it makes the slightest bit of difference to him or what happens next. When the mystery ship eventually disappears after accounting for two prize crews, it is engulfed in a watery haze.

These alarming goings-on were brought up to date with tales about the fate of aircraft. Bruce Gernon, an American pilot flying a light plane, was reported as being sucked

torpedo bombers took off from Fort Lauderdale on a routine patrol. The Flight Leader radioed that he was lost before communication with the ground ended. A rescue plane was sent up to look for them – and disappeared. A five-day search for the six missing aircraft produced nothing.

It was inevitable that Bermuda Triangle experts would start coming up with explanatory theories. The historically minded inclined towards the lost continent of Atlantis whose population, 10,000 years ago, developed a form of energy so powerful that they blew themselves to bits. The strange forces at work in the Triangle were the result of the

Atlantis generators – whatever form they took – relentlessly churning out energy. A clairvoyant named Edgar Cayce confidently predicted that Atlantis would resurface in either 1968 or 1969.

Charles Berlitz, pronouncing with the authority of one who is "fluent in 27 languages", wrote the best-selling *The Bermuda Triangle*, in which he picked up where Einstein left off in developing the theory of relativity. He speculated about a time anomaly in the Triangle "as if time at certain moments could project individuals from the present into the past or otherwise bend the continuum of time in a manner blending the past and the present – and perhaps the future as well." If the forces of gravity, energy and mass in a ship or aircraft met their equal in anti-matter – whoosh, they would vanish.

Perhaps because he found all this a bit difficult, the pastor of the Cathedral of Life Church in Torrance, California, the Rev. George Johnson, teamed up with Don Tanner, the religion editor of *The Daily Breeze*, to study the Book of Revelations, which they believed might provide a simple answer. The book, they pointed out, "tells where the redeemed go after death and shows the significance of water in the kingdom of God in contrast to its present role as a destructive and captive force."

Entrance to Hell: After painstaking research, they held up their verdict: the Bermuda Triangle was one of two entrances to Hell, the other being the Devil's Sea between Japan and the Philippines.

Larry Kusche, a librarian at Arizona State University, turned not to the Bible but to naval records and newspapers to track down as much as was reliably known about incidents attributed to the Triangle. In contemporary records which he thought would certainly have carried full reports of the *Ellen Austin* mystery, he could find no mention. Disappearances attributed to the Triangle might actually have taken place, he found, as far away as the Pacific, Ireland, Africa or not at all. He dug out a transcript of the radio traffic between ground control and the doomed US Navy torpedo bombers and concluded that, hopelessly lost, they had flown in formation for four hours until their

fuel ran out. The plane sent to look for them evidently exploded in an accidental fire 23 minutes after take-off.

Kusche's list of verifiable facts at the end of the day should have put a wet blanket over the Bermuda Triangle for all time. The percentage of aircraft and ships lost in the busy Triangle was no higher than anywhere else; the Triangle was only exceptional in the number of reported incidents which, on investigation, proved to be false. When ships or aircraft were lost, the weather was invariably bad.

His summary left no doubt about his position. "The Triangle is the ultimate example of the paranormal, pseudo-science, fictional

science and media run amok. It is the epitome of false reporting; deletion of pertinent information; twisted values among writers, publishers and the media; mangling of scientific principles; and the often deliberate deception of a trusting public." He was content to let it pass as a "manufactured mystery" but could not bring himself to condemn others who called it "an outright fraud or a rip-off".

However, there are members of the "trusting public" who still court the mystery of the Bermuda Triangle, just as there are those who will continue to believe, against all odds, in Father Christmas.

Left, there are no direct flights between Bermuda and Miami. Coincidence? **Right**, a rum business.

S. S. "Carribeau", Nearing Bermuda.

Mark Twain did it. So did Queen Victoria's daughter, Princess Louise. And US President Woodrow Wilson, not to mention Eleanor Roosevelt and literary types like Rudyard Kipling, Sinclair Lewis, Noel Coward and James Thurber.

What did they have in common? They wintered in Bermuda – despite the fact that today Bermuda is known primarily as a summer resort. In the days before the island became pre-eminently known for its pristine, eggshell-pink beaches and water sports, summer was the "off season", when hotels shuttered up and visitors headed home like the swallows to Capistrano.

Year-round resort: All that changed after World War II, when Bermuda evolved into a year-round resort with an emphasis on the spring and summer seasons. Now visitors, (holiday-makers are invariably known as "visitors" in genteel Bermuda, rather than as the crassly commercial "tourists"), are rediscovering winter in Bermuda, and, like that earlier genre of winter traveller, finding that Bermuda is more than sun, sand and sea.

In truth, winter in this tiny country tucked away in "the ocean's bosom, unespied", as 17th-century English poet Andrew Marvell put it, is more like spring in other parts of the world. Visitors are today invited to come to Bermuda for "our springtime festival", or "our extended season", which knowledgeable travellers realise is packed with complimentary attractions and activities, not to mention significantly reduced hotel and restaurant prices and a delightful lack of crowds and queues.

The impressive sight of the first longtail bird catching an upper air current off the South Shore beaches is, to those Bermudians who catch a glimpse of this national symbol, the heart-warming signal that spring is at hand. And more often than not, the sighting is in January. Spring arrives early in this, the world's second most isolated archipelago (and that's official – the only other place

further from any other scrap of land is St Helena, which undoubtedly explains why the British sent Napoleon into exile there).

Yet due west, the United States eastern seaboard is still in the snowy grip of winter. In Mark Twain's day, the author had to make the tortuous winter journey to Bermuda through storm-tossed seas which pitched the puny passenger ships about like matchsticks, moving Twain to comment acidly that "Bermuda may be Paradise but you have to go through Hell to get there." Today "getting

there" is a more civilised affair, thanks to the advent of stabilisers, which provide a smoother journey.

The primary joy of winter in Bermuda is that it is another way of life from the hectic summer season. The tempo eases back to half-time and the days are filled with languid walks on deserted beaches or inland nature trails. There's browsing through the unhurried streets of villages like St George's and Somerset. And evenings lingering over succulent Bermuda lobster (a large, warm-water crayfish that by law can only be caught and served between September and March), watching the Bermuda Regiment band re-

Preceding pages: Bermuda's official ceremonies often take place out of season. <u>Left</u>, the island was a winter haven in the 1930s. <u>Right</u>, off the island for the off season.

splendent in scarlet and gold uniforms, re-create the martial splendour of the Old Empire under floodlights on Hamilton's Front Street, or simply warming the feet in front of a toasty log fire while enjoying that distinctively Bermudian hotel experience, the cottage colony.

Warm weather buffer: Only a geographical and geological accident makes any of this possible. Bermuda stands alone as the world's northernmost coral island group, on the same latitude as Savannah, Georgia, but on average 10 degrees warmer, thanks to the benevolent intervention of the Gulf Stream, which surges northeastward between the southeastern US coast and Bermuda, acting

as an effective buffer between these sub-tropical islands and the frigid North American continent.

Day-time winter temperatures can reach as high as 23° C (73° F), with the average around 20° C (68° F). Golf and tennis addicts can exhilaratingly perfect their games without running the risk of the heat prostration of hotter climes.

The lanes and byways of the Bermudian countryside are already ablaze with flowers, and that choicest of Bermuda fruits, the loquat, is at its prime in February, when a golden hoard loads down countless trees. The ever-so-slightly tart loquat is an instant

roadside feast, one which Bermudians delight in transforming into jams, chutneys and a warming liqueur called Bermuda Gold.

Nature walks are at their best in winter, whether tramping the old Bermuda Railway, meandering through the backwoods and between sawn-away coral limestone cliffs, or on undeveloped country roads like Orange Valley in Devonshire, Greenfield Lane in Somerset, the western stretch of Spice Hill Road in Warwick or Ferry Reach Road in St George's. Many of the more "countrified" roads are exploratory pathways to all-weather attractions, ranging from antique-crammed mansions and museums to enormous subterranean caverns and formidable fortresses that once made these islands the "Gibraltar of the West".

Richard Hansen, associate director of public affairs at the White House, Washington D.C., put it rather well when he said: "In winter Bermuda appears to be a dream come true for the bird-watcher – observing the flight of the longtail from the cliff above Spanish Rock is worth nearly the cost of the trip, even for a non-bird-watcher like me – as well as the plant lover, those interested in the study of marine life, and the artist. The opportunities for enjoyment in these areas seem endless, and do not require summer temperatures. In fact, spring-like weather is more desirable." The Spanish Rock that Hansen talks about is the oldest surviving physical evidence of human presence in Bermuda. Spanish Rock is now part of the Spittal Pond Nature Sanctuary, one of a number of charming preserves protected by the Bermuda National Trust.

Just minutes away, up another wooded hillside, is Verdmont, a fine Georgian mansion typical of the museum homes that provide such pleasant explorations in winter. Another National Trust property, Verdmont's interior walls and typically Bermudian tray ceilings are sheathed in pickled pine and its wide, pegged floorboards are designed like those of a ship's deck. Indeed, much of the building done in Bermuda in centuries past was by trained shipwrights – witness, for example, the beauty of Devonshire Old Church.

Left, Bermudians wear winter clothes while visitors wear summer clothes. **Right**, skirling ceremony during the winter season.

Verdmont is notable for its large-hearthed kitchen, where many a Bermudian delicacy of old was cooked up. Some are still features of winter and spring holidays in Bermuda, notably the cassava pie, dating from earliest settler days, when it was created from ground cassava root flour, wild bird eggs and the pork from the wild hogs the Spanish left behind. Today it is Bermudians' traditional Christmas and Easter dish.

There are other peculiarly Bermudian rites that are linked with these and other off-season holidays, like the Gombey dancers on New Year's Day.

Good Friday is Bermuda's national kite-flying day, when thousands of colourful with fireworks, these are now banned – something that does not apply to the serving of the Bermuda sweet potato pudding, traditionally eaten for dinner at this same time of year, November.

These customs tend to highlight the increased folksiness of the island in winter, when Bermudians, always friendly and solicitous (start a conversation at your peril without declaring "Good Morning!" or "Good Afternoon!"), have time to be especially out-going.

High-pressure hosts: Indeed, many Bermudians believe the present-day decline in the number of winter visitors is necessary for a "recharging of batteries" after having played

creations of every size and shape take to the air. Most notable is the classic Bermuda kite, with a long mast and buzzers, which purists make in part from wild Bermuda sagebrush sticks. According to tradition, the cross-shaped kites are supposed to be a reminder of the resurrected Christ rising to Heaven.

Easter Sunday is another day to savour Bermuda's off-season scenic splendour, particularly at sunrise services which are conducted on tops of cliffs and in other spectacular settings. These are followed by the traditional serving of hot-cross buns and coffee. While Bermuda, with its deep British roots, used to celebrate Guy Fawkes' Day high-pressure host throughout the summer.

Winter is a time of renewal and replenishment, all part of the rhythm of a seasonal cycle that more tropical climes are denied. It's a time for sprucing up the house with paint and enjoying showers which top up the depleted underground water tanks virtually every Bermudian home needs for water; a time for scraping down the multi-hued boat hulls on the slipways on inlets and bays; and a time to wait with anxious eye for the first, inevitable sighting of the longtail returned.

Above, Good Friday is Bermuda's national kite-flying day.

DANCIN' IN THE STREET

A drumroll, loud as thunder. Far down the road they appear: young men in bright capes and masks, dancing a wild acrobatic step. There is a hypnotic swirl of sound and colour. Costumes are a combination of African tribal and American Indian; the head-dresses are crowned with peacock feathers. Children fall into line behind the procession, and the Gombeys roll on, dancin' in the street.

The Bermuda Gombey, or Masquerade, is the island's premier folk art. The troupe, always male, traditionally consisted of men and boys from the same family who passed on the techniques from one generation to the next. The Gombeys' noisy, always rhythmic presence personifies the winter season in Bermuda, for they perform most often around the Christmas season. During other cool months, the Department of Tourism organises regular indoor demonstrations for visitors.

The dance is West African in origin, but the unlikely combination of military music, British Mummers (who used song and mime to entertain), slavery rites, West Indians and American Indians, not to mention a touch of Mardi Gras, contribute to the distinctive Gombey heritage.

The word "Gombey" has a dual meaning. Not only does it describe a certain type of African drum, but in Bantu it means, literally, "rhythm". Louise A. Jackson, director of the Jackson School of Performing Arts and someone who has "observed, studied and travelled abroad with Gombey 'crowds' for close to 30 years," has written a lovely book which traces the roots of the dance through its different cultural influences.

In *Gombey* she writes: "African dancers have been known to use sculptured objects such as houses or boats on their heads, and all this has been seen in the Bermuda Gombey… American Indian influence on the Gombey dance is seen in the costume, character roles in the Gombey folk drama and use of Indian symbols." A tomahawk often rests near a dancer's shoulder during certain selected numbers.

In the past, the Gombey acted not only as an entertainer, but also as a social commentator and even a tour guide. It was common for one "crowd" to travel to another's "territory", a Christmas tradition adapted from the Mummers, and to make sardonic observations. Louise Jackson cites this song as an example:

All 'de way to Bailey's Bay
Fish and 'taters every day
All 'de way to Tucker's Town
Chew 'de whale an' blow 'de horn
All 'de way to Spanish Point
Half a gill and half a pint
All 'de way to Paget side
Nothing 'dere but foolish pride
All 'de way to Brackish Pon'
Cow-heel soup an' damaged corn.

Biblical rituals have also been re-enacted in dance and mime, which possibly relate to the conversion of slaves to Christianity. The British, too, were responsible for a bit of cultural integration, for Gombey musicians use not the traditional tribal hand drum employed by other ethnic groups but a snare drum played with sticks which was used by British soldiers when they were stationed in Bermuda. The triangle, fife and whistle are additional military instruments played.

The strongest influence on the contemporary Gombey is, however, from the West Indies. The Caribbean has its own "Goombay" dancers, and slaves or convicts imported from other islands to work at Dockyard brought their own traditions. Only the Bermudian Gombey plays the drums with sticks, however, which reinforces its unique status.

The Gombey tradition is, unfortunately, a diminishing art form, for the intricate rhythms and acrobatic dance steps require peak physical condition and tireless practice. Whereas in the past Bermuda was able to boast several regional troupes, economic pressures have meant that many dancers and musicians can only rehearse part-time. The performances staged mean hours off work, and a further reduction in wages.

During the winter, should a Gombey troupe come your way, it would be fitting to continue a time-honoured custom by offering a few coins as a "Christmas present" in return.

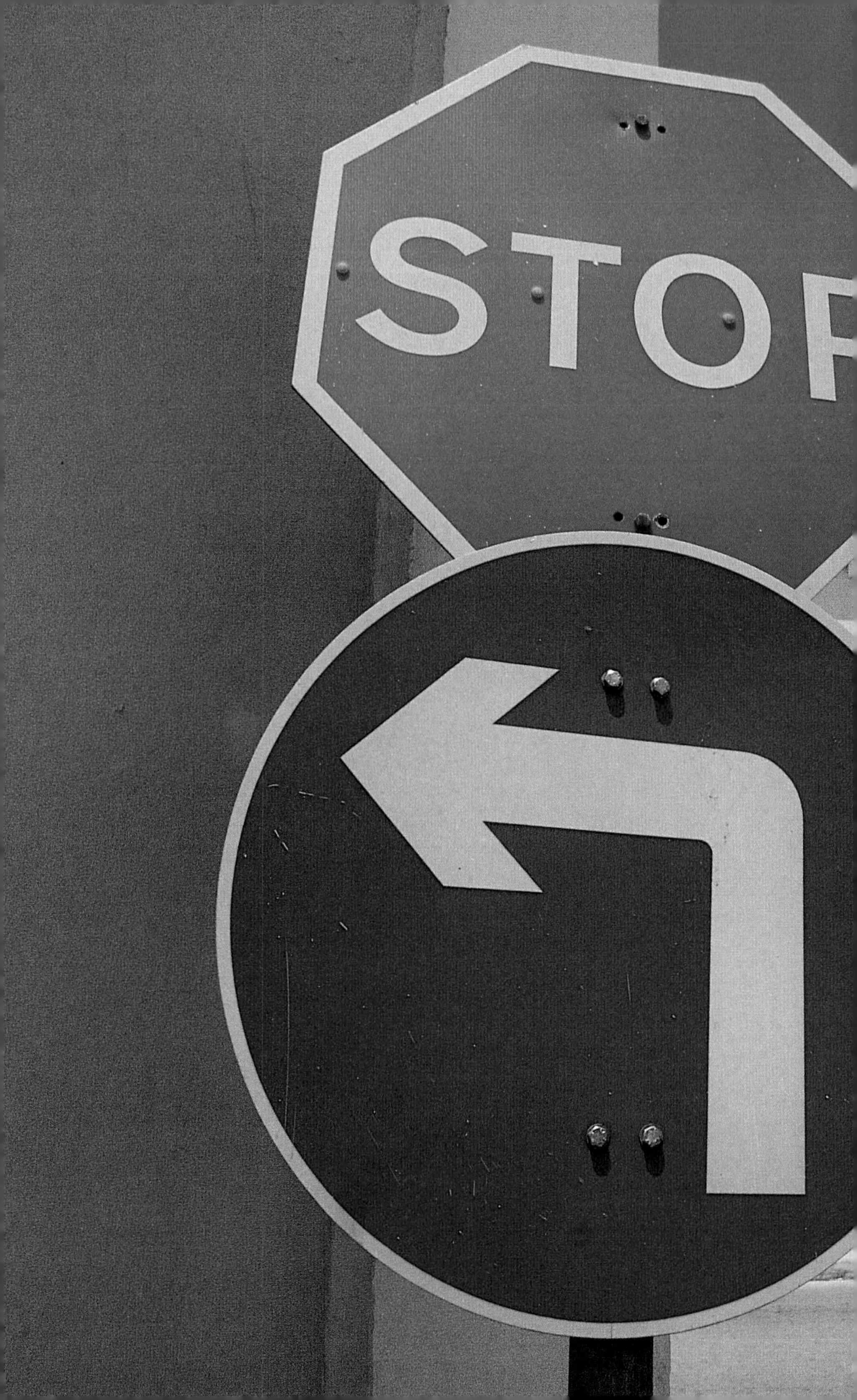
STO

PLACES

Bermuda's landscape is enormously varied. The popular image is, of course, of the island's pastel beaches and turquoise water. But there is more: from sophisticated towns to subterranean caverns.

This scenic variety makes Bermuda interesting. What makes Bermuda fascinating is that it is all contained within just a few square miles. In context, the island's diminutive proportions are exceptional: 50 times smaller than Rhode Island, America's tiniest state, and 561 times smaller than Belgium, one of Europe's most compact countries.

This mix in landscape extends throughout the island. Above ground, there are fields of flowers, some cultivated, some wild, and botanical gardens with exotic, mysterious trees. Below ground are the caves, rich in stalagmites and drippy stones which configure into a range of shapes, from Buddha to the Manhattan skyline. Into the sea, deeper still, the variety continues: Bermuda's crystal waters attract divers from all over the world, who study the fish and submarine flora.

Trails, both man-made and natural, are other distinguishing features, along with shapely domestic architecture, beautifully maintained nature reserves and fields used exclusively for agriculture. Just when it seems safe to assume the island consists mainly of beaches and countryside, it throws up a surprise, like an exclusive clothing store surrounded by trees and offering top-quality goods.

Quality shops are something the island knows about, shops which are found, for the most part, in Bermuda's quality towns. The capital, Hamilton, boasts a handsome cathedral, dignified municipal buildings and a range of businesses, often family-owned, which can trace their origins as far back as 1844. St George's, on the other side of the island, is older still; it was Bermuda's first village and sports a local town crier. The island has more golf courses per square mile than any nation in the world, and has one of the highest per capita incomes.

History, architecture, flowers and fine shopping – all contained in an area 14 times smaller than New York City. Coupled with some of the best beaches in the world, what more could a visitor ask for?

Preceding pages: schoolgirls in action; artful houses; snorklers on a South Shore beach; the graphic architecture of St George's; Hamilton's Front Street is lined with pastel buildings.

Bermuda

1,0 miles/ 1600 m

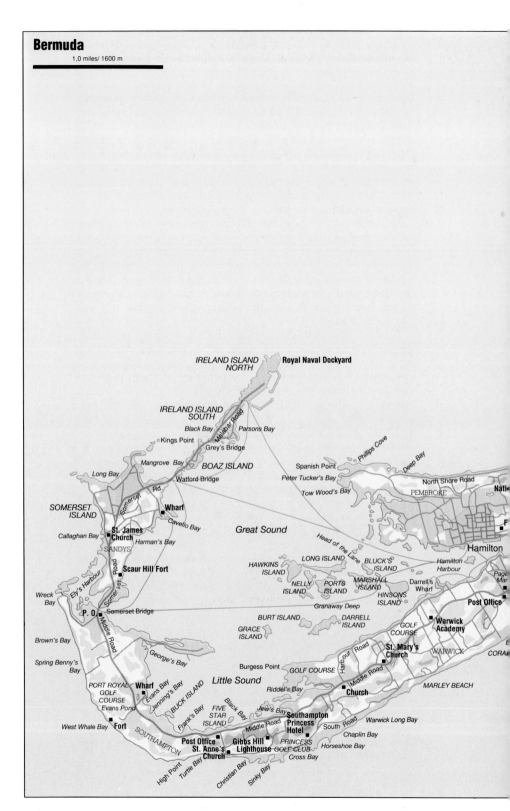

IRELAND ISLAND NORTH

Royal Naval Dockyard

IRELAND ISLAND SOUTH

Black Bay

Parsons Bay

Malabar Road

Kings Point

Grey's Bridge

Mangrove Bay

BOAZ ISLAND

Spanish Point

Phillips Cove

Deep Bay

Long Bay

Watford Bridge

Peter Tucker's Bay

Tow Wood's Bay

North Shore Road

PEMBROKE

Nati

Somerset Rd.

Wharf

Great Sound

SOMERSET ISLAND

Cavello Bay

Head of the Lane

Hamilton

Callaghan Bay

St. James Church

Harman's Bay

SANDYS

LONG ISLAND

BLUCK'S ISLAND

Hamilton Harbour

Somerset Road

Scaur Hill Fort

HAWKINS ISLAND

MARSHALL ISLAND

Darrell's Wharf

Page Mar

Ely's Harbour

NELLY ISLAND

PORTS ISLAND

HINSONS ISLAND

Post Office

Wreck Bay

P. O.

Somerset Bridge

Granaway Deep

Middle Road

BURT ISLAND

DARRELL ISLAND

GOLF COURSE

Warwick Academy

Brown's Bay

GRACE ISLAND

Harbour Road

St. Mary's Church

WARWICK

CORA

Spring Benny's Bay

George's Bay

Burgess Point

GOLF COURSE

Middle Road

MARLEY BEACH

PORT ROYAL GOLF COURSE

Wharf

Evans Bay

Jenning's Bay

BUCK ISLAND

Little Sound

Riddel's Bay

Church

Evans Pond

Frank's Bay

FIVE STAR ISLAND

Black Bay

Jew's Bay

Southampton Princess Hotel

South Road

Warwick Long Bay

West Whale Bay

Fort

SOUTHAMPTON

Middle Road

Chaplin Bay

Post Office

St. Anne's Church

Gibbs Hill Lighthouse

PRINCESS GOLF CLUB

Horseshoe Bay

High Point

Turtle Bay

Christian Bay

Sinky Bay

Cross Bay

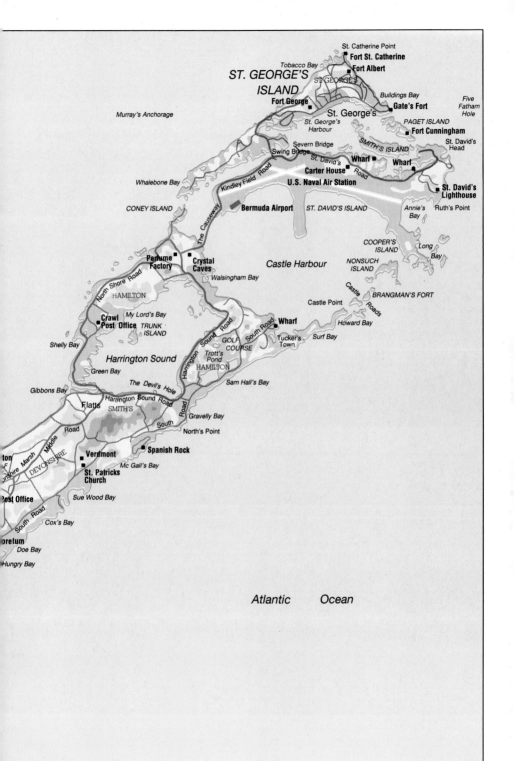

St. Catherine Point
Fort St. Catherine
Tobacco Bay
Fort Albert
ST. GEORGE'S
ISLAND
ST.GEORGE'S
Buildings Bay
Fort George
Five
Fatham
Hole
Gate's Fort
St. George's
Murray's Anchorage
St. George's
Harbour
PAGET ISLAND
Fort Cunningham
St. David's
Head
Severn Bridge
SMITH'S ISLAND
Swing Bridge
Wharf
Wharf
St. David's
Whalebone Bay
Kindley Field Road
Carter House
Road
U.S. Naval Air Station
St. David's
Lighthouse
CONEY ISLAND
The Causeway
Bermuda Airport
ST. DAVID'S ISLAND
Annie's
Bay
Ruth's Point

COOPER'S
ISLAND
Long
Bay
Perfume
Factory
Crystal
Caves
Castle Harbour
NONSUCH
ISLAND
North Shore Road
Walsingham Bay
Castle
Roads
BRANGMAN'S FORT
HAMILTON
Castle Point
My Lord's Bay
Howard Bay
Crawl
Post Office
TRUNK
ISLAND
Harrington Sound Road
GOLF
COURSE
Wharf
Tucker's
Town
Surf Bay
Shelly Bay
Harrington Sound
Trott's
Pond
HAMILTON
Green Bay
Sam Hall's Bay
Gibbons Bay
The Devil's Hole
Harrington Sound Road
Flatts
SMITH'S
Road
Road
South
Gravelly Bay
North's Point
ton
Middle
Road
Spanish Rock
DEVONSHIRE
nshire Marsh
Verdmont
Mc Gall's Bay
f
St. Patricks
Church
ost Office
Sue Wood Bay
South Road
Cox's Bay
oretum
Doe Bay
Hungry Bay

Atlantic   Ocean

HAMILTON

Like clever women and all successful actors, the town of Hamilton has two distinct characters – one for day and another for night. In daylight hours, the capital is the nearest Bermuda achieves to a bustling metropolis. The narrow streets beyond the harbour teem with shoppers and office workers, and there is a busy, urban ambience.

As dusk falls, Hamilton dons a different face. Streets which only hours earlier buzzed with the mosquito sound of motor scooters now echo to the clip-clop of horses' hooves. Perfume fills the air, the scent of night blossoms from nearby Par-la-Ville Park. Later on, the only sound will be the whistling tune created by tiny tree frogs, those invisible residents who provide the night-time chorus for all of Bermuda.

Hamilton covers an area of 177 acres (70 hectares), with a resident population of only 2,000. Because the town blends seamlessly into its parish, Pembroke, it seems larger than it is. This deceptive appearance is enhanced by the many interior arcades which meander off Hamilton's principal shopping streets. Turn a corner into what appears to be an alleyway, and find, instead, multi-levelled tiers of shops, restaurants and chic boutiques.

The unofficial boundaries might well be the Hamilton Princess hotel on the west, then extending all along Front Street and the waterfront to the round-about on the east, which serves as the gateway to Paget parish.

This roundabout is known to all Hamiltonians as the place to wave "hello" to Johnnie Barnes. Mr Barnes is a retired bus driver, sound of mind and sociable in spirit, who stands in the middle of the roundabout each morning to greet commuters on their way into work. Barnes is a notable Bermudian figure, whose radiant eccentricity and loyal presence at the roundabout, rain or shine, says a great deal about the island and its people.

The **Hamilton Princess** has played host to royalty, movie stars and charity events. It was also the scene of stirring espionage during World War II (see the one-page feature *Spies at the Princess Hotel*, page 71). Today, although life at the Princess is calmer, its ground-floor bar remains open late at night and is a local rendezvous for residents and visitors alike.

Near the Hamilton Princess is a shop called **Pegasus,** located in a Victorian house set back from the street in private grounds. Walk up stairs lined with hand-tinted engravings (authenticity seals intact) for the largest collection of antique prints and maps in Bermuda. The atmosphere inside is markedly old-fashioned. Prints and artworks are hung on the walls of several small rooms, so the feeling inside is rather like walking through a succession of (very cluttered) libraries whose stock just happens to be for sale. Purchases are rung up on an antique cash register.

Across the street are two facilities invaluable to sailors. Both **PW's marina** and **Miles supermarket** are so

Left, Johnnie Barnes greets each commuter, rain or shine. **Right**, the clip-clop of horses' hooves.

close to the water's edge it feels possible to sail right to their doors. Further along Pitt's Bay Road lies the capital's finest smaller hotel, **Waterloo House**. Built on a series of undulating terraces which end up by the sea, the hotel is one of the few places in Hamilton where outdoor tables are arranged so diners can enjoy the view of the harbour. For this reason – plus its excellent kitchens – Waterloo House is a popular lunchtime spot for both Bermudians and visitors.

Further along is one of the island's distinctive **moongates**, the round, limestone gates through which honeymooners are meant to walk to ensure good luck. This particular moongate leads to a parking lot for the bakery, so dedicated romantics are urged to try elsewhere for their luck.

A stone staircase opposite the Bermudiana Hotel (now closed) leads to the harbour and pretty **Barr's Bay Park**, which might well be considered a bit of the front yard of the **Royal Bermuda Yacht Club**. Members' boats dominate the landscape, and the view to the other side of the harbour is charming, glimpsed through the silhouettes of tall masts. (This on a cloudy day, of course. On sunny days and weekends, sensible members have sailed away.)

The **Bank of Bermuda** was founded in 1890 by a group of prominent merchants, although its head office is located in a modern, very ugly building right on the waterfront near Barr's Bay Park. A local ruling states that buildings cannot exceed the height of the cathedral, although at seven storeys high the Bank HQ must come close. For people who like to keep up with commerce, there is a direct Reuters line to New York, with up-to-the minute quotations from the world's major stock markets.

Less thrusting visitors will appreciate the dozen cubicles and queueing system which allows travellers' cheques to be cashed with ease. At the entrance to this feeder system is, however, a cryptic sign: "Save time. Don't wait. Please use our personal touch teller."

Personal touch tellers are nowhere to

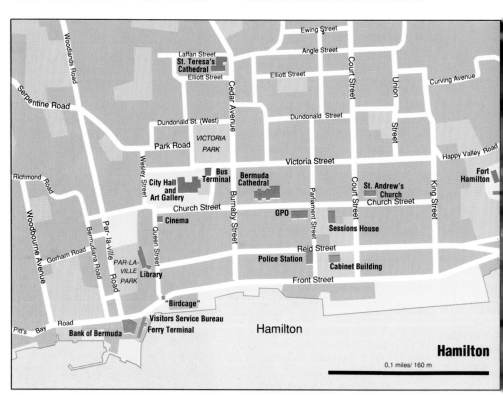

Hamilton

0,1 miles/ 160 m

Hamilton

be seen upstairs on the mezzanine, for it is collectors who flock to see the **coin collection** which traces Bermudian currency from the 16th century to the present day. Doll-like replicas of each monarch denote which coins were used under which sovereign, and many of them bear further scrutiny, especially the Bank's reserves of historic Hog Money consisting of seven one shilling pieces, seven sixpences and the rare threepences, of which only six others are known to exist. Note, too, the very British coins, which were standard currency until 1969, and the very American-style coins adopted only the following year.

The **tourist information office** (in the genteel vernacular called the **Visitors Service Bureau**) might be considered the hub of Hamilton. In one direction lies Queen Street, site of several historic buildings. At this junction, Pitt's Bay Road becomes Front Street, the premier shopping thoroughfare and "main drag" of Hamilton. Monitoring the ebb and flow of traffic is Bermuda's

Waterloo House is Hamilton's finest small hotel.

most famous moving postcard: the shorts-clad **"bird-cage" police officer.**

Next door to the Visitors Service Bureau is the **ferry terminal,** a pink building with candy-striped awnings. Buy a token from one of the machines inside, or from the receptionist. Bermuda's ferries are clean, efficient and run to schedule. If it's raining, a local passenger might well wipe your seat with her hankie before allowing you to sit down. It is from here, too, that glass-bottomed boats depart for short sightseeing cruises. When the cruise ships disgorge passengers only a few hundred yards away, and hundreds of people pour into Front Street, the low-key island hub-bub momentarily becomes "big town".

Refuge is only a few steps away. Down a rather tacky lane separating the Bank of Bermuda from the Visitors Service Bureau is a small promontory jutting out to sea. This is **Albuoy's Point** (also spelled Albouy's Point), a grassy park popular with office workers and their lunchtime sandwiches. The

point is said to have been named after a "professor of physick" who fought courageously against a plague of yellow fever which was over-taking the island in the 17th century. At dusk, this peninsula is probably the best place in downtown Hamilton to watch the sun set over the water.

Front Street follows the line of the harbour all the way from here to beyond the docks. The south side is a series of warehouses and terminals used by the cruise ships which steam directly into Hamilton. When not in use for their original purposes, these buildings in the winter months often serve as entertainment centres.

The other side, **Front Street West**, is a series of two-tiered pastel-coloured buildings. Walking on the brick pavement between these shops and their stocky, colonial columns, the pedestrian traffic divides into two lanes, for the regular pavement continues alongside. For such an orderly island, it seems logical that strollers would divide into two lanes as well, one heading west and

one east. No such division occurs, and a fair amount of jostling takes place, reassuringly confirming that Bermuda's formality throughout the island is self-imposed, rather than regimented.

This area signals the island's finest collection of shops. Many date from the previous century and family-owned businesses tend to remain in the family; it's not uncommon to be waited on by a Trimingham in Trimingham's. Goods are often British, and can offer substantial savings on similar items bought in the US, although canny shoppers will check current prices before stepping on the airplane.

Stores where the key-note is quality and service is a way of life include **Trimingham's** (established in 1844; general goods), **Bluck's** (1844; china and crystal), **Smith's** (1889; Burberry raincoats) plus Bermuda's oldest wine and spirits merchants, **Gosling's**, which dates from 1806. The **Irish Linen Shop** and **Pringle of Scotland** for fine cashmeres can be recommended, too. A selection of Bermudian goods is also

Front Street provides the island's best shopping.

mentioned in the *Travel Tips* section at the back of this book.

Two doors along from Trimingham's is a staircase. The paintings hanging in the upstairs corridor point the way to the **Masterworks Foundation**, a gallery whose task it is to purchase and then return to Bermuda works of art about the island which have found their way abroad. The walls hold beautiful scenes of St George's by American Ogden Pleissner, prints from copper etchings and, on the shelves below, a collection of posters and postcards which make perfect souvenirs. This is the place, too, to see genuine 1930s posters of Bermuda in its heyday as a winter resort. The Masterworks Foundation will shortly move to a room in the new National Gallery in City Hall.

If Humphrey Bogart's character Rick in *Casablanca* had opened a café rather than a bar, it would probably have looked very like the **Arcade Restaurant**, tucked away in the Walker Arcade further along Front Street. Established in 1945, the restaurant features lazy hanging fans, wooden chairs, tables with iron bases, and a slap-up menu which includes all-day breakfasts. The slightly seedy, slightly elegant ambience is matchless. The café is open from 7 a.m. to 4 p.m. or "whenever we feel like closing".

The **Walker Arcade** is Hamilton's prettiest enclosed shopping area. Lined with shops and offices, it widens into a courtyard complete with Spanish-style birdbath and terracotta tiles. It's a pleasant place to pause when making lots of purchases in the nearby shops.

While still inside the arcade, walk through the iron gates towards the **Windjammer Gallery's** Pocket Print shop for **Old Cellar Lane**. Before 1900 this alleyway was one of many stables, sheltering horses and carriages for patrons of local businesses in a sort of municipal "parking lot". Now, its whitewashed walls encompass two of the island's most interesting small shops. **The Old Cellar,** locked up tight at night by sliding stable doors, is, surprisingly, the island's only junk shop.

A sample of locally-produced goods.

THE BANKING BUSINESS

When Joseph Gibbons was studying for his honours degree in European colonial history at the University of Toronto, the last thing he imagined he would become was a banker. But when he was approached by Hamilton's Bank of N. T. Butterfield & Son Ltd., who were headhunting bright young Bermudians to enter the international side of their banking business, the idea seemed feasible.

Bermuda is now a world-recognised home for captive insurance companies, mutual funds and investment holding companies, and, not least of course, the business of international banking.

From early beginnings as an officer, Joe Gibbons is today the senior manager of the International Department, with dual responsibility for group business development, especially in the United Kingdom and European markets, as well as the day-to-day administration of the international group in Bermuda. He has a local staff of five, and the bank's international operations in London, the Channel and Cayman Islands, and Hong Kong also report to him.

"What I enjoy most about banking is working from a place like Bermuda, where we have a very sophisticated infrastructure and an interesting client base," he says. "We deal with major corporations and individuals who are wealthy by anybody's standards. Very often we are involved in transactions, as a conduit or service provider, which people read about in the financial press."

Joe is typical of many ambitious young Bermudians today who are prepared to work hard for both their own success and the success of Bermuda.

"Bermuda has a tremendous amount to offer apart from its reputation. We go for the top end of the market. We are expensive and becoming increasingly more so at a time when other jurisdictions are looking to our success and are competing with us, but it is our job to let potential clients or advisers know of the island's expertise. That is our competitive edge and that is where we have been successful."

Of the island's economic future, Joe Gibbons says: "If we are going to maintain our standard of living here in Bermuda, then international business will come to play an even greater role in our economy. I'm pleased to be part of that process."

There is a reason for this. The weather which makes Bermuda such an enjoyable holiday destination (bright sun, moist air) wreaks havoc on goods which have passed their sell-by dates, and even the smallest older items are snapped up by collectors. It is for this reason that old books and memorabilia about Bermuda can often be more easily obtained in destinations other than Bermuda itself. The Old Cellar compensates by having five rooms of amusing bric-a-brac and novel imported items, like Guatamalean worry dolls.

The best collection of old postcards which Bermuda can supply are found next door on the premises of the **Bermuda Coin and Stamp Company Ltd.** The staff are extremely courteous, even to browsers and non-philatelists, and a pleasing time can be had perusing the stock.

As one exits on to Front Street again, horses (the probable descendants of those that were once housed in the stables in Cellar Lane) can be found tethered by the waterfront opposite.

Visitors love to hire these horses and carriages by the hour and, at night, the horses' hooves on the quiet pavement make a sentimental sound.

Because a great deal of dining on the islands is confined to the larger hotels, it can be surprisingly difficult in Hamilton to find places serving casual evening meals. The **Cock and Feather** pub is one such place, with a terrace overlooking the harbour. Indoors, there's live entertainment until 1 a.m., which can be twinned with sampling the speciality of the house, a Cock-a-Doodle-Doo cocktail, made of a blend of cockspur rum, orange juice, coconut milk and "special spices".

Smack in the middle of the **Emporium Arcade** is a **bronze sculpture** by local artist Desmond Fountain. Appropriately, the sculpture is itself a fountain, crowned by the sylph-like figure of the former Miss World, Gina Swainson. This is one of two statues of Miss Bermuda 1979; the other one is located behind the **Windjammer Gallery** on the corner of Reid and King Streets.

As the sun sets, night sounds begin.

Chancery Lane lies tucked behind a series of offices – a steep, brick corridor which links Front Street to Reid Street. It's a pretty siting, with huge tubs of plants, and wrought-iron canopies with motifs of grapes supporting glass hurricane lamps. The atmosphere is vaguely Spanish, which perhaps accounts for the incongruity of a shop selling wares from Mexico. Wrought-iron gates lead to the headquarters of the United Bermuda Party; swap differences of opinion or champion the politics of your choice at **Dorothy's Coffee Shop**, a funky Bermudian café serving the improbable combination of peanut-butter-and-bacon sandwiches.

The "grapes motif" of Chancery Lane extends to the frontage of **Rum Runners** on Front Street. The building which houses this restaurant and pub has one of the most elaborate exteriors in town; its filigree wrought-iron balcony could have arrived by ship straight from New Orleans' French Quarter. Up the stairs, a gigantic nautical figurehead dominates the restaurant's entrance.

The lawns in front of the handsome, two-storey **Cabinet Building** are extremely pleasant at twilight, when tree frogs make their chirpy sound and scent is heavy in the air. This land has always been reserved for the public, a right which came about when the building was constructed around 1840.

At the very tip of the lawns is the **Cenotaph**, made of native stone, which commemorates those who died in both world wars. It's modelled on the Cenotaph in London's Whitehall, just opposite Downing Street. In many ways, Bermuda is more British than Britain: Remembrance Day is a public holiday on the island, whereas in England it is not. On that day, 11 November, wreaths are laid at the Cenotaph by families and friends in honour of the brave Bermudians who died.

The legislature of Bermuda was first established in 1620 to make laws for "the peace, order and good government" of the island. It is based on the system used in Britain and consists of Her Majesty the Queen, a Senate and a

Rum Runners takes a bow.

House of Assembly. Entrance to the **Senate Chamber** is up the green stairs of the Cabinet Building which is lined with portraits of Sir Thomas Gates and Queen Victoria at the time of her marriage. The 11 members are appointed by the Queen's representative in Bermuda (the Governor) in consultation with the Premier and the Leader of the Opposition. The Senate elects its own President and Vice President.

Each Wednesday, from November to June, the Senate meets to consider the legislation initiated in the House of Assembly. Visitors are allowed in to the Public Gallery to watch the proceedings, which take place under a very colonial ceiling and the ubiquitous wooden fans. Many world leaders have met around the circular table, from US President Dwight Eisenhower to Sir Winston Churchill; from President John F. Kennedy to Prime Minister Edward Heath. Margaret Thatcher and George Bush have also been recent visitors to Bermuda.

Black Rod, the silver-headed rod made by the Crown Jewellers, lies in a glass case. The rod represents the symbol of authority of the Head of State (the Governor). It is carried by an official (also called Black Rod) at the Convening of Parliament which occurs in late autumn. Black Rod leads the procession of Members of Parliament to the Senate Chamber for the reading of the Throne Speech by the Governor.

The long, low waterfront building on the corner of Front Street and Court Street was once the Town Hall. In 1795 the first municipal elections were held here, at the extremely reasonable hour of 9 o'clock at night. In the early 19th century it was the temporary home (11 years) for the House of Assembly, shortly after the seat of government was moved from St George's to Hamilton. The Town Hall was upstairs, sharing its premises with the customs warehouse on the ground floor. The building is now a government information office.

Opposite the docks, Front Street turns into **East Broadway** and begins to change in appearance. Distinguished

Two views of the Senate.

buildings give way to rather run-down properties and "wine merchants" become "liquor marts".

Further still, a building huddled low over the main road gives rise to speculative folklore. Was this building, now the residence of a respected local citizen, once the site of Hamilton's legendary brothel? This brothel, called "Queen of the East", employed girls, probably of French-Caribbean origin, and set them up as laundresses. "Doing the bedding" took on an entirely new meaning for curious and intrepid islanders, until the premises were eventually closed down. This tale is told in full (with perhaps an embellishment or two) in John Weatherill's novella of the same name sold in Hamilton bookshops.

Queen's tour: Bermuda's bird-cage landmark marks the junction of Front Street and Queen Street. If the first is noted for shopping, the latter is known for history, because several of the buildings on Queen Street are of notable importance. One of the first shops on Queen Street proper is the **Bermuda Book Store Ltd**, which contains the most comprehensive selection of books on Bermuda to be found on the island. Be sure to sneak a peek upstairs before leaving the shop. The upper floor sells pencils, notebooks, envelopes and other literary paraphernalia. The long room, with its wooden floors and ceiling fans, gives a pleasing sense of work-a-day colonialism.

Par-La-Ville Park is Hamilton's largest, most central public garden. Its gently undulating slopes provide variety out of all proportion to its modest size: there are palm trees, bird baths and flower beds containing plants with exotic-sounding names: "Flame of the Woods" and "Duchesse de Brabant". The gardens were laid out around 1850 as part of the estate of William B. Perot, and even though the gardens suffered still-evident damage in Hurricane Emily in 1987, there is a personal, almost cosy air about the grounds which belies their municipal status. Spick-and-span public toilets can be found by the Queen Street entrance.

Par-La-Ville-Park.

The park's original owner, William B. Perot, created a famous postage stamp for which collectors will now pay a fabulous sum (only 12 are still known to exist). Perot was Bermuda's first postmaster, appointed in 1821. He was a highly visible character on the island, collecting mail from the docks, storing it under his top hat, and making personal deliveries "at the drop of a hat".

Mail was sent by horseback from Hamilton to St George's on Mondays and Thursdays and made the return journey on alternate days. Somerset Bridge received letters on Wednesdays and Saturdays. Although a daily postal delivery commenced in 1842, just six years before Perot's stamp, some Bermudians think the mail service has decreased in efficiency since the days of horseback, hence the high proportion of post office boxes, which are used for personal collection.

A short walk past Perot's Post Office. The room in which the postmaster worked has been restored and is now called **Perot's Post Office**. An authentic feel prevails, from the brass candle-sticks to the wooden counter, where simple postal business is still conducted. In fact, the well-proportioned interior is a modern invention, for in Perot's day the premises were shared with an apothecary shop. Still, to sit on one of the tall wooden stools and to write a letter at the old-fashioned desks is delightful. It's worth taking time out to do this at the old post office, even if the letter you write has to be sent to someone you don't like.

William Perot lived next door in Par-La-Ville house, which is now the Bermuda Library and Historical Society Museum. The postmaster's passion for collecting exotic plants from all over the world led him to import from Demerara a rubber tree seed, and to plant it in front of the house.

The seed grew to the massive tree under which local residents now take refuge from the heat, but the tree hasn't always been a favourite. Mark Twain, on visiting the island, is said to have been disappointed in this exotic specimen, for in his view a "rubber tree"

BERMUDA SHORTS

Knowing full well what Bermuda shorts are may not prevent visitors from being taken slightly aback on first spotting the things in the full glory of the natural habitat, which is to say terminating at the regulation four inches above the knee of a bank manager or business executive who is otherwise at his desk conventionally turned out in jacket, collar and tie.

The slim fit of the celebrated shorts as they are now worn obscures their baggy antecedents. The inspiration was the tropical kit issued to British troops stationed in Bermuda. Soldiers did not start wearing shorts until this century, so the history of the Bermuda derivatives cannot be equated with, say, the Scottish kilt, which was adopted at the turn of the millennium by an eccentric Viking, known thereafter as Magnus Bare-leg.

Shorts bought as souvenirs in Bermuda in the latter half of this century were transported to the American mainland in tourists' suitcases and were there subjected to local impositions like ostentatious check patterns. Some of these foreign influences have been incorporated in later generations of the home-grown product, but the sober, plain colours of the classical style are closer in spirit to the original.

In Bermuda, these relatively austere shorts are not meant merely for leisure. They are considered equally suitable for a defendant in court, whose shorts may even be seen to lend dignity to the proceedings. The official position is summed up in the booklet *Bermuda: As a Matter of Fact*, which pronounces authoritatively on local etiquette: "Bermuda shorts are an acceptable mode of dress in the most conservative areas of Bermuda life (for men)."

The sting is in the parentheses: the circumstances in which Bermuda shorts may respectably be worn by women are much narrower. On the beach, certainly; while shopping, on condition that they are not significantly higher than four inches above the knee; on other occasions, only with circumspection. Bermuda, where nagging wives were once pointed towards the Ducking Stool, still has firm ideas about female decorum. Locally written tips for tourists invariably sound a splenetic note on one particular solecism, and that is women who wear hair curlers in public.

With the agitation caused by exposed hair curlers, it cannot be surprising that toplessness is entirely out of order. Club Meditérrannée, whose members can scarcely conceive of sunbathing any other way, went to extraordinary lengths to find corners of Bermuda which were suitably discreet. To no avail; vigilantes gave them no quarter and eventually, perhaps for other reasons as well, the hotel closed down.

It was seemingly ever thus, because in 1816 the *Bermuda Gazette* wrote of "an elderly gentleman of venerable appearance and correct manners" who took exception to women who wore dresses "extremely low in the back and bosom or off the shoulder." He sidled up beside them and stamped the exposed flesh with an indictment: "Naked but not ashamed."

It was actually the longer-suffering women of 18th-century Bermuda who first put local fashion on the international map. While the men were mainly interested in the palmetto tree for its heady juice, women plaited the leaves into hats. The most famous was Mrs Martha Hayward, a descendant of Christopher Carter, one of the Three Kings. She died in 1791 at the age of 114. An obituary in the *Bermuda Gazette*, having noted that "she desired to live longer, but when she understood her dissolution was drawing near, she resigned her mortal life without a groan," recorded she "platted palmetto hats for a living."

One of her hats was sent to Queen Anne as a present and started a fashion among English-women. For years every mail ship to England contained another consignment of palmetto hats. "English ladies are gradually extinguishing this tree in Bermuda" was a complaint recorded almost a century after the hat's introduction.

While it is doubtful that Bermuda shorts occupy the thoughts of modern philosophers, Bishop Berkeley was writing about the hats in 1725, albeit briefly. "Bermuda hats are worn by our ladies," he noted. "They are made of a sort of matting, which is the only commodity that I can find exported from Bermuda to Great Britain."

would surely bear a crop of hot water bottles and rubber over-soles.

The entrance hall of Par-la-Ville house contains antique furniture and framed portraits of Sir George and Lady Somers, plus pictures of the principal investors in the Bermuda Company after whom the island's parishes are named. The **Bermuda Library**, founded in 1839, contains an excellent reference division on the ground floor, with rare books about Bermuda and colonial America in its collection, although permission must be obtained to see them. The library staff are, however, unfailingly polite and helpful to both serious scholars and casual enquirers.

Of particular interest is a complete set of the island's first newspaper, from the inaugural issue printed on 17 January 1784, when the paper was known as the *Bermuda Gazette*, through to the daily edition of today's *Royal Gazette*. The lending library upstairs receives newspapers from America, Britain and Canada the day after publication.

The **Historical Society Museum** is a series of small rooms decorated in original style with hurricane lamps, cedar furniture and English china. The old pitch-pine flooring is authentically uneven; these planks were thought to have been imported by the Perots from the east coast of America. Pieces to note are the dazzling Waterford chandelier, dating to around 1840, a letter from George Washington "to the inhabitants of Bermuda", the Hog money, and the cedar table which dates from 1680. Donations can be placed in the box on top.

Near the corner of **Reid Street** is the **Phoenix drugstore**, "drugstore" in the American sense because pharmaceuticals play only a secondary role. The Phoenix is the place to buy magazines, cosmetics, scissors, cigarettes and all other holiday requisites. It's in the Phoenix, too, that a time-honoured ritual is played out. Around 3 p.m. the daily papers arrive from America. There is a flurry of activity as visitors and locals hurry to buy their copy of the *New York Times* or *USA Today*. Two and a half hours later, just before clos-

ing, the same flurry occurs, but this time for the British newspapers which are flown in direct from London – if you're lucky. Otherwise the papers arrive the following day.

This dual convergence of all things American and British extends even to the chocolate counter. Along one aisle are typically American candy bars: Baby Ruths, Reese's Cup, Mr Goodbar. Following on is a selection of typically British sweets: Cadbury's Fruit & Nut, Yorkie bars, Rowntree's Fruit Gums and Smarties.

Back on Queen Street, young people mill around the Kentucky Fried Chicken emporium, and into **Casey's**, a haunt for locals where tourists are welcome. The former is one of the few take-away restaurants on the island, and always does a roaring trade. Casey's serves inexpensive beer. This area tends to be the only street life downtown Hamilton offers during the evening (otherwise, go uptown towards Union Street). If teenagers aren't eating fried chicken, chances are they're queuing at

the **Little Theatre cinema** across the street. The Little Theatre tends to show American releases shortly after they premiere in the US and, as the show changes weekly, crowds are common.

Church Street, which stands at the head of Queen Street, was named for the only church in town – in 1844. This Methodist Chapel was torn down to make way for an addition to the **Hamilton Hotel**, which, sadly, has also been destroyed. The loss of the Hamilton Hotel is a blow to the history of an island where tourism is a primary concern, for the Hamilton was the first hotel on the island. Opened in 1863 to attract winter cruise passengers, it experienced both exceptional popularity and huge losses before finally closing its doors in 1945. The hotel is remembered fondly by islanders for two local "firsts": installing a lift (elevator) to soothe its weary guests, and wiring up the first electric lights ever to be seen on Bermuda.

The place where the hotel stood is occupied by the car park of **City Hall**, a grand-looking building with a profu-

The Hamilton Hotel was the first on the island.

Hamilton Hotel, Bermuda. Bedroom and private bath

sion of wind-divining instruments on top. The fountains just outside hold very large goldfish and the low stone walls surrounding the grounds are rarely empty of loungers. The lobby is rather austere. Portraits by Curtis Hooper, unveiled by the Duke of Gloucester, are the only furnishings. Upstairs, the formal atmosphere softens. At the top, a bright, airy room, like a loft in New York's SoHo, is the perfect place for the art exhibitions frequently held here.

City Hall is also the premier venue for the annual Bermuda Festival and its East Exhibition Room will be the site for the new **National Gallery**. This climate-controlled room will house a collection of Bermuda's best works of art as well as present a variety of exhibits from all around the world. A separate room will present pictures from the Masterworks Foundation.

It is possible to travel to almost anywhere on the island by pink, efficient public bus, all of which originate and terminate at the **bus terminal** next to City Hall. The fare structure is a slightly complicated one, however, as the island is divided into different "zones". You must have the exact fare in order to climb aboard a Bermuda bus, and for this reason it is helpful to buy a booklet of pre-paid tickets from the terminal office. Not only does this save fumbling for coins in a queue of people, but "bulk buying" bus tickets works out to be less expensive than paying for each journey individually.

Victoria Park, directly behind, has a sunken garden. Open-air concerts are held in the ornate bandstand, which was built to commemorate Queen Victoria's Golden Jubilee in 1887.

Church Street has had a chequered time with its religious centres. The Methodist Chapel notwithstanding, just over 100 years ago an arsonist burned not only the Anglican church but also the Roman Catholic church. The present **Cathedral of the Most Holy Trinity**, on the site of the original Anglican church, was consecrated in 1911. A mix of Gothic and Middle English architecture, it is constructed of local limestone

Victoria Park was built in 1887 for Queen Victoria's Jubilee.

Victoria Park, Bermuda.

quarried solely from Perot's Par-La-Ville estate. The pews of imported American oak have hand-sewn prayer cushions. The atmosphere is light and airy, avoiding the solemnity so often found in important churches. Perhaps, if you're lucky, someone will be practising on the organ during your visit, which heightens the sense of calm.

Hamilton's main **Post Office** sits on the corner of Church Street and Parliament Street. Whereas postcards and letters can be mailed from the more exciting Old Post Office in Queen Street, this is the place for the serious business of sending home packages and island souvenirs. The Post Office has a couple of telephones from which long-distance calls can be made without incurring the heavy surcharge levied by many of the island's hotels – but, alas, there is no fax machine.

The **Sessions House** was built on the highest hill in Hamilton. It is a conspicuous, dignified edifice, with a clock-tower boasting a 6-ft (1.8-metre) pendulum weighing just under 100 lb

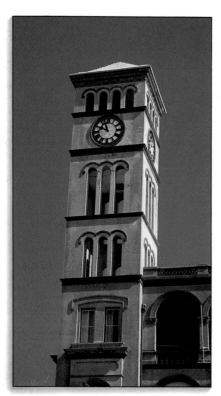

(45 kg). This handsome tower was erected to commemorate the Golden Jubilee of Queen Victoria in 1887; a terracotta medallion of the Queen's profile can be seen under an arch on the southern side. The large chamber in the House's upper storey is reserved for the use of the House of Assembly. In the chamber immediately below it, the Supreme Court holds its sessions.

The Bermuda Parliament first met on 1 August 1620. It is the oldest of all the parliaments of the British Commonwealth countries overseas, and the third oldest in the world, after Iceland and England. Parliament meets on Fridays from late October through July. On other days the public are welcome to view the **House of Assembly chamber** if the Serjeant-at-Arms is free to unlock the door.

Entry to the chamber is via a massive oak staircase. On either side are **sculptures**, carved in 1840 and originally part of the exterior of the Palace of Westminster in London. London's fog proved too damaging to the limestone figures, so they were removed to the gentler surroundings of Bermuda around 1930. The figure on the left is of King William II holding a model of Westminster Hall; the one on the right once accompanied another figure which was of King John.

The arrangement of the chairs in the chamber follows the pattern in Westminster's House of Commons: double rows of chairs facing each other with a central gangway between. On the wall flanking the Speaker's Chair hang two enormous portraits, one of King George III and the other his consort Queen Charlotte.

The Visitors' Gallery spans the back of the room. Visitors are encouraged to attend the sessions, but sun-worshippers should heed this warning posted on each public bench: "At the opening of each sitting, when the speaker enters, and on the motion to adjoin when the House rises, visitors are requested to stand. The Serjeant-at-Arms is empowered to maintain order and decorum in the galleries and may refuse admission to persons improperly clad."

The Sessions House. Right, scooter city.

194

"The government uses kilometres; we use miles," explained a taxi-driver on the route out of Hamilton. Five parishes surround the capital, none more than a few minutes away by taxi, bus or moped, and all roads do indeed sport signs giving distances in kilometres.

The five parishes are as different from one another as common practice is from official thought, and each one provides an enjoyable day out of town. Pembroke parish is domestic; Devonshire deep country. Paget has both the Botanical Gardens and Camden, the residence of the Premier. Warwick has the island's most spectacular beaches, while Southampton, far to the west, is perfect for walkers. All roads, whether travelled by miles or kilometres, lead back to Hamilton.

North Hamilton: Pembroke, the parish in which the capital resides, is primarily residential, its suburbs providing accommodation for the people who work in Hamilton. From Victoria Park north to the seacoast, houses tend to be small and rather tightly packed; the streets, too, are unkempt and there is even a spot of litter. On any other island, North Hamilton might be considered a slum, but Bermuda's high standard of living means this "slum" consists of tidy two- and three-bedroomed houses which are given a seasonal coat of paint.

The area around Union Street provides nightlife, mainly frequented by locals. Clubs come alive after midnight, when hotel dining rooms close and the staff, with a sigh of relief, slip out of their tuxedos and into their dancing shoes. The music is loud, the drinks are cheap and the clientele is primarily black and genial. While white visitors might feel more comfortable if accompanied by their hotel waiter or bartender – an invitation is sure to be issued – they will be warmly greeted even if they arrive alone.

Walking the streets of Pembroke, especially on a Sunday afternoon, shows a completely different side of life to the upscale cuteness of Hamilton's waterfront. The scene is suburban and peaceful, warm weather ensuring a constant flutter of domestic activity, from washing cars to painting houses, to children playing games in the streets devoid of traffic.

Behind Victoria Park lies **St Theresa's Cathedral**. This cathedral, with its notable Spanish flavour and decorative tower, is one of six Roman Catholic churches in Bermuda. It opened its doors around 1930 and was visited by the Pope at the end of the 1960s. His Holiness (Pope Paul VI) presented a beautiful chalice to the local diocese, which can be seen.

Beyond the cathedral lies the town's **tennis courts**, where matches are frequently held and where locals stay trim in order to present a pleasing picture in lightweight summer clothes. Black Watch Pass and Black Watch Well, although often shown on maps as part of Hamilton, are in fact best reached from the north, by following the North Shore Road and turning inland near Govern-

ment House. The importance of these sites is historical, rather than contemporary, and are only worth visiting if you happen to be in the area. **Black Watch Well**, at the foot of Langton Hill, was instigated by the Black Watch Regiment in order to replenish fresh drinking water during the great drought of 1849, and was so effective it can still be used today.

Black Watch Pass was built for a different reason. The steep cliffs of the North Shore were so impregnable that horses, carriages and carts full of supplies used to make the tortuous trip from Hamilton to the North Shore over the hills, adding hours and danger to any journey. In a remarkable feat of engineering, a pass was constructed in 1934, tunnelled through solid limestone. Although the pass is visually unremarkable, it is possible, just for a moment, to feel that you are not in balmy Bermuda but in some high mountain area. The air turns chill, and the steep stone walls with their tufts of spiky undergrowth are fleetingly impressive.

Government House is not open to the public, but its lawns are often meaningfully employed. It's not uncommon to see the grounds festooned with marquees, tables and even equestrian hurdles, as local sporting events are frequently staged here.

The North Shore Road, which extends through the parishes of Pembroke, Devonshire, Smiths, and Hamilton, concludes at its most westerly tip at **Spanish Point**. The early Bermudian settlers found the remains of a Spanish encampment on this spot, and the site takes its name from that incident. The Point can clearly be seen all the way from the West End of the island, but was primarily noted for the ships which crashed into it in the dark. Tiny **Spanish Point Park** offers wonderful views out to sea while on a clear day the wreck of a ship can sometimes be seen lying abandoned in the water.

East of Hamilton: Bermuda's isolated position in the Atlantic made the island particularly vulnerable to invasion and no fewer than 55 forts were built at

Sporting events are held on the lawns of Government House.

202

various times in self defence. **Fort Hamilton**, towering above the eastern edge of the capital, was constructed by the British to protect the approach roads into the city and to defend Spanish Point from attacks by sea. It is the finest example on the island of the mid-Victorian polygonal fort. In the 19th century, entrance was by a drawbridge, with another drawbridge linking the galleries to the main ditch. Today, the large 18-ton guns look out not at the advancing enemy but over flowering gardens.

The moat has been landscaped to provide an exotic tangle of flora which is reached by a labyrinth of underground passages cut from solid rock. Most weeks during the winter season a **skirling ceremony** is held, and bagpipers take to the ramparts with gusto. In the summer the tea room is open for tasty refreshments.

Not far from Fort Hamilton is the **Arboretum**, a 20-acre (8-hectare) oasis. Most of the trees planted here are for educational or scientific purposes, but this academic background does nothing to detract from its pleasing aspect. Bamboo or split-wood fences are used for protection around some of the trees, which gives an old-fashioned, rural flavour to the grounds.

Like its namesake in England, the parish of **Devonshire** has rolling hills and touches of green. But the graceful name is a new addition, as the parish was once known by the less attractive moniker "Brackish Pond". This was because of the large marsh which virtually covered it.

Bermudians like to point out a favourite landmark, the **Old Devonshire Church**, which lies just south of Middle Road, the thoroughfare which bisects the parish. The original church was constructed in 1716, on the site of an even earlier church, but the stark, rather plain exterior visitors see today was totally reconstructed in 1970, after an explosion on Easter Sunday. Valuable items were destroyed, but a few were salvaged and can be seen inside. Pieces of the church silver are said to date from the 16th century, which makes them

The communal tombs of Old Devonshire Church.

among the oldest pieces in Bermuda.

The earlier church was apparently just as popular as this reconstruction is now. A reprint in a local brochure gives this "thumbs-up" review from a guest staying with the Archdeacon in 1830: "In the afternoon we went to Devonshire Church which lies in a romantic valley near a large marsh, whence its name Brackish Pond. In front of the church is a venerable cedar, the largest I have yet seen and the church not having belfry the bell is suspended from a branch of this ancient tree.

"The Churchyard with its white-washed tombstones glistening amid the sombre foliage of the cedar, and the numerous winding paths, which all meet at the foot of the primeval tree that summons the natives to one loved spot, were scattered with groups of people. I remarked many more aged persons than I have seen elsewhere in Bermuda, they also looked healthier, in spite of the great marsh, and I have since heard that it is considered the most salubrious spot in Bermuda."

Banana Tree and Fruit - Bermuda

The island's "white-washed tomb-stones" are a notable feature on the landscape. At first glance Bermuda's **cemeteries**, with their massive vaults, appear to be similar to the above-ground funeral memorials found in marshy areas such as America's New Orleans. But in fact, these tombs recede deep into the ground, reaching, in some instances, to a depth of 10 ft (3 metres). The vaults can be family affairs, and what began as tradition has become a way of saving space. Bermudians are buried in cedar caskets shaped like Egyptian mummy cases; this replaces an even older type of coffin which was unique to the island. A year and a day must pass before a vault can be opened after a funeral.

North of the Old Devonshire Church lies **Palmetto House**, a National Trust property occasionally open to the public. It is a fine example of a "cross house", the architectural term for a house whose wings form the shape of a cross. The **Edmund Gibbons Nature Reserve** is situated in Devonshire along the South Road near the junction with Collector's Hill. Rare birds and exotic flora inhabit the marshy land, so visitors are advised to stick to the paths and to observe them from a distance.

Towards Devonshire Bay, on the South Road, is a lovely traditional Bermudian home called **Palm Grove**. The house is privately owned, but on certain days of the week the grounds are open to the public. There's a small aviary with tropical birds – very pleasant – but be sure not to miss the pond which lies just behind the house; imprinted on the bottom of the pool, incongruously, is a map of Bermuda.

Southeast of Hamilton: A short taxi ride from the capital in the parish of Paget lies the **Botanical Gardens**. This 36-acre (15-hectare) site has 15 permanent attractions, including an "Exotic House" of orchids and waterfalls under a partially shaded roof. The Botanical Gardens suffered severely during Hurricane Emily, which ravaged the island in 1987, but after extensive replanting it is now coming back to life.

Only one type of fruit, the prickly **Tropical resources.**

204

HURRICANE EMILY

At 7.30 a.m. on Friday, 25 September 1987, Bermuda was hit by the worst hurricane in almost 25 years. Packing maximum gusts of 116 mph (185 kph), the gale hit Bermuda with a forward speed of 45 mph (70 kph), three times that of a normal hurricane.

The island's only television channel and six radio stations were knocked out. Hundreds of trees and houses were destroyed, and estimates of the total amount of damage ranged from $15 million to $35 million.

Remarkably, there were no deaths and only minor injuries – mainly cuts, bruises and broken bones from flying debris.

The cruise ship *Atlantic*, carrying 825 passengers, broke its moorings at the docks in Hamilton, but the captain, Mario Palombo, said his crew never lost control of the 672-ft (204-metre) vessel, fending off driving winds by maintaining the ship's balance using engines and anchors.

"We've had many occasions during the year to take some decisions to avoid storms," Captain Palombo was quoted as saying. "We've also had many occasions to fight bad weather. But they have happened only at sea. That is completely different than being in port. There is no room to manoeuvre."

The Royal Gazette put out a special edition to keep residents informed of the damage. Many were without electricity or water, and stores quickly sold out of candles. The stores themselves use reserve generators in the case of power cuts, a practice which has now spread to the homes of private individuals.

According to the report in the *Gazette*, the storm's sudden intensification into a Category 2 hurricane from a waning tropical storm wasn't detected until four hours before Emily struck Bermuda. Mr Bob Case, of the Miami-based National Hurricane Centre, is quoted as saying the Centre underestimated Emily's strength. "We had such a great batting average with this storm – we forecast it as a hurricane, we forecast it would hit Hispaniola as a Category 3 hurricane and we forecast it would break up over the mountains of Hispaniola – that we may have become a little too confident about its predictability."

Mr Case were on to describe Emily as a small, compact, tightly knit hurricane. Her cloud canopy was 200 miles (320 km) across – relatively small compared to the 600-mile (960-km) spread of other hurricanes that have raged through the Gulf of Mexico. The Centre felt the tropical storm had only a 28 percent chance of striking. But Bermuda was hit by Emily's "strongest possible punch" with "downbursts" forcing its most violent conditions to ground level.

The National Trust properties Verdmont and Winterhaven suffered, as did many of the historic walls around St George's. About $100,000 worth of damage occurred to the Southampton Princess Hotel, when the hurricane shattered windows in 80 of the rooms. All members of the 700-strong staff, however, came in to clear up the debris. The dining room of the Mermaid Beach Club was blown out after being hit by a waterspout, and staff at King Edward VII Memorial Hospital treated 111 people for broken bones and other minor injuries.

The Premier, the Hon. John Swan, touring the Emergency Measures Organisation command post at Prospect, asked the public to be particularly helpful during this "distressing and trying time". There were several reports of bravery. At the island's only mental hospital, St Brendan's, staff organised the evacuation of scores of patients into another wing when the roof of the main hospital blew off. "It was a life and death situation," said one of the employees.

"I've never seen such chaos on Jubilee Road before in my life and I've lived here for 58 years," observed another Bermudian. By 8 p.m. that Friday night, less than 12 hours after Emily made her presence felt, the Fire Service had responded to 275 calls.

There were no incidents of looting after Hurricane Emily, which reflects well on Bermuda and her people. Speaking to the community at large, Mr Swan is quoted as saying: "It shows there is a collective effort being made to get the country back to normal. The damage is extensive and far-reaching but we are a determined people and we will achieve our goals."

pear, is native to Bermuda, but avocados, loquats and bananas all thrive in the sub-tropical fruit gardens. The Botanical's "Garden for the Blind" is unique among displays. Created in 1960, this enclosed, rectangular area is planted with blossoms recognised immediately by their taste and smell. There is lemon mint, lavender cotton, dandelion (including instructions as to how to cook it), plus spearmint and spices galore. Free tours of the gardens (which begin in the car park) are held throughout the year.

It's easy to be side-tracked on the way to **Camden**, the official residence of Bermuda's Premier, located deep in the boughs of the Botanical Gardens. The eye is constantly diverted by different plants, not least by a particular type of tree with a trunk so knarled and coarsened it looks like a dozen trees all entangled. The roots of this dazzling specimen, called a banyan tree, spread out towards the pathway and threaten to over-take with long, spider-like legs. Alice in Wonderland would feel at home walking through these grounds.

The lawns surrounding Camden itself are less ethereal, more genteel, in keeping with a residence which is used primarily for official entertaining. Built in the 1700s and looking rather like a colonial mansion in the American south, Camden contains elegant watercolours and items created by local craftsmen. The cedar panelling in the dining room and entrance hall, plus the furniture in the dining room, were the work of a local cabinet maker named Jackson, who lived in the mid-1880s. They took nearly 30 years to complete. Be sure to note, in the ornate dining room, not only the cedar moulding on the ceiling but also the cedar serving plates.

The view from Camden's verandahs, which were probably added in the 19th century, sweeps over the Botanical Gardens and all the way out to sea. It is a tranquil spot, when crowds are few, enlivened by the occasional cry of a peacock from the nearby aviary.

South of the Botanical Gardens lies **Hungry Bay,** a popular spot for visitors

The Botanica Gardens has 36 acres of trees and flowers.

206

and fishermen. In 1988 there were 301 registered fishermen in Bermuda, more than two-thirds of whom have their own boats. The life of a commercial fisherman is not an easy one, however, as local waters are in danger of being overfished, often by foreigners.

Alfred Birdsey is one of the island's best-known contemporary artists. His watercolours concentrate on landscapes and birds, with an overall effect, as described in the essay on art in this book, "as if a butterfly had brushed the paper on the wing, and a spider had tracked it after wading through an inkwell." Birdsey's Stowe Hill studio is called Rosecote, and a visit to the artist or his artistic offspring can be arranged by appointment. Birdsey's number is in the Bermuda telephone directory.

South of Hamilton: The **Harbour Road** borders Hamilton Harbour for several miles before coming to an end opposite Darrell Island, the green islet which was the site of Bermuda's first airport. Ferries ply the route regularly from the capital to this southern penin-sula, landing at an attractive spot called, appropriately, **Lower Ferry**. Some visitors consider the Lower Ferry area the ideal spot to stay on Bermuda, not only for the views of the capital across the sparkling waters, but also for sheer convenience. The sea is just a hike away if heading south; Hamilton with its shops and parks an approximately equal distance to the north. An evening spent in one of the capital's entertaining restaurants can be enhanced by a boat ride back to home base.

East of Lower Ferry is **Waterville**, the 18th-century headquarters of the National Trust. The National Trust, as well as owning some of the most distinguished properties on the island, also organises spring tours of private homes and gardens not normally open to the public. It's worth enquiring at the Visitors Service Bureau in Hamilton as to when and where these are taking place. **Clermont**, another handsome house in the area, was built in 1800. Chief Justice Sir Brownlow Gray, a later owner, became such a keen fan of tennis, a

Alfred Birdsey, with one of his watercolours.

British sport, that he ordered the construction of the island's first courts on an isolated piece of his property. One year later an enamoured guest named Mary Outerbridge, clutching a racquet and a rule book, sailed to the US, where she introduced tennis to the Staten Island Cricket Club in 1874. This marked the first time the sport had ever been played in America. Sir Brownlow Gray's grass court can still be seen.

Inland from Harbour Road is **Paget Marsh**, one of the island's most important and interesting nature reserves. Its open areas are of ecological interest owing to the number of endangered plants and trees contained within its 18 acres (7 hectares), but because of their fragile status an appointment is needed to walk around the site. Contact the National Trust at their headquarters in Waterville for details. The marsh has been enlarged by additional land presented to the Trust by the Society for the Prevention of Cruelty to Animals.

The South Shore: Bermuda's glorious coastline is most richly observed along the South Shore. No fewer than 23 beaches or coves comprise this coast, and the turquoise sea is rarely out of sight. Some beaches are attached to hotels, for this is also an area of lavish "colony cottages".

Colony cottages are hotels with fully serviced bungalows dotted throughout extensively foliaged grounds. The detached bungalows offer the seclusion of private houses, but provide the facilities of a luxury hotel. Bermudians are permitted to use the beaches attached to certain hotels, like Elbow Beach, in exchange for the payment of a small fee, but most local people don't bother. Their reluctance to do so is twofold. First is a genuine desire not to impose upon holidaying visitors. The second reason soon becomes evident: Bermuda's public beaches are spectacularly beautiful.

The 3-mile (5-km) stretch from **Warwick Long Bay** to **Horseshoe Bay** backs onto South Shore park to stunning effect: rippling blue water to the front, trees, greenery and nature trails

The South Shore contains 23 beaches and coves.

behind. During the summer, Bermudians observe their right to camp on this stretch of land (a privilege denied to tourists), for the summer is the only time locals will dip into the sea.

A joke is told that any time before Queen Victoria's birthday, on 24 May, the season is still officially "winter"; although before and after this date the beaches are dotted with sunbathing foreigners, Bermudians stay well away and bundled up.

The South Shore is meticulously maintained. Litter seemingly evaporates, and "beach sweepers" occasionally collide with early morning joggers. **Elbow Beach**, along the eastern edge, is said to be the longest strand on the island. No one seems to know, however, the origin of its distinctive name.

The area which stretches from Elbow Beach to **Coral Beach** was once known as the Sand Banks, due to the hills created by centuries of shifting sands. Information obtained by taking samples from the sand mounds has for a long time fascinated geologists, and the **Sand Banks** have provided important data on the early formation of the island.

Beaches serve different functions for different people. Hotel guests frequent the beaches on the eastern part of South Shore while Bermudians and many non-resident guests favour the beaches to the west, in Warwick. The more isolated **Church Bay**, near the parish of Southampton, is a popular spot for snorkellers, because there are wonderful specimens in this portion of the sea. Beware the red sponge and Portuguese man-of-war, which can sting. Otherwise, bathers have little to fear when swimming off the South Shore coast.

It is said that sailors can see the bright beam of **Gibbs Hill lighthouse** from up to 40 miles (65 km) away, an important, even vital, beacon for those negotiating Bermuda's reefs. The lighthouse is a commanding structure, made in Britain of cast iron and shipped to the island in pieces around the middle of the 19th century.

Visitors can clamber to the top via a series of steep steps, for the lighthouse

An island in the sun. Following page: nature in Bermuda is as rich under water as it is above the ground.

is open to the public every day of the week throughout the year.

The view from the top is one of the most impressive in Bermuda, as the lighthouse's beam shines from a height of 362 ft (110 metres) above sea level. A small walkway around the top offers an all-encompassing view, from Ireland Island at its western tip to St David's Head at its eastern. Faint-hearted fans should not despair, however: if the prospect of climbing 185 steps appears daunting, the panorama from Gibbs Hill, at the base of the lighthouse, is only marginally less spectacular.

Whale Bay is a public park reached by turning west off Middle Road in the parish of Southampton. The **Railway Trail** criss-crosses Middle Road several times in this area, so the parish is a popular one with walkers. Whale Bay Park slopes down to a beach which tends to be less crowded than its glamourous South Shore neighbours. In fact, much of Southampton is by-passed by visitors, a bonus to those in search of a tranquil holiday.

Whale Bay Battery lies in the park itself, a defensive fortress completed in 1876. Its function was to control access to the delightfully named Hog Fish Cut, a small channel which leads to the massive defences mounted at Dockyard on Ireland Island (now called the West End). A portion of an even earlier, semi-circular fort, can be seen in front of the Battery, as can the ammunition magazine and barracks, hidden behind an earthen rampart.

The northern end of Southampton is best known for the **Port Royal** 18-hole golf course, and for the US Naval Air Station Annex, located on a peninsula to the east. The strip of land which contains the military base was originally called Tucker's Island.

These acreages were the "overplus" from Norwood's Survey of 1616 which Daniel Tucker intended to have as his own. This is commemorated in the area by a street called "Overplus Lane". The story of the greedy governor of Bermuda and his quest for personal property is recounted in the history section of this book (*see page 53 onwards*).

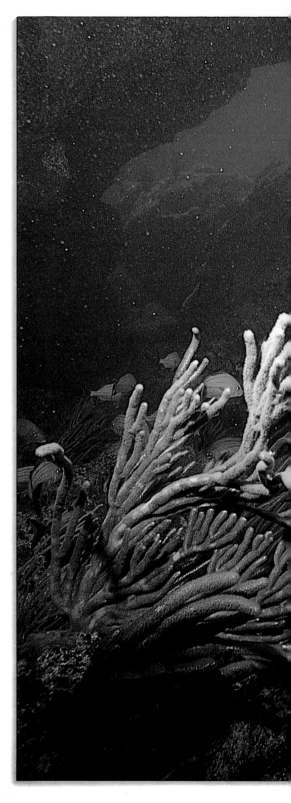

THE RAILWAY TRAIL

The railway sagas which tend to grip popular imagination are journeys chugging across Siberia, the American prairie or some such immense tract. Failing that, the mind's eye has passengers groping along corridors in dressing gowns because of some untoward incident at an international border at dead of night. Bermuda, a group of pocket-sized islands which collectively could not pack in more than 21 miles (34 km) of track, would not seem cut out for a railway, much less a railway saga, yet somehow it has contrived to end up with a healthy railway saga but no railway.

As visitors are the main beneficiaries of Bermuda's trainless railway system, they may wish to consider the evidence of the matter before passing judgement on this curious state of affairs.

Before World War II, it ought to be recalled, Bermuda was without motor vehicles; any journey beyond walking distance was, of necessity, by carriage or boat, often the latter because in the absence of cars there was no pressing need to do much about roads. The idea of a railway was brought up in 1899 and acted upon in 1922, by which time the local money had concluded it was crackpot and the funding had to be sought from abroad. The first train rolled on 31 October 1931, and the first-class passengers travelled in wicker chairs, *hoi polloi* on benches.

After the war, Bermudians were captivated by the novelty of the motor car and not inclined to stump up the £1 million required to make good "Old Rattle and Shake", who was thereupon sold off to British Guyana for further duties. Closer acquaintance with the problems associated with motor cars led to remorse, and with every passing restriction on the use of cars – some visitors would not be stretching their legs on this railway trail but for the ban on self-drive hire cars – Bermudians ask themselves whether they did the right thing. The soul-searching saga continues to this day.

The wrangling over the route of the proposed railway has turned out well for present purposes. Property owners wanted it nowhere near them, so the engineers were obliged to pick their way as far as possible along the shore. Ten percent of the track was elevated on 33 bridges, and as half of these cross water the line provides walkers with many splendid vistas. There are some tunnels and conventional railway cuttings, but on the whole the **Railway Trail** is as good a way to take in Bermuda as any. Lazy walkers may wish to remind themselves that trains avoid steep hills too.

The Bermuda Department of Tourism publishes a free guide to the Railway Trail. It is not now continuous because certain sections, especially round **Hamilton**, were taken up by new roads. The department's map indicates points of access for walkers arriving by bus and helpfully recommends stretches which, having been negotiated at a dawdling pace for anywhere between 1½ and 3 hours, will deposit

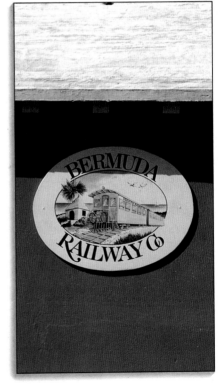

Preceding pages: island art in Somerset; the Devonshire coast. **Left**, a local resident. **Right**, the Bermuda Railway Co. is a chain of chic boutiques.

them at a point where they can conveniently catch a bus back to their hotels. Parts of the trail are open to self-propelled visitors on motor scooters and are safe spots for novices to familiarise themselves with the controls.

Guests staying in the resort hotels along the south coast are within walking distance of the section of the trail which forms the spine of the **Paget-Warwick-Southampton isthmus** between the South Road roundabout on the outskirts of Hamilton and Somerset village. Moving in that direction, the trail connects soon after a 450-ft (135-metre) tunnel with roads leading to spectacular **Elbow Beach**. Take along your bathing costume.

There follows a fine opportunity to reflect on the architectural features of old Bermuda houses which prompted Ralph Adams Cram, the American architect, to observe: "I wonder if Bermudians realise how unique, charming and distinguished are these dwellings, great and small, of the 17th and 18th centuries. They are absolutely indige-nous, built almost automatically by men of instinctive good taste."

The points to look out for are the wedding-cake roofs draining precious rain into a domed tank designed to keep it cool. The small, square outbuildings with pyramid roofs are butteries, a slight misnomer because they were used to store all perishables before the invention of refrigeration.

A group of allspice trees beyond the **Belmont Golf Course** conceals the small Warwick Pond bird sanctuary. The so-called **Khyber Pass** is a bit of harmless hyperbole, less Rudyard Kipling than chain gang, because this is where much of Bermuda's building stone was and is quarried. There is a clear distinction between the lower sections, which were worked by hand, and the bigger swathes cut above by modern machinery.

Tribe Road 7 meanders down through the **South Shore Beach Parklands**, a possible diversion from the trail which must be weighed up, if time is short, against another further along,

A train on opening day, 31 October 1931.

to **Gibbs Hill lighthouse**, beyond which the trail hugs the inside of the arc forming **Little Sound** against a backdrop of dunes and rock formations.

Readers of the history section of the book may now like to put themselves into the shoes of the 17th-century surveyor, Richard Norwood, under instructions from the autocratic governor, Daniel Tucker, to keep an eye open for desirable agricultural land which Tucker felt ought to belong to him, by hook or by crook.

Norwood, a blameless party to all this, began to recognise when he reached this section what he thought Tucker had in mind. Norwood's judgement was vindicated by the fact that, while agriculture in Bermuda generally was made unviable by prohibitive American tariffs, most of the 600 acres (245 hectares) which are still worth farming are in this region.

The scandal created by Tucker's machinations was Bermuda's 17th-century Watergate. It was known as "Overplus" and survives as the name of

the lane which bears sharp left to take trail-walkers on to **Middle Road** and thence to **Somerset Bridge**, "the smallest drawbridge in the world". It was probably built in the year (1619) that Tucker was grudgingly awarded a small share of his Overplus claim. The centre section of the bridge, 22 inches (55 cm) wide, is opened by hand in order to let a sailboat mast pass through.

Visitors staying in or near the capital should be aware of the chance to take a ferry from **Hamilton** to **Somerset Bridge**, either to backtrack on the sections described above or to advance along the remainder of the trail to picturesque **Somerset village**, a walk of less than 2 miles.

This stretch, however, could easily occupy a whole morning or afternoon because there is much of interest: historic **Fort Scaur**, clear views of **Ely's Harbour**, **Spanish Point** and (in the distance) **St George's**, as well as the 43-acre (17-hectare) **Heydon Trust Estate** and the **Springfield** and **Gilbert Nature Reserve**. The Somerset bus termi-

Train crossing trestle bridge at Baileys Bay.

nal at the end of the trail is the original railway station.

The Railway Trail running from Hamilton to St George's and beyond begins at **Palmetto Park**. Shortly after, it passes near **Palmetto House**, a lovely 300-year-old home. Sitting on the North Shore facing the sea, Palmetto House is built with its wings in the shape of a cross, a common architectural feature of its time. When the British army was stationed nearby, the house was used as a golf course clubhouse. Walkers of the Railway Trail are welcome to visit Palmetto House, but special arrangements must be made in advance. The National Trust headquarters at Waterville can advise.

The hillside along **North Shore Road** down to Flatts village has many examples of the Bermuda cedar which was so vital to the colony's early development. The tree is different from more common types of cedar, the most important from a shipbuilding point of view being the exceedingly fine grain which is watertight without the need for

seasoning. Many cedars were deliberately sacrificed by burning in the interest of exterminating a plague of rats which in the 17th century threatened to devour practically everything. The rats were an unsuspected part of a consignment of grain provided by a pirate.

The implications, justifiable or not, of the pole on **Gibbet Island** at the entrance to **Flatts Inlet** are discussed in the *Small Islands* chapter of this book (page 275). Trail walkers might anyhow like to imagine (or not, as the case may be) poles along this stretch of shoreline adorned with the quartered bits of Indian John, incompetent burglar and failed murderer. Witches, too, met their (flaming) end on this island.

The attractions of **Flatts Village** are gentler. The tide, racing through the narrow passage to **Harrington Sound**, has boats bobbing at their moorings. Bermuda's Aquarium in the same village contains nearly 100 species of fish in several tanks, the largest being a 40,000-gallon (150,000-litre) reef tank. The grounds around the Aquarium house birds and animals – flamingoes, macaws, giant tortoises, etc – and there are special facilities for children.

The trail contains through **Shelly Bay Park** and **Nature Reserve** and along a fine stretch of wild coastline which may work up a thirst quenchable, on reaching **Baileys Bay**, in the stylishly tatty **Swizzle Inn**, which also does nourishing snacks and meals at reasonable prices.

The crossing from **Coney Island** to **Ferry Point** is the boundary between Hamilton Parish and historic St George's, the change heralded by the remains of two **ancient forts**. The shoreline is different, too, suddenly bleak and in winter lashed by gales. The bodies of soldiers who died from yellow fever were brought to this place and buried in the **old cemetery**.

Astor's Halt is the nostalgic terminus of the Bermuda railway proper. It was here that a private line took over for the descent into St George's. Trail walkers could do worse than absorb the view from **Sugerloaf Hill** before making the descent.

This banyan tree, spotted on the trail, orginally came from tropical India. Right, the trail is within walking distance of good beaches.

THE WEST END

Bermuda consists of an East End and a West End, names which owe much to the island's British homeland, for these terms also define specific areas in London. Bermuda's West End has little to do with Parliament, art galleries and theatreland, however, and much to do with maritime activities.

The parish of Sandys, plus the islands of Somerset, Watford, Boaz and Ireland, have long been dominated by the great naval base at **Dockyard**, and even today, warships replaced by ferryboats and the barracks by bijou attractions, the tug towards Dockyard is strong. There is only one road (with a variety of names) and it, too, ends at this historic site – specifically, in front of Bermuda's Maritime Museum, with its important collection of exhibits.

Along the way to Dockyard, though, are lovely churches, surprising shopping, and pastel-painted Victorian mansions which echo the past. The Railway Trail, the scenic nature track which follows Bermuda's now-abandoned attempt at railway transport, is particularly attractive through Somerset and the parish of Sandys.

But perhaps most fun of all is the ferry ride from Hamilton. There are three ferry stops along this part of the island, conveniently located near sites of interest. It is an apt reminder of Bermuda's early history that most visitors choose to arrive at the West End by boat.

The ferry from Hamilton to Somerset Bridge, the first stop, squeezes through a channel called Timlin's Narrows before threading a picturesque path past a series of islets and rocky outcrops. More than 30 of these islets are scattered around **the Great Sound**, which is the basin formed by the left "hook" of Bermuda. Most are residential or barren, but a few are used by locals for recreational purposes, like camping trips or nature hikes. Curiously, for Bermuda has few indigenous animals, this northeast section houses a virtual menagerie – islets with names like Goat Island, Bird Island, Goose, Partridge and Cat Islands. Perhaps the settlers who presumably named them were homesick, or just hungry.

The ferry from Hamilton docks at a tiny white shelter, empty save for a (working) telephone and palm trees on the horizon. Closer scrutiny of the shelter reveals that "Greg 'n' Ruby" and "Jennifer & Becky was here" earlier.

A few minutes' walk down a tree-lined lane leads to **Somerset Bridge**. This bridge, which connects Somerset Island to the mainland of Bermuda, is said to be the smallest drawbridge in the world. Its 22-inch (55-cm) draw is opened by hand to allow boats to pass through. The bridge is a much-loved and well-photographed landmark, and even appears, sailboat at the ready, on the Bermudian $20 bill.

Sandys is an attractive parish, with marinas or boatyards at most strategic inlets, and stone staircases which lead off the main road sporting mysterious signs saying "Eleseum". The people of the West End are fiercely independent.

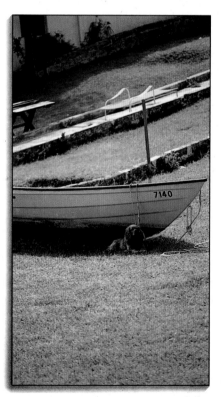

eceding ges: school ys; Dock- rd was the and's most ιbitious ilding heme. Left, ιngrove y. Right, s a dog's e.

During the American Civil War, when the rest of Bermuda supported the South, the defiant residents of Somerset threw their hats in with the damned Yankees of the North.

Both were united, however, in defence of Queen and Country. **Scaur Hill Fort** is built on the highest point of Somerset Island. Its construction in the 1870s was strategic; with a view that stretches in all directions and far out over **Ely's Harbour**, enemy armies advancing towards the royal naval base at Dockyard would be spotted well in advance of attack.

This vista from Scaur's high ramparts can still be admired through a telescope thoughtfully provided. Also on display are the remains of a Moncrieff Disappearing Carriage. The British were usurped as caretakers during World War II, when American troops used the fort as a US Marine outpost and nicknamed it "Cockroach Gulley". The fort is a fine spot for a picnic (no cockroaches in evidence) and tables are scattered throughout its grounds. If you go for a walk on the northern side of the slope facing the Sound, look for an isolated marker which states, rather wistfully: "London 3,076 miles".

Sandys parish is bisected by **Somerset Road** which, although pleasant, is clearly not intended for pedestrians. Skirting the high walls of Scaur Hill Fort while negotiating the deep curves of the narrow lane, a hapless footsoldier might well end up impaled on one of the (albeit historic) stone walls.

A winding uphill lane off Somerset Road leads to the **Heydon Trust**, one of Bermuda's few private parks. The park's owner, a Christian charitable trust, allows the public to wander through its 43 acres (18 hectares) from sunrise to sunset every day.

Even on a Saturday afternoon, the grounds are blissfully quiet: cardinals and butterflies flit through groves of banana trees and benches are provided in order to pause and savour the views. The vegetation is too lush, however, to allow for more than coy glimpses of the sea and lingering is best enjoyed further

Scaur Hill Fort.

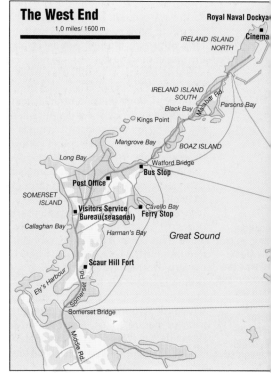

The West End

Royal Naval Dockyard

1,0 miles/ 1600 m

IRELAND ISLAND NORTH

Cinema

IRELAND ISLAND SOUTH

Black Bay

Parsons Bay

Kings Point

Mangrove Bay

BOAZ ISLAND

Long Bay

Watford Bridge

Bus Stop

Post Office

SOMERSET ISLAND

Visitors Service Bureau(seasonal)

Cavello Bay

Ferry Stop

Callaghan Bay

Harman's Bay

Great Sound

Scaur Hill Fort

Ely's Harbour

Somerset Bridge

Middle Rd

up the hill where the path levels off.

Tiny **Heydon chapel** is a squat, white building in traditional island style, with an interior almost monastic in its simplicity: whitewashed walls, three pews and a modest altar of cedar. Built before 1620, the chapel is thought to be the Somerset church mentioned in Norwood's Survey of 1616.

A stone tablet outside reads in part: "Lift up a song to Him/Who rides upon the clouds". A bare wooden cross stands on the crest of the hill with sea views encircling it. White sails flutter in the blue ocean far below, for the chapel is so elevated it is on a par with the horizon. Looking around, the simple charm of the church and the all-encompassing scenery does inspire. Just for a minute, it seems almost possible to "ride upon the clouds".

From Somerset Road **St James' church** appears perfectly proportioned. Whitewashed tombs flank a long driveway; beyond is the slate, grey-and-white facade of the church and behind it, the sea. Although an earlier wooden

structure probably existed on this site, much of the present church dates from 1789. Inside, although attention is rightly drawn to the handsome organ and polished cedar doors, the rear of the church also offers interest. A long wooden balcony with connecting stairs on either side takes up the rear wall. This modest construction was presumably for the black members of the community of St. James'.

Unusually, there is only one stained-glass window. Perhaps this is due to the lightning which struck the church in 1937, toppling the grand spire into the nave. Whatever the reason, cheerful sunlight floods into the room from colonial, arched windows, avoiding the gloomy atmosphere of so many religious buildings.

The pretty pink building with brown wooden shutters at the entrance to Portland Lane is a seasonal **Visitors Service Bureau**. Just beyond are the equally colourful (white and mustard green) walls which lead to **Kingdom Hall**, the church of the Jehovah's Witness. In

Perfectly proportioned St James' church.

fact, several of the buildings in this little hamlet consisting of a bakery, a grocery and an Italian restaurant are painted in pale ice cream colours; most notable is the pink and blue **Somerset Cricket Club**. To one side of the club is a cricket pitch and the engagingly named **Bat 'n' Ball Lane**.

Springfield is a perfect example of colonial architecture. Formerly the private home of the Gilbert family, its grounds have been turned into the **Gilbert Nature Reserve**, which includes 5 acres (2 hectares) of unspoiled land which is open until dusk. A walk around the back of this National Trust house reveals the original entrance to Springfield, plus a series of fascinating outbuildings: a kitchen, a slave quarters and a buttery. All now have other functions, either as a nursery school or private apartments or, in the case of Springfield House itself, as the Somerset branch of the **library.**

Although the library has only around 150 regular visitors a month (it's open three days a week) and the lack of air conditioning does the books little good, a rustle through the tumbling, cluttered shelves with its attractive blue reading lamps could unearth undemanding holiday reading. Even better is a cooling respite on the library's verandah, thought to have been a later addition to the house, which looks out over the lawns, acres of banana plants and the nature reserve.

The road towards **Long Bay Beach and Nature Reserve** leads to what is possibly the most incongruous and picturesque store in all of Bermuda, the tiny **Irish Linen** shop. Walk through a flower arcade of bougainvillea to purchase exquisite tablecloths, sheets, handkerchiefs, and christening dresses, all of finest linen. The shop is actually **Torwood**, the 18th-century family home of the owners of Bermuda's linen stores, and it was in the cellars of this mansion that the idea of importing fabric from Ireland, then selling it embellished with embroidery, was conceived.

At the time, 1949, finances were simple. The linens were sold at what-

Left, street signs. **Right**, the Irish Linen shop was a family home.

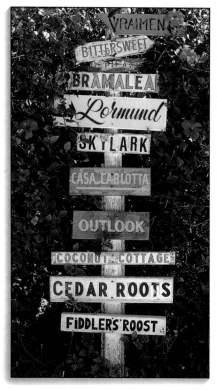

ever the owners felt was a fair price. The wooden packing cases from Ireland were offered to local farmers for chicken coops, and pound notes were known to have been carried off and buried by the family poodles. Tea was served in the drawing room at four o'clock for customers and staff. Now, the busy shop at the corner of Front and Queen Streets in Hamilton handles the majority of the family business, but it is infinitely preferable to buy beautiful goods within sight of a rose garden rather than of rush-hour traffic.

Further along, again deep in jungle-like vegetation, is a bucolic version of **Trimingham's**, selling that establishment's range of classy and classic sportswear.

Mangrove Bay is a curving sweep of idyllic beach from which, in summer, it is possible to hire sailboats, rowing sculls, motorboats, kayaks, snorkelling equipment, even rafts and fishing tackle. Mangrove trees (*Rhizophora mangle*) were once so plentiful they gave their name to this tranquil little lagoon but, although the species still exists on other parts of the island, it cannot now be found near the bay itself.

Hugging the northern shore of Mangrove Bay is **Somerset Village**, a tidy hamlet dominated by Sandys Boat Club and a restaurant-cum-tavern called the Country Squire. Visitors with money to spare can find much to choose from in the small selection of boutiques and craft centres. A good place for souvenirs is a former meat market called the Old Market, where it is possible to buy "discreetly sensual, memorable" locally produced cologne.

A welcome throw-back to the 1950s, when American kids went to sox hops and drank malteds at the local drugstore, is the **Somerset Pharmacy**. In the rear of this shop is a glorious soda-fountain with gleaming chrome stools, a Coca-Cola dispenser and quick snacks ranging from hot dogs (now microwaved) to, on cooler days, chilli. Even tastier is the home-made black-eyed pea soup, where a steaming bowl costs only pennies. If Elvis had been Bermudian,

High fliers.

he would have hung out at the Somerset Pharmacy.

Somerset Village also marks the beginning of Bermuda's **Railway Trail**. If you plan to walk any of the trail, this is the place to begin.

Just before Watford Bridge, a detour down East Shore Road leads to the **Gladys Morrell Nature Reserve**, a 2-acre patch of unspoiled land presented to the National Trust in 1973.

The three islands, **Watford**, **Boaz** and **Ireland South**, which link up to Somerset like a slightly accusing finger, point the way for the most important site in the West End: **Dockyard**. Bermudian street names like Honeysuckle Lane give way to stout English names (Victoria Row), emphasising the importance of the massive British naval base at Dockyard.

Until the **Watford Bridge** was built around the end of the 19th century, workers at the massive Dockyard had no idea whether they would be able to arrive at work, or even return home again, so erratic was the ferry service.

The erecting of this unassuming bridge contributed in no small measure to the defence of the country.

Crossing from Boaz (Gates Island in Bermuda's history books) into Ireland Island South, the road divides and encircles **Lagoon Park**, a beautiful open space with a central watery refuge for wild birds and nature trails which criss-cross much of the island. The road to the south is the scenic route, travelling in a narrow band between the lagoon and the sheltered sea before arriving at a beach cove and picnic site known as **Parson's Bay.** The main, northern road passes near two evocative burial grounds, the 19th-century **naval cemetery** and the equally historic **old convict cemetery**, where labourers who built Dockyard were laid to rest.

At the beginning of the 19th century, when Britannia ruled the waves, the Royal Navy needed a safe haven in the Atlantic. The Crown wanted to keep an eye not only on French privateers but also on the Americans who, after their successful revolution in 1776, closed all

Pottering around in Dockyard.

ports to the British. Bermuda was the obvious site and, in 1809, **Dockyard**, the most ambitious building scheme in which the island ever engaged, was begun. It was none too soon.

The fleet that attacked Washington DC in 1814 set sail from here, and there has not been a major war since in which Dockyard has not played a role. Over 9,000 slave labourers and English convicts toiled for 39 years under intolerable conditions to construct the wharfs, workshops and outbuildings which were to become the bastion of British power in the Western Atlantic. After the British pulled out of Bermuda in 1951, the Georgian buildings were abandoned, and it wasn't until the 1990s that the commercial potential of Dockyard was fully exploited.

Plans are now afoot to turn the site into a vast upscale recreational complex, consisting of shops, fine restaurants, a well-appointed marina, workshops and craft centres.

A tour of Dockyard is fascinating. It begins in the large building opposite the

Keep, where the barrels of drink were once kept. This building is now the premises of the **Dockyard Craft Market** and it is the pungent smell of cedar, rather than ale, which fills the air, emanating from a wood-turners' shop in the corner. The most complete collection of island crafts in Bermuda can be found at this market, from stained glass examples of indigenous birds, to cunning Gombey dolls in a variety of shapes and forms. Across the breezeway was the **Smithy**, with its huge fireplace of hard local stone.

Another fireplace is located in the lobby of the **Cooperage Theatre**, which several times daily shows a 30-minute audio-visual presentation called "Attack on Washington". (On certain nights the Cooperage Theatre turns into the **Neptune cinema** and shows non-historic, Hollywood-style movies.)

The grassy expanse in the middle of the complex was the **Vittling Yard**, where all supplies for the base were stored. It's a stately spot, surrounded by imposing two-storey Georgian build-

A wife shops while a husband flops.

THE SALVAGING OF THE *SEA VENTURE*

Allan (Smokey) Wingood is a former diver for the Maritime Museum. A chance opportunity to go helmet diving at the age of 14 was to prove a turning point in his life. Decades later, having survived some of the worst battles of World War II as a bomber pilot, and having retired from his successful commercial diving/underwater construction company business, Mr Wingood would prove that the remains of a shipwreck lying off the south-eastern tip of the island were those of the historic ship the *Sea Venture*.

"Cousteau did the same thing," Mr Wingood says. "He was in the air service of the French navy and with a gas engineer called Gagnan developed the aqualung."

Smokey (a soubriquet he earned at the age of seven when he was caught smoking behind the barn) was so enamoured of his first underwater experience that he resolved to get his own diving helmet. But since a manufactured one was beyond his financial reach, the schoolboy was determined to build his own. Working in their spare time, he and a friend crafted the helmet from a steel paint tin, affixed a lead collar to it and, after many failures, managed to insert a watertight glass face panel in it without breaking the glass. There was no fancy air supply, and hence no air hose.

Small wonder, then, that his father, "was always under the impression I was trying to kill myself," Mr Wingood laughs.

With the outbreak of World War II, Smokey joined the Royal Air Force and was presented with the Distinguished Flying Cross "for bravery and devotion to duty" by King George VI at Buckingham Palace. Back in Bermuda, the time had come for Smokey to realise a long-cherished dream: to form his own marine construction company. Eventually, he wound up diving for the Bermuda Maritime Museum, which triggered a lasting interest in marine archaeology.

In 1958 an American diver, Edmund Downing, discovered what he claimed was the wreck of the *Sea Venture* off the coast of St George's. With the island's 350th anniversary looming the following year his find seemed too convenient to be believed. Two decades would pass before Smokey Wingood pressed for an investigation of Downing's find with a view to proving or disproving his theory.

"To all intents and purposes the *Sea Venture* was never lost because the flat on which the ship sits is called Sea Venture Flat," Mr Wingood explains. "The wreck is located three-quarters of a mile from the shore off the most southeasterly point of Bermuda – and those are the things given in a contemporary account of the shipwreck."

Smokey formed the Sea Venture Trust and successfully obtained permission to be the sole diver on the wreck, promising that it would be a proper archaeological investigation which included the services of a recognised marine archaeologist. The Maritime Museum would take possession of any artefacts Mr Wingood brought up.

The project soon became an all-consuming passion, taking Mr Wingood and his wife to many countries for research at their own expense. Shards of pottery from the wreck were trekked around the museums of England until finally one in Plymouth confirmed that they matched similar shards which had been excavated in the Plymouth and Bristol areas, and which conformed to the period when the *Sea Venture* foundered.

Further confirmation came from Mr Ivor Noel Hume, chief archaeologist in colonial Williamsburg, Virginia, who reported that the Wingood shards matched pottery he was excavating in Martin's Hundred, near Jamestown, Virginia – where, incidentally, the *Sea Venture* had been sailing in the service of the Virginia Company before foundering on the reefs of Bermuda.

"So now it has been accepted internationally that the wreck is the *Sea Venture*, and Downing was right," Smokey says proudly. "How many other countries can say they have found the wreck of the ship that founded the colony?"

Mr Wingood has since written papers on the *Sea Venture* project for various nautical publications. Queen Elizabeth II recognised his work by awarding him the Queen's Certificate and Badge of Honour in her 1989 Birthday Honours list.

ings with arched windows. If you walk to the middle of the lawn and look towards the Cooperage, it's possible to see a large house on the right. This was the **Commissioner's House**, where all materials, like the Welsh slate roof, and we are told, marble fireplaces, mahogany woodwork and even domestic fittings, were shipped 3,000 miles (5,000 km) from the UK.

The convicts were paid three pennies a day for their back-breaking labours: one penny went towards food, one penny towards housing and the sole remaining penny went into their pockets. Ironically, overlooking the massive dockyard area is one of Bermuda's contemporary prisons. It is interesting to speculate what modern inmates must think when gazing down on the well-heeled visitors below. This prison will probably be moved to a less public site when Dockyard becomes fully operational as a tourist complex.

As a reminder of past glories, there is occasionally still a small naval presence berthed in the **South Basin**. On the far

side of the harbour are blue-and-white terminals for cruise ships. Nearer the dock are modern "tenders", which transport passengers from the cruise ships into Hamilton.

One of the later buildings to be constructed at Dockyard was the **Great Eastern Storehouse**, a handsome building with twin towers. Its facade is smoother than earlier buildings, presumably because, over the years, the convicts learned their trade. In front of the storehouse are the **King's Steps**, with the intriguing engraving "William IV Rex". No one is quite sure why the markings are retained, as he never came to Bermuda.

Because local stone is too porous to construct an ample dry dock, three ships towed the **floating dock** from England in 1869. Behind the Eastern Storehouse is a building with an intriguing history. The **Sail Loft** was built in 1860. Its handsome floor was made of teak to prevent splinters from getting into the sails. But by the time the building was completed, steam power had virtually

Vittling Yard: over 9,000 convicts laboured to build Dockyard.

replaced sails, and the loft saw little action in its intended function. The loft later had a brief but rowdy period as a dance-hall.

The **ramparts** offer wonderful views out to sea; directly below is reclaimed land. One huge, echoing warehouse is now the premises of the **Island Pottery**, with a small factory in the back where it is possible to watch potters at work. The **Bermuda Arts Centre** was opened by Princess Margaret in 1984. A non-profit organisation run by volunteers, the centre holds a changing exhibition every month.

The most important building at Dockyard was undoubtedly **the Keep**, with its moat, drawbridge, watergate and inner lagoon, where small boats were loaded with munitions and supplies for larger ships at anchor. The Keep was the last line of defence in the protection of Dockyard, should an enemy successfully pass the other massive fortresses protecting its approaches by land and sea. This handsome building (actually, series of buildings) is now the **Bermuda Maritime Museum**. There are exhibits on diving, navigation, shipping, whaling, plus a separate, very interesting walk around **the Keep's ramparts**, which are a towering 30 ft (9 metres) high.

The Maritime Museum vividly illustrates Bermuda's intimate connections with the sea. According to the publication *Life at Sea*, published in 1750, at any one time one-third of the adult male population was manning the island's sailing vessels. Strict regulations governed the number of free men aboard these ships, to ensure that enough manpower remained at home to prevent slave uprisings. But slaves went to sea, too, usually as crew, but occasionally rising to positions of power. They were also allowed to vote.

Privateer sloops carried the largest crews, often manned by ex-pirates, but the risk on board was so great, either from each other or from enemy privateers, that every man, regardless of status, voted on whether to do battle. Coming almost 200 years before black people played a significant role in political decisions, this is a striking example of the irregularities of life at sea.

To many people, the most fascinating room in the Maritime Museum is the **Treasury**. The exhibit of shipwreck archaeology features Bermuda's treasures, retrieved by Teddy Tucker and others from the island's reefs. Most of the booty is Spanish, like the gold bar weighing 984 grammes (35 ounces), as the Spanish were "easy victims". They sailed to the Old World laden with treasures from Spain's "New World", South America. Bermudians happened to be on hand. Archaeologists are particularly excited when "pieces of eight" are discovered. Over 2,000 of these silver coins have come to light, which provide important clues as to the date and source of the wreck being salvaged.

The Treasury's caretaker is Douglas Little. With his ruddy features, sailor's hat and peg leg, this man is the epitome of a sea-faring Bermudian. The fact that Mr Little is a confirmed landlubber should in no way cast doubt on the veracity of the Maritime Museum.

Dockyard took 39 years to complete. Right, Douglas Little, caretaker at the Maritime Museum.

HARRINGTON SOUND

Harrington Sound is a salt water lake almost 6 miles (10 km) long. It is ringed by nature reserves and natural caves, many of which form Bermuda's premier tourist attractions. The surrounding area is lush and extensive. Much of Harrington Sound lies in Hamilton parish, which bears no relation to the capital, but Verdmont, the most interesting of Bermuda's historic houses, lies in neighbouring Smith's.

Verdmont was built around 1710 in the style of a small English manor house. This peach-coloured home was in continuous residence until fairly recently, when it was sold to the National Trust. The last owner, a Miss Lillian Joell, never bothered to modernise the property, preferring instead to live by oil lamps and cook by kerosene, right up to the middle of this century. Inside, the floorboards are bare and a little bit scuffed, the walls are peeling in places, as if a hand too busy with other matters attempted to slap on a coat of paint.

This adds, rather than detracts, from Verdmont's charm, for its cosy atmosphere is in direct contrast to the French-polished formality of many historic homes around the world. Rumours are afoot that the National Trust plans to "smarten up" Verdmont's interior, which would be a great pity.

Verdmont is approached by a flag-stoned path, wonderfully fragrant with wild flowers. To appreciate its proportions, go around to the south side, as the house was constructed to look out over the sea. Verdmont's four great chimneys, two at either end, allowed for a fireplace in each room; the cedar balcony replaces a Victorian portico and was added by restorers.

The gardens are delightful, skimming down to the sea in graceful undulations. Although the volunteer guide claims the shrubberies date from the 18th century, which means they would have weathered many a gale, this is a romantic view; they were in fact planted by the National Trust from several varieties

which grew on the island at the time.

Inside, much of the furniture, assembled from other island properties, is of Bermuda cedar and made by local craftsmen. The wooden armchair in the dining room, called a "Cromwellian", is probably the oldest piece, and pre-dates Verdmont by 50 years.

Although there is much to see in the sunny drawing room and the library with its fine roll-top desk, the real charm lies upstairs in the nursery. Strewn around a miniature canopied bed is an eccentric collection of Victorian toys including a rocking horse with no ears and a horse-headed tricycle, quite the reverse of modern cycles, for it was propelled by the arms while steering with the legs. A Dresden doll lies in a baby cradle – rare for its day and even more valuable now – for the doll has brown eyes rather than the regulatory blue.

Modern parents, please note: a slim volume discovered in the nursery's bookcase, *Etiquette for Little Folks*, published in Boston in 1856, reads in part: "Modesty is a polite accomplish-

Preceding pages: minimalism is memorable; Devil's Hole, possibly the first tourist attraction. Left, Verdmont. Right, engaging children.

ment, and generally attendant upon merit. It is engaging, in the highest degree, and wins the hearts of all with whom we are acquainted. None are more disgusting in company than the impudent..."

East of Verdmont lies **Spittal Pond**, the island's largest wildlife sanctuary. Unlike other reserves, which can be visited only by special permission, Spittal Pond's 60 acres (25 hectares) are open daily to the public. About 25 species of waterfowl choose to winter in Bermuda, and most of them opt for this open space with its large pond suitable for swimming. Spectators are requested to keep to the pathways.

Another nature reserve lies nearby: the **H.T. North Reserve** at the western end of Mangrove Lake on the border of Hamilton parish. Bermuda's reserves are not just of interest to ornithologists, however, for in addition to exotic birds there are many examples of rare flowers, which thrive on the protected land.

Situated high on a hill between Spittal Pond and the south shore is **Spanish Rock,** the starting point for an intriguing little tale. When the early colonists arrived in Bermuda they found, carved into this rock, the initials "TF" or "TFC", plus a date: 1543. Historians are divided over whether the initials stand for the Spanish adventurer Theodore Fernando Camelo, or whether the engravings were left by Portuguese explorers who might also have visited the island. Modern thought seems to favour Señor Camelo, hence the name. A cast of the inscription, taken from Spanish Rock, can be seen in the foyer of the Bermuda Library, but as the original initials have now been wiped out, a bronze plaque taken from this cast now marks the spot.

Knapton Hill Road leads to **Devil's Hole** and its **Aquarium**, the island's first tourist attraction, established in 1834. The "hole" is actually a natural pool where, for the price of an admission fee, it's possible to fish with hookless lines for sharks, Moray eels, fish, and loggerhead turtles.

Entrance is, eccentrically, through

Sonesta Beach hotel.

the Angel Wings café (avoid fish on the menu), but the best possible description of Devil's Hole has been written by its owner and is posted out front. It reads: "The beauties of nature abound around a pool of 32 foot depth of clear blue water alive with the silent movement of beautiful and ferocious fish invites relaxation and rest or arouses the spirit for sport fishing." Enough said. The nearby rock in Harrington Sound is called, appropriately, **Turtle Island**.

Devil's Hole marks the beginning of a circular route around the Sound which can be made on foot, by moped or, for the privileged, by car. Heading north up Harrington Sound Road, the first junction reached is the village of **Flatts.** Rumour has it that Flatts was once a smugglers' cove, and its position, on a spindly neck of land which leads to the open sea, would lend credence to this theory. It is now a popular stopping-off point for yachts, whose tall masts make ghostly silhouettes at sunset.

All in all, Flatts is a very pretty spot, with a tasteful blend of new and old buildings painted a variety of ice-cream colours. The new buildings, although attractive, replace an elegant hotel whose loss is mourned by Bermudians, an example of the island's increasing capitulation to commerce.

The Bermuda Aquarium, Museum and Zoo, all located within the same grounds, has its own landing dock for the loading and unloading of animals. The cool verandah of the **Bermuda Aquarium** is a perfect place to observe the comings and goings of Flatts. The interior of this sea-green building is ultra modern, belying its opening date of 1928. Fish tanks are filled with unfiltered salt water and coral prised from the seabed. It's evident that a great deal of thought has gone into making life agreeable for the fish, all of whom are native to Bermuda. For example, a reef tank with an artificial tide has been installed for species that need the ebb and flow of the sea.

Visitors select a wand-like instrument and wander from tank to tank listening to an audio commentary on

Island ceramic; scooting around Flatts village.

exotic specimens such as the peacock flounder who lies down so that he can see: both eyes are on the same side of his body. Sea-horses trot merrily through smaller tanks, but the darker side of marine life is not overlooked.

In one tank, which covers an entire wall, swim barracuda, a dusky shark which can grow up to 12 ft (4 metres) in length, a huge hawksbill turtle and assorted other fish. The shark's dinner is these "other fish", who form excited little schools to protect themselves. It is quite disturbing to have a front-row seat at mealtime, for the smaller fish, trapped in a glass corner, are close enough to reveal their terror seconds before being gobbled up. Children love this spectacle, however, and egg on the shark with glee.

Other animals seem happy enough. Charlotte and Archie, the resident harbour seals, gave birth on 23 June 1989 to a pup named Calico, who can be seen waddling in a pool just outside the Aquarium. In the **Bermuda Zoo**, a reptile walkway provides views of tortoises, lizards, terrapins and alligators in "natural" settings. The Galapagos tortoises, an endangered species, were first bred outside their native island in the Bermuda Zoo.

Inside the terrestrial room of the **Natural History Museum**, it is possible to watch a movie (through a porthole) of a recent attempt to duplicate the success of the Beebe Project. This was an experiment conducted in 1934 by Dr William Beebe to descend deep into the ocean off the coast of Bermuda to document fish never seen before. Dr Beebe, director of Tropical Research for the New York Zoological Society, descended over half a mile (800 metres). The local (when the movie was made) attempt was less successful, but a replica of the original Bathysphere, the "underwater laboratory" which Dr Beebe used for his feat, can be seen outside the museum.

Leaving Flatts, Harrington Sound Road temporarily becomes the continuation of **North Shore Road**, the long, unswerving, and fairly traffic-free

Old-fashioned exterior but with modern facilities.

boulevard which begins at Spanish Point in the parish of Pembroke and extends all the way to the greenery of the delightfully named **Coney Island**. It is a beautiful route which parallels the Railway Trail, and this stretch offers some of the finest scenery to be found in the parish of Hamilton.

Both **Shelley Bay**, with its beach, nature reserve and park, and Shelley's eastern neighbour, **Baileys Bay**, are named after early Bermudian settlers. **Crawl Hill**, just before Baileys, is the highest point in Hamilton parish and worth a short stop for the view.

Within the Baileys Bay area is a series of tourist attractions like a busy **pottery**, a **glass-blowing workshop**, an **ice cream parlour**, and the **Swizzle Inn**, a well-known hostelry serving up copious quantities of the island speciality, rum swizzles. Until recently this was also the home of the Blue Grotto Dolphin Show, but no longer. It is said that when one of the dolphins passed away the other died of a broken heart, so the grotto is now closed.

One of the best attractions can often be smelt before it can be seen: the **Bermuda Perfumery**. Surrounding the working perfumery are gardens where passion flowers and Easter lilies, used in the production of scent, grow in sweet-smelling profusion.

Much of the grounds have been given over to a **Nature Trail** which, in full bloom at the height of spring, provides an aphrodisiacal walk in miniature, for the entire route is just over one-third of a mile and can be covered in 12 minutes. The trail is laid out in a series of gradients which belie its tiny proportions and, although still suffering from hurricane damage, rambles past fat sago palms, which look like hairy pineapples, and Bird of Paradise flowers.

The trail is really quite charming and, at its deepest part, known as "the Jungle", it would be easy to believe the real world were far away, were it not for the incessant buzzing of scooters accelerating to get to the top of a steep hill nearby. It might be best to pretend the sound is the buzzing of bees, rather than

In the swim: *Holacanthus tricolor*, or Rock beauty.

scooters, to preserve the ambience.

Towards the Palm Grove are two smooth grey trees which even knowledgeable horticulturists have been unable to identify. In 1986 the perfumery offered a reward of BD$100 (plus perfume) to the first person to identify them correctly. To date, although there have been more than 100 attempts, these hardy specimens of the *Leguminosae* family remain the "Mystery Trees". The trail can be muddy, so wear rubbersoled shoes.

Scents and sensibility: The Bermuda Perfumery began in a wooden shed in 1929, started by Madeline Scott, a keen gardener, and her husband Herbert, a chemical engineer. In 1931 a 200-year-old farmhouse became the new home for Scott's burgeoning business, which was the cultivation of Easter lilies. Additional construction in 1934 produced the building which now houses the perfumery – a series of rooms, displays and glass bottles, like an oldfashioned laboratory, which culminates in the modern "factory" upstairs.

All the flowers for the colognes and after-shaves – except for two, which grow wild – are cultivated in the surrounding gardens. The fragrances include Oleander, Jasmine, Passion Flower, Frangipanni and the top sellers, Easter Lily and Bermudiana. In honour of the perfumery's 60th anniversary, in 1989, a new scent, Paradise, was added to the list.

Church Bay in Harrington Sound is so named because of **Holy Trinity Church**, one of the oldest on the island. It lies very near the water, presumably so that, in 1623 when the church was built, worshippers could arrive by boat. The region around Church Bay is riddled with caves. For centuries cave exploration was a popular activity, for it was commonly believed that gold and precious diamonds had been hidden by extinct tribes.

Pot-holers should note that some caves can be reached only on hands and knees; others are underwater. It is claimed that a team of local divers discovered one cave full of blind shrimps.

The Bermuda Perfumery uses local flowers.

Other caverns are accessible, like the cave attached to the Grotto Bay Beach hotel, which has been turned into a lounge bar (wear waterproof clothing to avoid the drips). The **Amber Caves of Leamington** lie in the grounds of the Plantation Restaurant, a nice spot for lunch. Occasionally "packages" are offered which include a meal at the Plantation and free entry into the caves.

The most breathtaking of the lot is undoubtedly the **Crystal Caves**, located, appropriately, on Crystal Caves Road, a tranquil cul-de-sac which winds through a small plantation of palms and open fields. The caves were discovered in 1907 by two small boys pursuing a lost ball which had rolled down a hole in the ground. Further exploration revealed an enormous cavern surrounding an underground lake of clear water. Although the 120-ft (37-metre) descent was originally made by ladder, today the lake can be reached by a gently sloping path and a few steps.

The interior is astonishing; an underground cathedral of crystal and water.

As Cahow Lake is salt water, with two tides a day, there is constant movement. This movement creates ripples which, together with underwater spotlights, causes the water to shimmer in shades from turquoise to midnight black. Two of the stalagmites are over 1 million years old, while other rock formations are reflected in the water in fascinating shapes – the Manhattan skyline, for instance, or a very watery Buddha.

The climate underground is cool in the summer and warm in the winter, for the temperature remains constant at 68° F (20° C). The Crystal Caves might well be Bermuda's premier visitor's attraction and should not be missed. And no, the boys never did get their ball back.

Between the Crystal and Leamington Caves lies **Walsingham Bay**, linked to the 19th-century Irish poet Tom Moore, who arrived in Bermuda to take up a government post and wreak havoc with the hearts of young ladies. Moore had achieved considerable fame in Britain, and at one point was even mooted as Poet Laureate of Ireland. According to

William Zuill, in his booklet *Tom Moore's Bermuda Poems*, the Bermuda position was merely a fee-paying job and, after four months (and several scandals), Moore returned to Ireland and literary achievement.

Moore spent some time at **Walsingham House**, which had in its grounds a calabash tree. From this memory Moore composed the lines: *'Twas thus, by the shade of a calabash-tree, With a few, who could feel and remember like me, The charm, that to sweeten my goblet I threw, Was a sigh to the past and a blessing on you!*

Moore spent many more hours in the town of St George's than he did at Walsingham House (see *The East End,* page 258), so it remains a mystery as to why this particular spot should claim his name. Nevertheless, Walsingham House is now an elegant restaurant called **Tom Moore's Tavern**, and a very pretty spot it is, too.

The east coast of Harrington Sound, directly opposite St George's parish, was well known in Bermuda's history.

The area around **Castle Harbour** was designated by governor Daniel Tucker to replace St George's as the island's new capital. He proposed to call it Tucker's Town. Whether the plan actually got off the ground or remained a figment of the governor's greedy imagination is unknown, but **Tucker's Town** is now an exclusive residential area where properties change hands for several million Bermudian dollars.

Tucker's Town is surrounded by golf courses. The public **Castle Harbour Golf Club** is to the northwest, and the private **Mid Ocean Club** is towards the spectacular rock formations, the **Natural Arches**. The Mid Ocean is Bermuda's oldest golf course, designed by an American champion in 1921. The famous or merely wealthy flock to suffer the challenges of its fairways, which overlook the sea and undulate towards two separate bodies of water, **Trott's Pond** and **Mangrove Lake**. Eisenhower met Churchill at the Mid Ocean, but it remains unrecorded as to which world leader had the greater handicap.

Tom Moore and his muse.

Bermuda, Tom Moore's Calabash Tree.

NOTES FOR NERVOUS DRIVERS

Bermudians have cars. Visitors have motor scooters. This idea – clear, direct, and wonderfully discriminating – has kept many a holidaymaker off Bermuda's roads entirely.

A shame, really, for some of the island's best-kept secrets are hidden down tiny lanes or halfway up hillsides where buses never tread and taxis are uncalled for. The solution leads back to motor scooters.

Just why the thought of hiring one of these innocuous vehicles – mopeds, scooters, cycles or bikes – should inspire such fear in the hearts of visitors is surprising. The maximum speed limit is a perfect 20 mph (35 kph). Bermudian drivers are infamously polite and tolerant. They would no more dream of harassing a novice cyclist than they would contemplate the idea of swimming in the sea before May. Old ladies riding to market have been known to create a queue of six cars unable to pass, which may give cause for complaint, but drivers never, ever honk. In the local vernacular, it's simply not done.

Bermuda's petite size makes it ideal for scooter touring and so do Bermuda's scooters. Many "beginner bikes" do not come equipped with rear-view mirrors. This technical oversight is a godsend to nervous drivers, for it becomes physically impossible to see, and as a result become intimidated by, any queues of impatient cars building up behind.

Anyone who can ride a bicycle can drive a moped. Only two things need to be considered: hiring a scooter, and choosing the inaugural route. Rental centres are widespread and usually charge by the day, with prices decreasing the more days the bike is hired out. No driver's licence is required.

Most centres include an introductory lesson, but instructors tend to be rev-happy teenagers unconversant with a beginner's fears. Be firm. Ask to be shown again. Ask if he or she will watch as you wobble around the forecourt. Check the brakes. For a faster response when slowing down, ride with the fingers of the left hand resting on the rear brake lever. Helmets must be worn at all times, and it's wise to take a sweater in the summer or a leather jacket in the winter; the air can get chilly. Bermudians always drive on the *left-hand side* of the road.

The route a nervous driver selects for that all-important first run can make or break the decision to ride again. There are many choices around the island, from the peace of the Railway Trail to the clockwise-charm of Harrington Sound, where drivers who overshoot their intended destination need only keep going in a circle before coming across the turning again.

One tried-and-tested route is to drive the distance from Hamilton to St George's – at least half the distance of the entire island – without stopping. This circuit is nicknamed the "Go For It Route" for it caters to people determined to conquer their fear of the roads, but who are basically cowards at heart.

The "Go For It Route" is travelled in about 40 minutes. It involves a couple of right-hand turnings to get out of Hamilton (plotted in advance), a few dodgy moments while checking out roadsigns, and then levels off at the North Shore Road. The North Shore is every nervous driver's dream. It runs in a straight line to your precise destination. It is relatively free of traffic, certainly compared to the bus-fumed South Road, with scenery pleasant enough to be appealing but not so awe-inspiring as to divert from the mission at hand: getting to St George's.

The time involved is an excellent introductory length. The tedious business of stopping, starting, and winding through traffic over, exhilaration sets in, along with the realisation that anything difficult has already been accomplished. The long smooth road ahead – every sign pointing to St George's – is intoxicating.

Once in St George's, park the scooter by the harbour. Then lock it: insurance against theft is not included in the rental. Walk swiftly to the White Horse Tavern, and indulge in a well-earned brandy.

For the faint-hearted, buses lead straight back to Hamilton but victors will want to stroll around town to sober up cheerfully, and will never use public transport again.

THE EAST END

Progress in Bermuda – in terms of a bridge here, a causeway there, nothing too radical – has blurred but not quite obliterated the distinctive characteristics of individual islands. **St David's**, which together with **St George's** (the island, as opposed to merely the town) makes up the bulk of the eastern wing of Bermuda, retained an extraordinary degree of cultural insularity until – and even after – the 1930s, when a bridge finally replaced the old ferry link with the other islands.

A St David's man, probably with features revealing North American Indian blood, may still claim a closer identification with that island than Bermuda as a whole, although such a remark ought not to be taken too literally. The issue is parochial pride rather than festering secessionist tendencies. E. A. McCallan's highly enjoyable memoirs, *Life on Old St David's*, published by the Bermuda Historical Society and found in local bookstores, rattles on as if the rest of Bermuda scarcely existed.

The bridge which joined St David's and St George's – the two names are respectively those of the patron saints of Wales and England – was pointedly named after the Severn Bridge between the two British neighbours. There used to be the odd character who, living at either end of Bermuda, would boast of never having been to the other. The constant flow of traffic on an uninterrupted road right across Bermuda now makes such claims sound less quaintly defiant than gratuitously silly.

Nevertheless, while time and communications have eroded the barriers, Bermudian loyalties are divided between Hamilton and St George's, with even smaller pockets of allegiance to hamlets like Somerset and Flatts. The instincts which, for example, steered sympathies into one or other camp during the American Revolution and later in the Civil War, as well as in domestic disputes, are not yet ready to be buried.

"The harbour of St George is one of the most beautiful and secure harbours in the world," a Dr Theodore L. Godet noted in 1860. In his medical opinion, Bermuda was ideal for "natives of cold countries who, from general delicacy of constitution, are unable to undergo active continuous labour with exposure," but St George's was an exception. Dr Godet, it should be noted, was a West Ender. "The streets are extremely narrow," he sniffed, "which is a great disadvantage, as the accumulation of much confined air is occasioned thereby, which consequently renders the town unhealthy."

What was true of **St George's** then is not much changed now, and it is difficult to understand what the good doctor was going on about. No building was higher than two storeys, the population was measured in hundreds, and refreshing breezes swept in from thousands of square miles of open ocean.

The narrow "streets" which worried Dr Godet are, for modern visitors, aesthetic assets with appealing names like **One Gun Alley**, **Shinbone Alley** and

Preceding pages: St George's; a reflective portrait of children. **Left**, Bob Burns, Town Crier. **Right**, a hoax happened in the Town Hall.

Featherbed Alley. Old Maid's Lane, for example, was once Cumberland Lane; the nickname was inspired by the number of spinsters who coincidentally happened to live there. Their strenuous efforts to resist the creeping use of the new name included the erection of a sign upon which "Cumberland Lane" was writ emphatically large.

Although their rearguard campaign proved futile, they may have derived some posthumous consolation from the lane's later role as a kind of Juliet's balcony in Bermuda's most celebrated romance. It involved Nea, wife to one of the indomitable Tucker clan, and the visiting Irish poet Tom Moore who, until eclipsed by the man himself, had a precocious, Byronic reputation in English society. He first caught sight of young Nea walking down the lane and that set him off:

And thou, when at dawn, thou shalt happen to roam
Through the lime-covered alley that leads to thy home

With Moore bringing round little notes with lines like "Sweet Nea! let us roam no more" the House of Tucker put its foot down. He was banished from the house, although presumably not even the Tuckers could deny him the right to gaze up Old Maid's Lane with a throbbing heart. His infatuation later received official blessing, or at least recognition, with the naming of an adjacent lane after Nea.

A **bust of Tom Moore** is to be found in a small, walled garden very near the **Bridge House**, home to several governors and to Bridger Goodrich, hero to some and pirate to others, not least Thomas Jefferson. The house is now an art gallery and shop selling original art, prints and old postcards.

The Tuckers had another, grander house at the corner of Water Street and Barber Lane, the latter a reference to a freed American slave named Joseph Rainey who escaped to Bermuda at the outset of the Civil War. He and his French wife lived and worked in the kitchen of the **Tucker House**, he as a barber and she as a dressmaker. He

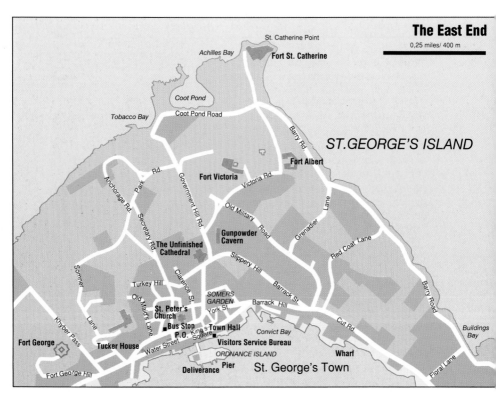

planned to return after the war and pursue a career in the Church, but went into politics instead and, unprecedented for a black man, was elected to the House of Representatives in 1870. The Tucker House is now a National Trust property housing a museum and the building itself has many important architectural features (see *Island Architecture*, page 89, for a guide to Bermudian style).

The **Carriage Museum**, across the road from the Tucker House, with its large collection of buggies, surreys and shays, could almost be regarded as a monument to Bermuda's resolute, but ultimately futile, resistance to the introduction of the motor car.

St George's rich anecdotal history, admirably set down in William Zuill's 1946 *Bermuda Journey* and works by the tireless Mrs Terry Tucker, who married into the family from Britain's Isle of Wight, greatly enhances what most visitors would anyhow wish to do in the town, which is simply to stroll about. From the beginning of the 19th century, most of Bermuda's development was concentrated around Hamilton, which replaced St George's as capital in 1815, a bitter pill for St Georgians. The differences lay in the harbours. Reefs made the approaches to St George's treacherously narrow and as ships grew larger they could not cope. The channels were progressively widened but it was always too little too late.

Visitors – and, one suspects, most St Georgians – now relish the commercial neglect which left the town much as it had always been. The alleys have not expanded beyond the width needed to roll a barrel. The concessions made to that World War II intruder, the motor vehicle, were minimal. St George's is practically as old as Jamestown, the first European settlement in America, and it feels as unaffectedly pristine as any town in the New World.

Gravity draws the winding alleys in the old part of the town down to **Kings Square**, a.k.a. Market Square, which resembles a film set in the absence of jarring anachronisms. It is the invariable fate of a photographer's travelling

companion to pose contritely in the preserved pillory and stocks.

Although the **ducking stool** was used even-handedly for petty offenders of either gender, it is best remembered (or resented) as a summary lesson for wives who nagged or were otherwise tiresome. A certain Goodwife Prosser, evidently an appalling creature, was forever being shown her errors – on one occasion her foul-mouthed behaviour warranted no fewer than six successive dips. The stool is still wheeled over to the water's edge for practical demonstrations, although the wet seat once occupied by petulant wretches like Goodwife Prosser now tends to be filled by a volunteer, possibly an attractive member of the crew of a visiting yacht or a selflessly dedicated employee of the Department of Tourism.

Bob Burns, the ubiquitous **Town Crier**, has an entry in the *Guinness Book of Records* to verify the all-conquering volume of his voice. The **Visitors Service Bureau** on the water's edge is well-stocked with information about St George's; a "Bermuda Journey" slide-show is presented in the Town Hall, and an entertaining history of the town by David Raine, a contributor to this book, is on sale in the Bridge House. The bureau can also help with accommodation in the area.

Added to all this, the congenial Town Crier shows visitors around and is not horrified by an invitation to pull up a stool in, say, the venerable White Horse Tavern, across the square from the Town Hall. The Mayor puts down his pen at about 11 o'clock some mornings, bedecks himself with the chain of office, and emerges into the square specifically to meet and chat to visitors.

A great deal of Bermuda's turbulent early history evolved in and around Kings Square. Chronologically, a walking tour ought to begin with the replica of *Deliverance* on **Ordnance Island**, a former British army arsenal. A certain amount of educated guesswork went into the reconstruction of the ship because the original was improvised out of the salvage from *Sea Venture*, the **Before... and after.**

260

ship which struck a reef while carrying some of the first settlers to Virginia. *Deliverance* (and a second vessel, *Patience*) took a year to build, during which time some of the delayed settlers began to wonder whether Bermuda, without hostile Indians, might be a better bet than Jamestown, Virginia, their original destination.

The interior of the ship is tiny, with little headroom and even less space for sleeping. Conditions during the 14-day journey to Virginia must have been intolerable. Those who stayed behind set up camp on Smith's Island. The choice of St George's as the main settlement was made by the governor in charge of Bermuda's first intentional settlers who, attracted by contrary reports reaching England about these supposedly dreadful dots in the mid-Atlantic, arrived in 1612 – just as the "three kings", as those who held the fort came to be known, were planning to leave.

The islands were then thickly wooded with cedar and palmetto trees which were an easy source of building materials. The **Town Hall**, focal point of Kings Square, was built of stone some 200 years later and was used for all sorts of non-municipal purposes, including entertainment.

In his book, *Bermuda Journey*, Zuill recounts a splendid hoax. The hall was packed to capacity in anticipation of *Ali Baba and the Forty Thieves*, a production staged by a certain Professor Trott. The audience, growing restless with a delay well beyond the advertised starting time, cheered with relief when the professor's head at last poked through the curtains to say: "Now you see me and now you don't", or words to that effect. Still nothing happened; in due course the head re-emerged with the same comforting, though somewhat enigmatic, message. This baffling routine was repeated a third time, but yet again without result.

The mood of the audience degenerated from impatience to anger. The professor's head failed to reappear. Ticket holders eventually barged through the curtains to find a bare stage:

Café viewing.

no Professor Trott, no sign of any preparations for *Ali Baba* and absolutely no chance of a refund. The evening ended in chaos and no explanation was forthcoming until, two days later, "Professor Trott" put in another appearance – on this occasion, in the police court, where he was charged with the theft of a safe while his theatre-loving victims were, of course, otherwise occupied.

The disgruntled audience very likely filed across the square to the **White Horse Tavern** for a drink. The pub was no stranger to bizarre practices. It was once the home of John Davenport, a paranoid entrepreneur who kept his money in arrowroot kegs in a basement fortress to ward off a world which, he felt, was out to rob him.

Which of the kegs contained the money was a secret entrusted only to his manservant, who was required to accompany Davenport down to the basement each day and hold up a candle while he bored a gimlet into the relevant keg. The hardness of metal beneath a layer of arrowroot was sure confirmation to both men that all was well.

This ritual was followed until Davenport's death, when his executors had to sort out the kegs. They were removed one by one over several days, emptied and, in the case of those riddled with gimlet holes, the contents counted. The final tally was an astonishing £75,000 in gold and silver. Today, the White Horse is the place for a refreshing glass of beer, but don't forget it is illegal to take drinks outside onto the square itself.

Another building of interest in the square is the **Confederate Museum**, formerly the Globe Hotel and, for the duration of the American Civil War, the headquarters and home of the Confederate agent, Major Norman Walker and his wife. Their portraits hang on a wall in the museum. The Union was represented in St George's by a consul, Charles Maxwell Allen, whose fairly frequent abuse at the hands of locals who favoured the Confederacy did not dissuade him from eventually settling in Bermuda after the war.

Local support for the southern states

The White Horse Tavern.

did not necessarily reflect high moral principles. There were fortunes to be made out of blockade-running trade with the south, a prospect which turned St George's into a rip-roaring magnet for adventurers, some in the "gentleman" class, others not. "Dr Blackburn" was definitely in the latter category. Ostensibly a philanthropic physician, he was actually a Confederate agent who collected the infected clothing of the victims of a yellow fever epidemic then sweeping Bermuda with a view to making poisonous presents of it to the civilian population in the North.

The museum has a fine collection of war memorabilia, including an antique Victorian seal press and a large wall-map, designed by noted local artist Desmond Fountain, of the blockade-running routes.

The beautifully preserved **St Peter's** above Kings Square was no ordinary parish church during Bermuda's early days; more often than not, it was centre stage for bruising battles that might have nothing to do with God and relig-

ion. The conflict between the established church and the Puritans in England did surface in ferocious local microcosm, but there were also purely secular vendettas which could explode in the middle of a service and lead to brawls. The church was later used as a courthouse for a while, the scaffold being conveniently situated down the hill on Ordnance Island.

The first church on the site, a thatched hut, was replaced by a more substantial structure in 1619. The basis of the existing building goes back to 1713. One way or another, St Peter's is "the oldest Anglican church in continuous use in the western hemisphere."

The altar is of local cedar, much darkened since it was made in 1624, the year before the parish was presented with its silver chalice by the Bermuda Company in London. The triple-decker pulpit is 17th century, as is a massive set of communion silver, the gift of King William III and engraved with his initials. The walls are lined with commemorative tablets whose inscriptions

provided a colourful, though necessarily selective, commentary on the passing show. The memorials are not always in strict proportion to the achievements of the people they eulogise. A specially commissioned sculpture by John Bacon, a big name in his time, glorifies Colonel Campbell, whose tenure as governor in 1796 lasted all of 12 days before he succumbed to fever.

St Peter's was very nearly lost to future generations. Its condition in the 19th century led to a campaign for something rather better, and in 1874 work commenced on what was to be a fine neo-Gothic cathedral. As the roof went on and the tower rose, so did the cost. The restoration of St Peter's began to look more and more sensible and the new project was summarily abandoned.

The hulk of the **Unfinished Cathedral**, a spiritual *Marie Celeste* sprouting undergrowth between blocks of masonry just as the departing workmen left them, has assumed the nobility of an ancient monument and is photographed by visitors more assiduously than would have been the case had it ever been completed.

The **State House**, east of Kings Square, was built in 1620 with immense limestone walls, the first stone building in Bermuda. To the discomfort of members of the Assembly who convened there, it served a secondary role as a gunpowder magazine. The governor was prevailed upon to place this potential bomb elsewhere and, with a fine disregard for his own safety had it installed in the grounds of his residence on Retreat Hill.

The danger came from an entirely different quarter – from the Tuckers who, in concert with others, stole the powder in order to sell it to a grateful General Washington during the American Revolution. The enraged governor promptly restored what little powder was left to its former place in the State House, poignantly above the heads of some of those whom he suspected of complicity. A later magazine has been converted into a bunker-like restaurant and bar, the **Gunpowder Cavern**.

The Unfinished Cathedral, like a spiritual *Marie Celeste*.

St George's lost its State House when the capital was moved to Hamilton, and the building was given over to the Masonic Lodge at a peppercorn rent, a ceremony which is re-enacted annually with much pomp and circumstance. The present **post office** also has connections with the American Revolution: it was a hell-hole of a prison for captured rebels.

Not far from the State House is the **Somers Garden**, named after Sir George Somers, the doughty admiral who was among the Jamestown settlers wrecked on Bermuda in 1609. It is his statue, arms exuberantly aloft on sighting Bermuda after the fearful passage in *Sea Venture*, that stands near the replica of *Deliverance*.

Although Sir George was paid the tribute of having the Somers Islands named after him (before they became "Bermuda"), the disposal of his mortal remains after his death in St George's in 1610 was not as ceremonial as might have been expected of this revered pioneer. His heart was removed for local burial; the rest of him had to be shipped back to England disguised as general cargo in deference to seafaring superstition about transporting bodies. Some years later, Governor Butler discovered an overgrown patch where the heart had been buried. He put matters right with a stone tomb and an epitaph of his own composition. A second Somers memorial in the park was added in 1876 by one of Butler's successors, Governor Lefroy. A rather macabre exhumation of the Somers tomb in 1819 produced a broken bottle, a pebble and a few bones.

A little cottage, known as the **Gwynn House**, stands well back from the road in the western part of the town as a monument to less glorious memories. In 1826 Joseph Gwynn, a hot-tempered tailor, armed himself with a pistol to settle a score with the local magistrate, who had just sent his son to prison. Unable to locate the magistrate, Gwynn shot dead his blameless brother-in-law. Gwynn was seen leaving the scene of the crime and there was never any doubt about his guilt.

He seemed to vanish, however, and

Red, white and blue: St George's had connections with the American Revolution.

the elderly Mrs Gwynn purported to be as nonplussed as anyone else. She took her loss badly, refusing to leave a rocking chair for days on end while she nursed her grief. A soldier on guard duty at Fort George happened to train his telescope on the distraught woman only to witness a furtive ritual whereby she checked that the coast was clear and pushed the rocking chair aside to reveal a concealed trap door. A pair of hands reaching up for a plate of food gave the game away.

The police hurried round but Mrs Gwynn, back in her customary position, refused to budge. She was lifted bodily in her chair and the hapless Gwynn fished out. The *Bermuda Gazette* described how he was "launched into Eternity" at the conclusion of a trial, the execution being staged, as was often the case, at the scene of the crime, near the entrance to the Somers Garden.

The Printery in Featherbed Alley is a historical landmark in its own right – the ancient press is kept in working order – but there is additional interest in the small shuttered window in the side of the building, which was once used as a jail. Carole Holding, a local watercolour artist, has a working studio nearby. A short distance from the Printery are the **St George's Historical Society Museum**, with its fine cedar furniture and interesting relics, and the **Old Rectory**, built in 1705 by a repentant pirate and later, but only temporarily, actually used as a rectory. The Rectory's churchyard contains many old headstones; be sure to see the slaves' graves to the west, behind the wall.

The geography of eastern Bermuda was turned topsy-turvy by the huge landfill operation which created the World War II military base and, as a by-product, **the Bermuda airport**. Many of the smaller islands around **St David's** were swallowed whole and the shape of St David's was changed beyond recognition. Operations on the **American base** are usually routine anti-submarine surveillance flights, but the NASA tracking station becomes a busy hive whenever there is a space shot. Bermuda takes on the responsibility of tracking space craft across the Atlantic Ocean almost as soon as they blast off from Cape Canaveral.

The base remains US property until the lease (part of the Churchill-Roosevelt Lend Lease agreement) expires in 2040. Parts of the base are open to the public on Wednesdays, the two attractions being (for locals) Bermuda's only **McDonald's** and the **Carter House**, the oldest residence in Bermuda, home of the descendants of one of the "three kings" (see *Beginnings*, page 37, for their story) and a perfect example of the distinctive, indigenous architecture.

Entering the base is not entirely straightforward: visitors will need their passports, a moped or scooter and protective goggles which, unlike helmets, are not normally issued as part of the standard hire. There is a shuttle bus service on the base but, in a classic example of military logic, it may not carry visitors on Wednesdays, the only day of the week when they are allowed on the base to begin with.

Apart from the special arrangements

Left, St David's lighthouse. **Right**, Elliott Darrel.

that need to be made to visit the Carter House, using St George's as a base to explore the east end of Bermuda on a scooter is a sound and convenient proposition.Guest houses in the old town are elegantly comfortable, and rooms invariably have private baths.

The excursions possible from the town are either a circular drive which begins clockwise around St George's Harbour and then turns back on itself past **Gates' Fort**, then to **Buildings Bay** (where *Deliverance* was built) and ultimately to Fort St Catherine, or the road which follows the southern shore of the harbour across to **St David's lighthouse** without encroaching on the naval base. The reward at the end of the latter journey ought to be a meal at the splendidly eccentric **Dennis's Hideaway** where the Falstaffian proprietor will serve up a selection of Bermudian specialities, some of which are available nowhere else: shark hash, conch fritters, mussel stew, and so on.

The trip around the eastern extremity of St George's could be attempted on foot because, if fatigue sets in, there are short cuts back to base. This route is steeped in Bermuda's earliest history: the doomed *Sea Venture* approached the islands from this quarter, and although the history books paint a vivid picture of Sir Thomas Gates leaping ashore with a cry of "Gates – his bay" there are no clear signposts to the spot in question. It is, in fact, the tiny bay beneath the fort which bears his name.

Bermuda was fortified over 400 years with the finest defences available; as the islands were never attacked in earnest, many of them survive in exceptional condition and, as an example of 19th-century military architecture, **Fort St Catherine** cannot be bettered. The 11-inch (28 cm) guns, capable of firing 400 lb (180 kg) projectiles, are in excellent order, as are the mechanical magazines which fed them.

The fort is open daily, including Sundays; a video programme shown at frequent intervals gives a fascinating insight into the development of this "Gibraltar of the West".

A sign of the times.

A Chef's Touch

Dennis Lamb is one of Bermuda's best-known restaurateurs – not because his establishment is *haute cuisine*, but rather because it isn't. Dennis's Hideaway, as his St David's Island eatery is called, has a rustic charm not to be found anywhere else on Bermuda.

Guests will not find glittering chandeliers or custom-made drapes within the little waterside cottage. Rather, the elaborately patterned carpeting is recycled from a luxury hotel, the oak refectory table was purloined from a shipwreck during World War II, and some of the nearly new chairs were retrieved from a dump site.

Guests will, however, find a proprietor whose natural charm is legendary, and who can cook up a bunch of local dishes like no one else.

Dennis began his cooking career as a small boy growing up in a household where no distinction was made between the sexes when it came to doing chores. Like his forebears, Dennis cooked and ate food which was grown on the local farms or caught in the nearby sea.

Since turtles were plentiful around St David's and shark was another much-favoured local delicacy, Dennis soon learned all there was to know about preparing seafood, which features exclusively on the menu.

"I used to get a lot of tips from my mother and father and write them all down," he remembers. "I'd make up apple pies, corned beef hash, codfish cakes and fish chowder and freeze them." It is that background which he has parlayed into a successful business which has seen governors, politicians, actors, yachtsmen, tourists and locals flocking to enjoy his cuisine.

Over the years, Dennis has been a jack of all trades, working in everything from farming to fishing, construction, skippering a pilot boat, as a chef during World War II and operating the old swing bridge which once connected St David's to St George's.

"I used to have to wind that thing in and out by hand," he says, thinking back to those long ago days. "Sometimes, when there was a heavy wind,

I'd rig a sail up on it and let it swing by itself!"

He also worked on constructing the new swing bridge, and told the divers exactly where in the waters beneath it they would find two old "Walk Your Horses" signs. "When they brought them up I sold them back to the Public Works Department and they are still affixed to the new bridge to this day," he says.

But it is as a superb cook of such local delicacies as conch fritters, hashed shark, turtle steak and fish chowder that Dennis has made his mark. "After the war a lot of people wanted me to go and cook for them, but I said 'No, the next time I cook it will be for myself'."

And so it was that, at the age of 45, Dennis built the cottage and began the business that has been his livelihood for the past 21 years.

The strictly seafood menu includes lobster, fresh fish, conch stew, mussels, fish chowder, shrimps and scallops. Just sit down and ask for "the works" and Dennis will bring to your table an unforgettable sampling of everything.

"I used to fish myself for my business, but I can't any longer," he says. Instead, he relies on local fishermen to do it for him.

Married at 19, Dennis has raised six children. His son Graham, better known as "Sea Egg", works with him in the restaurant, which is now on its way to becoming a family business.

A few years ago Dennis remarried, this time to a Filipino lady, and adopted her young daughter. "I have had a wonderful life," he says of his rich and varied existence. "If I had it to live over again there's not a thing I'd do differently."

A unique individual who is, quite literally, larger than life (Lamb's physique is an occupational hazard of being a good cook), Dennis admits that the business, which is open seven days a week, is a lot of work. But retirement is far from his mind. "I've got to be doing something," he declares firmly.

Typical of many islanders who are proud of their homeland, he grows impatient with those who speak only of its problems. "They talk of a better Bermuda," he fumes. "But how much better can it be? We are truly blessed. I love this island and everybody in it."

THE SMALL ISLANDS

When Spanish sailors in Christopher Colombus's time came up with the name "Isle of Devils", their use of the singular noun when referring to what were manifestly many islands set a precedent whereby the early names – e.g., Bermudas or Bermuda, Somers Island or Summers Islands – were casually either singular or plural. Consistency was introduced with general recognition of "Bermuda", and that was taken to mean the main islands lying in close formation in the shape of a fish hook and all the smaller ones.

The exact number of smaller ones was a folkloric toss-up, rather like the number of churches on a Greek island. The confident claim is all too often "365" – fortuitously, of course, one for each day of the year. Sure enough, Bermuda was said to have 365 islands.

It is not in the spirit of such claims to go out and coldly count the things, although in Bermuda the writer Terry Tucker, never one to leave a stone unturned, almost did. She arrived at 120 islands, some masquerading under more than one name. A government survey using different criteria later settled on 181 islands, Cockroach Rock being just large enough to escape the ignominy of being classified officially as a rock.

A typical complication in getting everyone to agree on the number is **Cooper's Island**, which features in Bermuda's history as a suspected treasure trove and favourite nesting place of the amazing cahow but ceased to exist as an independent entity when St David's was expanded to accommodate the naval base and airport. **Longbird Island** suffered a similar fate. Pre-war air traffic consisted of flying boats which used **Darrell Island** as a base.

As Mrs Tucker demonstrated in her survey, a copy of which (*Islands*) may be consulted in the Historical Society Museum in Hamilton, the small islands collectively have a large and varied story to tell. There are no organised island tours as such. The ferries which ply across the Great Sound between Hamilton and the western parishes pass close to some islands, while visits to others may be possible during the course of other activities like scuba-diving or sailing.

The first settlements were at the eastern end of Bermuda (the "three kings" preferred **Smith's Island** but were overruled in favour of St George's), and the islands straddling the entrances to St George's and Castle Harbours had to be fortified quickly because a Spanish invasion was thought to be imminent. The first fort to taste action when two Spanish merchantmen poked their noses in was the one that became known as King's Fort on **Castle Island**.

The result for the home team could easily have gone the other way: only one cannon was in working order, the ammunition stock amounted to three balls, and the floor was perilously covered in spilled gun powder which, amid the bangs and flashes and noise, miraculously did not explode.

Things were apt to go wrong on Castle Island. A rally to drum up support for the hopeless cause of Captain Miles Kendall, a drunkard seconded to the post of governor in 1615, was to be kicked off by the ceremonial firing of a cannon. Kendall's campaign manager, as it were, a Lieutenant Wood, sailed over to the island to confirm the arrangements. He checked the readiness of the cannon by poking a metal-tipped pike down the barrel. His scraping caused a spark which ignited the charge. The efficient Wood, who could not have been in a worse position, was blasted bodily into the channel.

He was pulled out of the water in a sorry state and died the next day "to the extreme passionate grief of the Governor and the dismay of his confederates." On a later occasion, a night-firing exercise at King's Fort sent shells whistling around a startled Bolivian warship that was innocently in the vicinity.

Fort Cunningham was built on **Paget Island** as a precaution against the newly independent, belligerent United States.

It was designed as "the strongest colonial structure of its kind in the British domain." The cost of importing millions of bricks, iron and stone from England because the local limestone was considered too fragile caused members of the House of Commons to ask whether it was being made of gold. The forts on Castle and Paget Islands are not readily accessible, but a telephone call to the curator at Fort St Catherine will advise on the possibility of special arrangements.

Visitors canny enough to select a renegade captain on one of the glass-bottomed boat trips might find themselves recipients of a journey through unexpected waters. Locations pointed out on this trip can be fascinating, like the rock nicknamed **Sin Island**, so-called because of its popularity as a venue for yachting parties, and the privately owned **Denslow's Island**. Denslow's Island is named for W. W. Denslow, who lived in Bermuda around the turn of this century. Denslow was the under-rated artist who created –

Denslow's designs from around the turn of the century.

perhaps in the large house with its handsome tower which he built – the characters depicted in *The Wizard of Oz*.

The Wonderful Wizard of Oz, as the book was first known, was written in 1900 by talented journalist-cum-children's-writer L. Frank Baum. The success of this book was due in no small measure to the characters drawn by William Wallace Denslow, the first person to visualise Dorothy, the Cowardly Lion, the Scarecrow and the Tin Woodman. Denslow's highly individual drawings have been remarkably enduring, establishing forever the way these characters are envisioned, almost a century later. The popularity of *Oz* produced 13 sequels by Baum, many additions to the series by another author after Baum's death, several stage productions and, of course, the movie extravaganza starring Judy Garland. In each of these cases, excepting a grown-up Dorothy to allow for Garland's singing talent, Denslow's influence on the characters can clearly be seen.

Visitors under their own steam in self-drive or skippered hire boats ought to make enquiries before landing on any of Bermuda's small islands. Barging through a nature reserve could upset years of painstaking work; **Nonsuch Island** is a case in point. The approved camping sites are on **Port's**, **White's**, **Darrell** and **Coney Islands**.

Passengers on the Hamilton to Somerset Bridge ferry pass, on the port side, **Burt** and **Darrell Islands**. The former was once used as an isolation station for passengers arriving from smallpox areas and at the turn of the century, together with Darrell and others in the group, as a camp for Boer prisoners of war. Most of them seemed to pass their time quite happily in the carving of souvenirs which found a ready market among tourists.

One of them, however, decided to swim for freedom. It is hard to say what he had in mind, particularly when he had gone as far as he could on Bermuda and, poised on the beach for the last leg, realised there was still some way to go before reaching Pretoria.

W. W. Denslow's remarkably enduring characters.

The end of the war created the problem of Boers who refused to take the oath of allegiance which would have seen them on a ship home, wouldn't take jobs locally to pay for their keep, and declined offers of free passage to the port of their choice. They were dubbed the "Irreconcilables" and remained a lugubrious presence in their wide-brimmed hats and long beards until forcibly removed in 1903.

The Boer prisoners left behind on **Burt's Island** the grave of a man named Skeeter. He had murdered his wife and thrown her body into the sea weighted with an 80-lb (36-kg) boulder. That was the last anyone saw of her for some time, but then a hurricane freakishly washed the body ashore, the boulder still attached. The judge stipulated that Burt's should be the place of execution and burial and added the provision that the boulder in question should serve as the condemned man's headstone.

Governors and judges made full use of the islands in this way and would probably have regarded the use of

Trunk Island in Harrington Sound as a hermit's retreat as rather wasteful. One half of what is now known as **Ordnance Island** in St George's, where the *Deliverance* replica stands, was once "Gallows Island", handy for those sentenced to death in St Peter's Church, when that was used as a courthouse, or afterwards in the State House.

The island was originally two, and these formed the basis of Bermuda's second example of sharp real estate practice, the first being Governor Daniel Tucker's devious dealings in the so-called Overplus scandal. An American entrepreneur bought the islands, which were individually not much use for anything bar a scaffold, filled in the channel separating them and sold his creation at a vast profit. The British Army later took it over as an ammunition dump.

A second Gallows Island, renamed **Gibbet**, is to be found at the entrance to Flatt's Inlet. In 1681, a slave named Indian John, who had been taken prisoner in New England, was responsible for one of Bermuda's less competent capital crimes. He broke into the Orange Grove mansion, stole a gun and hat, started a fire and crept outside again with the intention of shooting the occupants as they fled. Instead, the family woke up and put out the flames without difficulty.

A look in the shrubbery revealed Indian John wearing his new hat. He made a full confession, leaving Governor Florentius Seymour to do the necessary. Indian John was to be "executed at or by the Gibbet at the Flatts mouth and there to have his head cut off and be quartered and the head and quarters put upon poles at such remarkable places as the sheriff shall think fit."

A pole which is visible from the road running past the island is said by some to be the very one on which Indian John's head was displayed. To suggest otherwise – it looks like an ordinary pole holding up a navigation light – may be construed as the sort of scepticism which reduces the number of Bermuda's islands to less than the magical 365.

Footsteps to nowhere. Right, a seascape of sea grapes.

TRAVEL TIPS

GETTING THERE

Note: Unless a separate exchange code is shown, all telephone numbers are for Bermuda, country code 809.

BY AIR

Bermuda can be reached in less than two hours from the East Coast of America and in less than seven hours from the United Kingdom. There is a free baggage allowance of two checked-in cases and one carry-on case of specified sizes and weights.

Flights from the US:
American Airlines – direct from La Guardia (New York), Boston and Raleigh/ Durham, North Carolina.
British Airways – direct from Tampa, Florida.
Continental Airlines – direct from Newark (New York).
Delta Airlines – direct from Boston and Atlanta.
Pan Am – direct from J.F.K. (New York).
US Air – direct from Baltimore, Maryland.

Flights from Canada:
Air Canada – direct from Toronto with connecting services from all of Canada and the New York/Bermuda carriers.

Flights from the United Kingdom:
British Airways – 6 flights a week from London.

Flights from other countries:
British Airways – direct and connecting flights from the Bahamas, West Indies, South America and Europe.

BY SEA

There is a free baggage allowance for normal personal luggage.

From the US:
Weekly services:
Royal Viking Line *Royal Viking Star* from New York (May–October).
Bermuda Star Line, Inc. *Queen of Bermuda* from New York (May–October).
Royal Caribbean Cruise Line *Nordic Prince* from New York (May–October).

Other weekly schedules with one or two day stops in Bermuda include Chandris Lines' *Americanis* and *Galileo* from New York (May–October).

Periodic sailings of other cruise ships leaving the US and UK ports are also available; check with a travel agent.

TRAVEL ESSENTIALS

VISAS & PASSPORTS

A return or onward ticket or other document of onward transportation to a country which, at that time, the passenger has right of entry, is required by all visitors. Most *bona fide* visitors with a confirmed return ticket and a place of accommodation will have no difficulties with Bermuda Immigration Control. There is a special Secondary Immigration Control section at the airport to deal with any unusual circumstances posed by arriving visitors.

Bermuda Immigration authorities may restrict the length of stay. For example, in the case of passengers arriving with an open return ticket, a time limit will be imposed. Persons wishing to enter Bermuda for the purpose of residence and/or employment, or for indefinite periods, will not be permitted to land at all, unless they have prior authorisation from immigration authorities to do so.

Passports are required by all visitors from countries which require a passport for re-entry purposes or for entry through another country to which, at that time, the passenger has right of entry. Married women whose identification documents are retained in their maiden name but who are travelling under their married name should also carry a marriage certificate or certified copy as further proof of identity.

Proof of citizenship and identification: all travellers must carry with them proof of citizenship and personal identification relevant to their return to their own country or for re-entry through another foreign country.

Visitors from the United States are required by Bermuda Immigration authorities to have in their possession any one of the following items:

a) a passport which, if expired, should be of sufficiently recent date that the photograph resembles the bearer;

b) a birth certificate, issued by a competent municipal authority with a raised seal, or a certified copy;

c) a US re-entry permit;

d) a US voter's registration card that shows the bearer's signature, along with some photographic identification;

e) a US Naturalisation Certificate;

f) a US Alien Registration Card.

Note that a driver's licence is not acceptable proof of citizenship.

Visitors from Canada are required by Bermuda Immigration authorities to have in their possession either a valid passport, a birth certificate or certified copy, or a Canadian Certificate of Citizenship plus proof of their Landed Immigrant Status.

Visas are not required for entry into Bermuda except for nationals from the following countries: Albania, Argentina, Bulgaria, China (People's Republic of), Cuba, Czechoslovakia, Germany, Haiti, Hungary, Iran, Iraq, Jordan, Kampuchea (Cambodia), Laos, Lebanon, Libya, Mongolia, North Korea, Philippines, Poland, Romania, South Africa, Soviet Union, Sri Lanka, Syria and Vietnam.

Any of the above nationals who are permanent residents of the US or Canada, holding a valid US Alien Registration Card or valid proof of Canadian Landed Immigrant Status plus a valid passport, do not require a visa to enter Bermuda. However, persons requiring visas to enter other countries on departure from Bermuda must be in possession of the respective visas before arriving in Bermuda.

Visas may be obtained from the Visa Section of any British Embassy or other British Foreign Service establishment abroad, e.g a consulate.

MONEY MATTERS

Legal tender is the Bermuda dollar (BD$) which is divided into 100 cents. Before 31 July 1972, the Bermuda dollar was pegged to the pound sterling; it is now pegged, through gold, to the US dollar on an equal basis: BD1$ = US1$. US currency is generally accepted at par in shops, restaurants and hotels, with many cashiers automatically returning change to visitors in US dollars – a helpful gesture which negates the need to change money again at the airport if departing for the US.

Exchange rates for all other currencies are liable to the usual fluctuation; current rates can be obtained from any bank and many hotels. Credit card transactions or any other banking matters involving foreign currencies are subject to these exchange rates.

Travellers cheques in US dollars are accepted everywhere, and with much more grace than in most cities in the US. Proof of identity is rarely required, but carry your passport just in case. Major credit cards, too, are welcome in most hotels, shops and restaurants.

HEALTH TIPS

Visitors on a short-term holiday have little to fear when it comes to health matters. The island is extremely clean and all beaches, hotels and restaurants meticulously maintained. Despite the island's "garden" appearance, the climate is quite kind even to hay fever sufferers; pollens of most noxious weeds tend to be blown out to sea. Insects and snakes are virtually non-existent, due to Bermuda's isolated position in the Atlantic Ocean.

Swimmers should, however, beware of two sea creatures which can cause nasty stings: the red sponge and the Portuguese man-of-war. The sea egg (urchin) leaves a series of pinprick-sized holes in the feet if stepped upon, so tread carefully or wear plastic sandals.

The island's long-term health problem is, however, a serious one: AIDS. According to a news report released by CANA-REUTER in late 1989, more than one in every 200 people has symptoms of the virus. Drug users and homosexuals have been the main victims; but, the report continues, figures show that 18 percent contracted the virus through heterosexual activity. Tread carefully and wear condoms.

WHAT TO WEAR

Bermudians tend towards fairly formal attire, both in the day-time and in the evening. Casual "resort wear" and shorts are acceptable on the beach and around pool areas but, when shopping in Hamilton, women are encouraged to wear skirts, not trousers. Most restaurants and clubs ask men to wear a jacket and tie after 6 p.m., and women should don informal evening attire.

Bermuda shorts are perfectly OK for men, accepted but less OK for women, and short shorts (and bare feet) are out of the question in public areas. So are women in hair curlers.

It is an offence to ride cycles or appear in public without a shirt.

WHAT TO BRING

During certain seasons, Bermuda imitates its mother country, Britain, in having an uncertain climate. Islands have notoriously unpredictable weather patterns, and during the change-over months (mid-November through December and late March through April), Bermuda can experience anything from hot sunshine to chilly winter gales. Poor weather blows away quite quickly, however, so it is sensible to bring a combination of clothes, preferably in coordinating colours, so that you can add or subtract layers.

During the warmer months (May to mid-November), women should bring summer-weight sports clothes, cotton dresses, swimsuits, a light, dressy wrap for the evening, plus cocktail-type outfits to wear when dining out. Men should bring similar-weight sports clothes, a swim suit, plus a lightweight suit or sports jacket and tie for evenings. Both sexes should bring a raincoat or wind breaker, especially important when riding on chilly motor scooters.

During the cooler months (December to late March) men and women should bring light woollen or autumn clothes, a warmer jacket, a raincoat and a wind breaker, plus a swimsuit for those undoubtedly warm days.

CUSTOMS FORMALITIES

Visitors may bring, duty-free, all clothes and articles for their personal use, including sports equipment, cameras, golf bags, etc. Plus, 50 cigars or 200 cigarettes or 0.454 kgs (1 lb) tobacco, 1.137 litres (1 quart) liquor, and the same amount of wine. Visitors are also permitted to bring in duty-free approximately 20 lbs of meat, although other foodstuffs may be dutiable up to 22.25 percent of their value.

The importation of all fruits, plants and vegetables is strictly regulated and these may be held for inspection. Import permits are available from the Department of Agriculture, Fisheries & Parks, P.O. Box HM 834, Hamilton, Bermuda HM CX.

Animals arriving without proper documentation will be refused entry and returned to the port of origin. There is no quarantine facility.

Visitors entering Bermuda may claim a BD$30 duty-free gift allowance.

Importation of, possession of, or dealing with unlawful drugs (including marijuana) is an offence. Anyone contravening the Misuse of Drugs Act is liable to fines of up to BD$10,000 or 5 years' imprisonment or both. Conviction on indictment carries a maximum penalty of a fine or imprisonment for life, or both. Customs officers may, at their discretion, conduct body searches for drugs and other smuggled goods.

The importation of any firearm, part of a firearm or ammunition into Bermuda is forbidden except under the authority of a licence granted by the Commissioner of Police. Such a permit will not ordinarily be granted, except to visiting rifle club members attending a sports meeting on the island.

Spear-guns and a variety of dangerous weapons including verey pistols or signal guns are treated as firearms, but antique weapons manufactured 100 years or more ago can be imported if the importer can show they are genuine antiques. It is a serious criminal offence to import firearms or ammunition into Bermuda without a licence, and anyone seeking to do so may be imprisoned or heavily fined.

RESERVATIONS

Anyone arriving in Bermuda without accommodation booked prior to departure runs the risk of being turned away at the border; immigration officials at Hamilton airport regularly enquire as to where you will be staying. Always arrange your holiday through a reputable travel agent, or, if booking independently, be sure to secure proof of accommodation before leaving home.

Reservations for dinner are required at all of Bermuda's restaurants except for the most casual establishments. Some of the more popular restaurants get booked up days in advance, so arrange plans early.

EXTENSION OF STAY

Applications to extend a length of stay must be made in person at the Immigration Headquarters at 30 Parliament Street, Hamilton, tel: 295 5151. A fee may be charged for processing an application. It is extremely difficult to obtain permission to work in Bermuda, and anyone seeking employment is advised to obtain a job before visiting the island.

ON DEPARTURE

All visitors not in direct transit are taxable under the Passenger Tax Act of 1972. Air passengers are obliged to pay BD$15 on departure; ship passengers must pay BD$40, collected in advance by the cruise ship company. Children up to the age of 11 pay a reduced fee, and those under two years of age are exempt.

US Customs pre-clearance is available in Bermuda for all scheduled flights. All passengers departing to the US must fill out written declaration forms before clearing US Customs in Bermuda. These forms are available at all hotels, travel agencies and airlines on the island. Be sure to arrive at the airport at least one hour before departure, as clearing customs is a time-consuming business.

There is no duty-free shop at Bermuda airport. Bottles of spirits bought in island shops specifically for taking abroad are delivered to the airport for passenger pick-up at a booth located beyond the customs hall.

Visitors are permitted to take back merchandise, duty-free, up to the following amounts:

US citizens: purchases worth up to $400 after 48 hours on the island and every 30 days following. Although duty-free allowances vary from state to state, US citizens are allowed to import 1 litre (33.8 oz) of liquor every 30 days.

Canadian citizens: purchases worth up to $100 after 48 hours and any number of trips per year, or $300 after seven days once every calendar year.

UK citizens: purchases worth up to £32. Plus, 200 cigarettes or 100 cigarillos or 50 cigars or 250 gms of tobacco, as well as 1 litre (33.8 oz) of spirits or 2 litres (67.6 oz) of fortified wine and 2 litres of table wine. Plant materials which will propagate in the UK cannot be imported without prior permission from British authorities.

GETTING ACQUAINTED

GOVERNMENT & ECONOMY

The structure of Bermuda's government is based on the British system. Queen Elizabeth II is the head of state, represented in Bermuda by a governor who is assisted by a deputy governor. Both are appointed in London.

The governor selects the premier, nominating a member of Parliament who is the leader of a major party. Considerable power rests with the premier, who in turn appoints a cabinet.

Bermuda has 11 ministries. These are the Departments of Tourism; Education; Transport; Works & Housing; Finance; Community & Cultural Affairs; Health & Social Services; Labour & Home Affairs; Youth, Sport & Recreation; Environment; and Legislative Affairs.

GEOGRAPHY & POPULATION

Bermuda is 600 miles (965 km) east of Cape Hatteras (North Carolina) on America's east coast. It consists of seven islands linked by inter-connecting bridges, and measures 22 miles (35 km) in length. It is 21 sq. miles (54 sq. km) in area. The widest point is about 2 miles (3 km) across.

The population at the last census (1980) was 54,670 but this is thought to have risen to approximately 57,000. Around 60 percent is black and 40 percent white, with a sprinkling of Portuguese.

TIME ZONES

Standard time in Bermuda is Greenwich Mean Time minus four hours. Daylight Saving Time is in effect from the first Sunday in April to the last Sunday in October.

CLIMATE

Bermuda is a semi-tropical island and the Gulf Stream, which flows between Bermuda and North America, keeps the climate temperate. Yet, surprisingly, it has two seasons

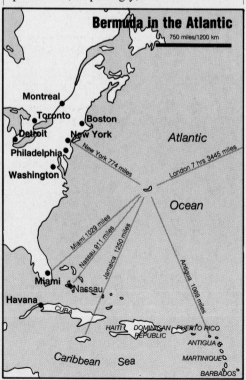

Bermuda in the Atlantic
750 miles/1200 km

Montreal
Toronto Boston
Detroit New York
Philadelphia
Washington

Atlantic

New York 774 miles
London 7 hrs 3445 miles

Ocean

Miami 1029 miles
Nassau 911 miles
Jamaica 1250 miles
Antigua 1069 miles

Miami
Havana Nassau
CUBA
HAITI DOMINICAN REPUBLIC PUERTO RICO
ANTIGUA
Caribbean Sea MARTINIQUE
BARBADOS

and two "changes of season". The thermometer rarely rises above 85° F (29.5° C) and there is often a cool breeze at night. Most accommodation is air-conditioned.

Bermuda's spring-like weather lasts from mid-December to late March, with an average temperature of around 70° F (21.1° C). December and January are often warm enough to go swimming. Summer temperatures prevail from May to mid-November, with the warmest weather in July, August and September.

CULTURE & CUSTOMS

Bermuda feels very British, in some ways even more so than Britain. Everyone drives on the left, calls soccer "football", and many still engage in the time-honoured tradition of afternoon tea. Policemen wear hard-topped "bobby" helmets, and the Queen's Birthday is an official holiday.

But Bermuda is also American. Most of its consumables are ferried in from the east coast. The currency is pegged to the American dollar. And many Bermudians will repair to the United States when they want a quick weekend break.

The language is British English, often spoken with a North American accent. This is due to the large number of Bermudians who pursue higher education in Canada or the United States.

WEIGHTS & MEASURES

Although the metric system is usually employed in shops, imperial weights and measures are used in everyday conversation.

ELECTRICITY

Electricity is 110 volts, 60 cycles A.C. This is standard throughout the island.

BUSINESS HOURS

Most stores are open Monday–Saturday 9 a.m.–5.30 p.m. Some shops, however, choose to open at 9.15 a.m. and may close at 5 p.m., so it's wise to enquire first. On Sundays, almost nothing remains open.

All Bank of Bermuda branches (except at the airport) are open Monday–Thursday 9.30 a.m.–3 p.m., Friday 9.30 a.m.–4.30

p.m. The airport branch is open Monday–Thursday 11 a.m.–4 p.m., Friday 11 a.m.–4.30 p.m. All other banks are open the same hours as the Bank of Bermuda, except on Friday when they close at 3 p.m. and reopen from 4.40 p.m.-5.30 p.m. The Bermuda Commercial Bank at the airport is open Monday–Friday 11 a.m.–4 p.m.

HOLIDAYS

Bermuda observes the usual New Year's Day, Good Friday, Labour Day, Remembrance Day and Christmas Day and Boxing Day (26 December) holidays. Public holidays which fall on a Saturday or Sunday are normally observed the following Monday. Please note that on these holidays *all* shops and businesses, and many restaurants close.

Three public holidays are special to Bermuda. The specific days may alter slightly from year to year, but tend to be celebrated around the time of the dates shown:

24 May: Bermuda Day
18 June: Queen's Birthday
2 and 3 August: Cup Match & Somers Day

RELIGIOUS SERVICES

For such a small island, Bermuda has a number of churches of all denominations: Anglican, Jehovah's Witness, Christian Science, Pentecostal, Jewish and Muslim are just a few. Consult the Yellow Pages of the Bermuda telephone directory for addresses. Weekend editions of newspapers often give times and places for religious services.

COMMUNICATIONS

MEDIA

Print: Bermuda's only daily newspaper is *The Royal Gazette,* which is published Monday–Saturday. Everyone reads it, regardless of whether they agree with its opinions or not. Outspoken, critical, occasionally sensational and often hard-hitting, the *Gazette* is the only real "voice" in print on the island.

There are three other newspapers. *The Bermuda Sun* (published Friday) is a weekly tabloid; *The Mid Ocean News* (also published Friday) is a weekly broadsheet with colour comics and is the *Gazette's* sister paper. *The Bermuda Times*, bi-weekly on Friday, places less emphasis on hard news and more on community events.

British newspapers can arrive as early as 5 p.m. on the day of publication (otherwise the following day), while North American newspapers arrive around 3 p.m. on the day of publication.

Bermuda Business is a glossy monthly magazine aimed at the business and financial sector, while the long-established *The Bermudian* tends to feature articles on the arts.

Three free magazines aimed at tourists are *This Week in Bermuda*; *Preview*; and *Bermuda Weekly*. These publications provide useful calendars of events and activities.

Radio and TV: Radio station VSB-1160 (AM) offers the excellent BBC World Service between the hours of 12.30 p.m. and 7 a.m. During the remaining hours the station is devoted to island music and information which might be of interest to tourists. Other AM radio stations include: ZBM-1340; ZFB-1230; VSB-1450; VSB-1280. There are three radio stations on the FM frequency: ZFB-FM-95; VSB-FM-106; ZBM-FM-89. Good for hurricane news is the Government Emergency Channel on FM 100.

Two Bermuda television stations are linked to American national channels. Channel 9, ZBM, shows programmes from CBS; Channel 7, ZFB, shows programmes from ABC. Channel 13, VSB, is devoted to information and news, while Channel 4 is the local Bermuda channel.

Many hotels also have cable television, and even small guesthouses will usually show a video movie most evenings.

POSTAL SERVICES

Postcards, stamps and letters can be bought or mailed from picturesque Perot's Post Office on Queen Street in Hamilton. The main post office for Bermuda is on the corner of Church Street and Parliament Street in Hamilton.

Postal rates:

Airmail USA and Canada: letters (10 gm)-50¢; postcards-50¢; air letters-50¢.

Surface mail: letters (20 gm)-35¢; letters (50 gm)-50¢; postcards-30¢.

Airmail Europe: letters (10 gm)-60¢; postcards-60¢; air letters-50¢.

Surface mail: letters (20 gm)-35¢; letters (50 gm)-50¢; postcards-30¢.

TELEPHONES/CABLES/FAXES

Most hotels and guesthouses have a fax machine, but they also add a service charge on calls made from hotel rooms. Telephone calls are charged according to the time of day the call is made.

USA: Full rate is in effect 10 a.m.–7 p.m.; discount from 7–11 p.m. and 7–10 a.m., and the rock-bottom economy fare applies from 11 p.m.–7 a.m.

Canada: Full rate 7 a.m.–9 p.m.; discount rate from 9 p.m.–7 a.m. No economy rate.

UK: Full rate 7 a.m.–6 p.m.; discount rate 6 p.m.–7 a.m. No economy.

Area codes:
USA: dial 1, then regional code, then telephone number.

Canada: dial 1, then regional area code, then telephone number.

All other countries: dial 011, then country code, then regional area code, then telephone number.

Country codes:
UK: 44

France: 33
Germany: 49
Hong Kong: 852
New Zealand: 64
Singapore: 65
Australia: 61

Cables, faxes and telexes can be arranged by calling 295 1815.

EMERGENCIES

SECURITY & CRIME

On the whole, Bermudians are very honest people. That fact, coupled with the knowledge that there are few ways a criminal can actually leave the island, means that belongings and possessions are safer than in almost any other country in the world. In the unlikely event that a crime occurs, the emergency police number is tel: 295 0011.

MEDICAL SERVICES

To obtain an ambulance tel: 236 2000; to contact a hospital tel: 236 2345. This is the number of the King Edward VII Memorial Hospital, at Point Finger Road, Paget. The Ladies' Auxiliary at this hospital are on hand to help overseas visitors in poor health with any problems they might experience. The Yellow Pages of the Bermuda telephone directory lists dentists and doctors.

GETTING AROUND

ORIENTATION

Once a group of seven islands connected only by boat, Bermuda is now fully linked from east to west by a series of bridges. When the term "The Bermudas" is employed, this includes all the smaller islands located along the shores of its major islands. These small islands are used as camp-sites and recreation grounds, some are privately-owned and some are mere lumps of rock.

Bermuda roughly forms the shape of a fish hook. It is divided into nine parishes (districts), seven of which are named after the principal investors in the Bermuda Company: Robert Rich, Earl of Warwick; William Herbert, Earl of Pembroke; Sir Thomas Smith; Sir Edwyn Sandys; James, Marquis of Hamilton; William Cavendish, Earl of Devonshire; and Henry Wriothesley, Earl of Southampton. The two other parishes are Paget, on the South Coast, and St George's, with the same name as its principal town.

The capital, Hamilton, is not located in the parish of Hamilton, but in the parish of Pembroke. The area commonly referred to as "The East End" is St George's parish, while "The West End" is Sandys parish, centred around the village of Somerset and the Great Naval Dockyard.

RECOMMENDED MAPS

The pink "Handy Reference Map" distributed free by the Department of Tourism is attractive (hand-drawn), and very serviceable. Many visitors will not require another.

Walkers, and anyone who plans a comprehensive tour of the island, might like to invest in a copy of *Bermuda Islands Guide*, a book of 24 maps which shows the different parishes in large, easy-to-read and carefully labelled detail. Obtainable locally, it is an excellent reference.

AIRPORT/CITY

Bermuda's airport lies on reclaimed land in the parish of St George's. Ironically, the view upon landing is probably the most unsightly the island offers. Visitors should not be disappointed, however, for within minutes of leaving the airport things improve immeasurably.

Except for anyone staying in St George's, the first real view of Bermuda is seen when crossing The Causeway, a narrow bridge linking St George's with Hamilton parish. Surrounded by turquoise sea on all sides and, on the horizon, pastel houses shimmering in bright sunlight, only the most jaded of travellers could fail to be excited.

Taxis are plentiful and located just outside the airport. It takes around 30 minutes to travel from the airport to Hamilton, and the fare is under BD$20. As in New York, the taxi meter spouts out a receipt for handy reference. Drivers are honest and won't rip off unsuspecting tourists, and the islands contain so few roads that it's virtually impossible to take "the scenic route" to bump up any fares.

Airport limousines are 8-seater mini buses which serve the smaller hotels. A 26-passenger coach serves the larger hotels, making several stops along the way. Pre-arranged bookings can be made, tel: 293 2500.

DOMESTIC TRAVEL

By Road: Bermudians drive on the left-hand side of the road. The speed limit is 20 miles (35 km) per hour. No one ever speeds, or ever honks their horn, except in greeting. There is no private car hire.

By Bus: buses are frequent and very good, with comprehensive schedules (they almost always run on time) but a complicated fare system. The island is divided into 14 different "zones" of about 2 miles (3 km) each, with different fares charged according to how many zones are crossed.

You must have the exact fare in order to climb aboard a bus which costs BD$1.25 for the first 3-zone ride. It's helpful to buy a booklet of pre-paid tickets. Not only does this save fumbling for coins in a queue of people, but "bulk buying" bus tickets works out less expensive than paying for each journey individually.

Books of tickets (called tokens) are available from the bus terminal on Church Street, Hamilton, next to City Hall, or from any post office. Schedules, which include a list of where to catch buses to popular tourist sites, are available either from the bus terminal or from Visitors Service Bureaux.

By Ferry: ferries are fun and reliable. They, too, run to schedule but, contrary to popular myth, do not wait if they see a latecomer scrambling to board. Be on time. The Hamilton/Somerset/Dockyard route is a popular day excursion, calling in at diminutive Somerset Bridge, and passing near the pretty village of Somerset before arriving at the westernmost tip of Bermuda, Dockyard. It's a perfect way to see the small islets located in the Great Sound. The fare is BD$2 each way; cycles, which can be taken on board, cost another BD$2.

The Hamilton/Paget/Warwick ferry goes past White's island with its sailboats moored in the harbour, and is the only public transport available to points in Paget and Warwick parishes on the southern side of Hamilton Harbour. The fare is BD$1 each way.

The main ferry terminal is in Hamilton Harbour, right by the Visitors Service Bureau.

By scooter/motorcycle: for a comprehensive briefing, see the feature *Notes for Nervous Drivers* on page 251.

Scooters can be hired by the hour, by the day or by the week. You must be 16 years of age, but pillion cycles can be rented for carrying small children. Scooter shops are located all around the island. Rates vary, but the daily fee tends to be from around BD$20 for a single seater; from BD$29 for a double seater and just under BD$40 for a top quality model. A deposit of BD$20 is required for a helmet (which must be worn), lock and key. The deposit is refundable on the safe return of the bike. Rates include third-party insurance, delivery and collection, service in case the bike breaks down, and the first tank of petrol. Rates decrease the longer the bike is hired.

By Taxi: taxis may be hired by the hour,

day, or mile (a day is considered to be six consecutive daylight hours). Rates per cab are the same for any number of passengers, from one person up to a maximum of six, for normal transportation and general sightseeing. All taxis are metered and the tariffed is fixed by law. If a taxi sports a blue flag, it belongs to a qualified tour guide.

On Foot: walking the trails and parks in Bermuda is fascinating; walking along public roads is frustrating. Walls and hedges can be high, obscuring vision, and scooters whizzing around corners appear without warning. It's best, too, to refrain from hitch-hiking, not because it's dangerous, but because it's considered unmannerly.

WHERE TO STAY

The Bermuda Department of Tourism publishes a series of excellent brochures regarding accommodation. It is worth getting hold of these brochures for a list of the complete range of establishments, which number only 90 (if all are fully operational) on the entire island.

Because accommodation is strictly controlled, there are no poor quality establishments. Even the most modest guesthouse is efficiently run and provides more than basic amenities, invariably in an attractive setting.

This attention to detail comes at a price, however. Accommodation is expensive. Just how expensive is difficult to gauge until the bill is tallied up, as surcharges and taxes are numerous. Service charges, telephone charges, third person occupancy charges, even energy charges are common, even in the smallest hotels. This is not an attempt to rip off the tourist, but one way to maintain high standards and to attract equally high-class visitors. In a phrase – there are no cheap hotels in Bermuda. But there are no doss-houses either. If you can't afford to stay here, you can't afford to be here.

Fourways INN

RESTAURANT, COTTAGE COLONY & PASTRY SHOP

WHAT THE PROFESSIONALS ARE
SAYING ABOUT US

"Fourways Wine List is strong on noble Bordeaux to accompany the Menu's classic selection of roasts and steaks.... Tops among the justly famed desserts are the individual Souffles: Grand Mariner, Strawberry, Chocolate, and the newest Specialty, Bermuda Black Rum. This, with an extra dash of rum and whipped cream poured into the broken crust, was a real treat." -- ***Gourmet Magazine***

"The Fourways Inn on Middle Road in Paget Parish ranks as the Island's Creme de la Creme; every dish is served with gourmet perfection. The Fourways Restaurant is housed in a luxurious 18th Century residence, now freshly outfitted for elegant dining (the Wine Cellar is unequalled on the Islands)." -- ***Vogue***

FOURWAYS INN

"Already known as one of Bermuda's best restaurants, the Fourways' reputation is now enhanced by a cluster of 10 great houses spread over hillside gardens adjoining the luxurious dining area. Visitors are housed in attractively furnished, climate controlled Suites extending out to sunny terraces in full view of the secluded fresh water pool." -- ***Better Homes & Gardens***

FOURWAYS COTTAGES

THE GRILL

PASTRY SHOP

GOURMET STORE

"Fourways, the Island's newest star Restaurant in Paget Parish, is a fantastic treat; excellent food; good wines; soignee, speedy service." -- ***Palm Beach Illustrated***

We invite you to discover us yourself!

FOURWAYS INN,	THE FOURWAYS GRILL	THE GOURMET STORE	THE PASTRY SHOP
COTTAGE COLONY	Windsor Place	Windsor Place	Washington Mall
AND PASTRY SHOP	Queen Street	Queen Street	Reid Street,
Middle Road Paget	Hamilton	Hamilton	Hamilton
Tel: 236-6517	Tel: 295-4086	Tel: 295-4085	Tel: 295-3263

The Department of Tourism and the Bermuda Hotel Association recommends using the services of a professional travel agent. It is important to have previously-booked reservations before arriving, as it is common for immigration authorities at the airport to ask where you'll be staying. If booked into a smaller guesthouse, you can change once on the island, but as there are so few places from which to choose, shopping around isn't always that easy. Visitors Service Bureaux will, sometimes, recommend inexpensive *(sic)* Bed & Breakfast accommodation which isn't on any official list. So if you find yourself in an area you like and want to stay locally, it *is* worth asking around.

All room rates are subject to a 6 percent Government Hotel Occupancy Tax, to be paid on check-out. A two-day deposit is required by a majority of hotels, which may be non-refundable if cancelled less than 14 to 21 days before the arrival date. Any service charge indicated is in lieu of tips and is added to the bill for room and board only. It does not cover bar charges, extra meals, etc. Most hotels accept major credit cards, but a few smaller guesthouses don't have the facilities to cope. Always check in advance.

Hotel dining rooms tend to serve excellent food, and meal plans are commonplace. MAP (Modified American Plan) means room, breakfast and dinner. AP (American Plan) means room, breakfast, lunch and dinner. BP (Bermuda Plan) is room and full breakfast. CP (Continental Plan) is room and light breakfast. EP (European Plan) means room only. Meal plans work out considerably cheaper than dining out in different restaurants each night and are definitely worth considering.

HOTEL CATEGORIES

Bermuda's 90 hotels and cottages are grouped in nine different categories:

Resort Hotels (Elbow Beach, Sonesta Beach, Marriott Castle Harbour, Southampton Princess) offer splendid views over the sea, resort facilities and private beaches, swimming pools, beauty salons, nightclubs and all that you would expect from a luxury hotel.

Small Hotels (Glencoe, Newstead, Pompano Beach, The Reefs, Rosedon, Somerset Bridge Hotel, Waterloo House) tend to be more private, with personal touches and an individual flavour about them. They usually have a swimming pool or beach; many have dining rooms and bars. Planned activities and sports facilities are limited, although specific requests can often be accommodated by talking to the manager.

Cottage Colonies (Horizons, Lantana Colony Club, Fourways Inn, Cambridge Beaches) are uniquely Bermudian, consisting of main club houses with a dining room, lounge and bar, with cottage units spread throughout extensive grounds. There is usually a pool or beach. Cottage colonies offer the privacy of a home with the comforts of a hotel. Unbeatable and very expensive.

Clubs (Coral Beach; Mid Ocean Club) are exclusive hotels requiring an introduction by a member.

Large Housekeeping Cottages and Apartments (Astwood Cove, Marley Beach Cottages, Pretty Penny, Surf Side Beach Club) tend to be separate cottages, self-contained and self-catering. Most have a pool and/or a beach.

Small Housekeeping Cottages and Apartments (Garden House, Ocean Terrace) tend to have tiny kitchenettes and a nearby public beach.

Large Guesthouses (Oxford House; Fordham Hall) are often old Bermuda mansions modernised into guest rooms. A few have dining rooms and a pool.

Small Guesthouses (Hillcrest; Pleasant View; Salt Kettle) are usually private homes offering casual accommodation.

Small Houses (South View; Wainwright) offer a combination of bedrooms and housekeeping units, some with communal kitchen facilities.

FOOD DIGEST

For an insight into eating out on the island, see the feature on page 133 by Charles H. Webbe called *Food For Thought*. Here are the addresses and telephone numbers of the restaurants he recommends:

Angle Street Deli
Angle Street
Hamilton
Tel: 292 5246

Black Horse Tavern
(no address; call for directions)
St David's
Tel: 293 9742

Checkmate Diner
Court and Dundonald Streets
Hamilton
Tel: 295 7840

Conch Shell Restaurant
Emporium Building
Front Street
Hamilton
Tel: 295 6969

Dennis's Hideaway
25 Battery Road
St David's
Tel: 297 0044

Fourways Inn
Middle Road
Southampton
Tel: 238 0510

Green Lantern Restaurant
Serpentine Road
Pembroke
295 6995

Hog Penny
5 Burnaby Street

Hamilton
Tel: 292 2534

Il Palio
Main Road
Somerset
Tel: 234 1049

Little Venice Restaurant
Bermudiana Road
Hamilton
Tel: 295 3503

Lobster Pot
6 Bermudiana Road
Hamilton
Tel: 292 6898

MacWilliams Restaurant
Pitts Bay Road
Pembroke
Tel: 295 5759

Margaret Rose Restaurant
The St George's Club
Rose Hill
St George's
Tel: 297 1200

Momma Stella's Kitchen
Ex-Artillerymen's Club
Victoria Street
Hamilton
Tel: 295 9897

Newport Room
Southampton Princess Hotel
South Road
Southampton
Tel: 238 8000

New Woody's Restaurant
1 Boaz Lane
Boaz Island
Somerset
Tel: 234 2082

Once Upon a Table
Serpentine Road
Pembroke
Tel: 295 8585

Paraquet Restaurant
South Shore Road
Paget

Ariel Sands
BEACH CLUB

*A*riel Sands is an attractive cottage colony overlooking the ocean in Devonshire Parish. The main clubhouse has lounges, bar, dining room and terrace with panoramic ocean views. Fresh water as well as natural ocean swimming pools, private beach, and tennis court feature on the property. Relax in plush comfort and enjoy breathtaking vistas. All Ariel Sands accommodations are in charming Bermudian cottages that have private patios, lovely ocean views, and offer great flexibility for individuals, couples, or families.

Ariel, Shakespeare's magical sprite from "The Tempest" stands off our beach. The stainless steel figure was created by world famous sculptor; J. Seward Johnson.

Indulge yourself – we offer a superb protected beach, a reef teaming with fascinating sea-life directly off-shore.

Our tennis courts are floodlit and our central location makes golf an easy game at nearby courses.

ARIEL SANDS BEACH CLUB
P.O. Box HM 334, Hamilton HM BX Bermuda
Tel: 809-236-1010/800-468-6610/800-225-2230
Fax: 809-236-0087
Owners: *The Dill Family*
A Member of Bermuda's Small Properties Ltd.

Represented by
SELECT RESORTS INTERNATIONAL
1820 The Exchange, Suite 350,
Atlanta, Georgia 30339 USA
Tel: 404-955-9565
800-541-7426
Fax: 404-859-0250

THE RMR GROUP INC.
Taurus House, 512 Duplex Avenue,
Toronto, Canada M4R 2E3
Tel: (416)-485-8724
Fax: (416)-485-8256

**MORRIS KEVAN
INTERNATIONAL LIMITED**
International House, 47 Chase Side,
Enfield, Middlesex EN2 6NB
Tel: 081-367 5175
Telex: 24457   Prestel: 546968
Fax: 081-367 9949

KNIGHTSBRIDGE
1290 Worcester Road, Framingham,
Massachusetts, 01701 USA
Tel: 508-879-8100/800-225-2230
Fax: 508-879-8157

nce-upon-a-time, all of Bermuda

was like Grotto Bay Beach. Beautiful

pink beaches and relaxing gentle surf.

Then the big hotels got even bigger. And

cottages remained...cottages. But, there's

still a place where you can discover the

best of Bermuda. Grotto Bay Beach. Acres

of spectacular gardens. Private beaches.

Gracious dining. Oceanview balconies.

Watersports, tennis & nearby golf. In short,

everything an island jewel is meant to be.

Treasure
The Moment

Memories of your Bermuda vacation, captured in 18kt & 14kt gold and Sterling Silver.

For one of a kind originals, stop by and discuss your ideas with one of our jewellers.

Tel: 236 9742

Plantation Restaurant
(excellent restaurant close
to the Amber Caves)
Bailey Bay
Hamilton Parish
Tel: 293 1188

Show Biz Café and Bar
66 King & Reid Street
Hamilton
Tel: 292 0676

Swizzle Inn
Baileys Bay
Hamilton Parish
Tel: 293 9300

Tavern on the Green
Botanical Gardens
Paget
Tel: 236 7731

Tom Moore's Tavern
Walsingham Lane
Baileys Bay
Hamilton Parish
Tel: 293 8020

Waterlot Inn
Southampton
Tel: 238 0510

THINGS TO DO

TOWN

The Department of Tourism has written two leaflets perfect for anyone who wants to savour the urban flavour of Bermuda's two largest towns, Hamilton and St George's. These are both called *A Self-guided Walking Experience* and include illustrations, opening hours and admission prices to all premier attractions.

COUNTRY

Trails, nature reserves and beaches are the finest outdoor attractions Bermuda can offer. A leaflet called *The Railway Trail* is available from Visitors Service Bureaux, and gives tips on things to look out for while taking this walk.

The most important nature reserves open to the public are Paget Marsh (Middle Road, Paget); Spittal Pond (South Road, Smith's); Gladys Morrell (East Shore Road, Sandys) and the Gilbert Nature Reserve (Somerset Road, Somerset, Sandys). All reserves are open daily and all year round, but please keep to the paths provided.

Over half of Bermuda's coastline consists of beaches. Some are private, but many are not. The best way to find good beaches is by sampling as many as possible. John Smith's Bay, on the South Shore, Smiths, usually has a lifeguard during the summer months, a rarity. It also has take-away food on the beach itself. Astwood Park, further along the same shore in Warwick, is a lovely picnic spot (tables provided) with a cove suitable for inshore snorkelling. At the secluded eastern end of the cove is a smaller beach. Chairs and umbrellas are provided at the private Elbow Beach Hotel, where a BD$3 fee will secure a towel and changing room as well. Snacks and cold drinks are nearby at the Surf Club. Elbow Beach also has a public section, with take-away food in the high season.

WATER SPORTS

The number of activities (April-November) in which visitors can engage while above, on top of, or actually in the water is vast. You can go para-sailing, scuba-diving and snorkelling; hire motor boats, sail boats, windsurfers, paddle boats, rafts, rowing sculls and even yachts.

A number of cruises are offered, from glass-bottomed boat tours to observe Bermuda's highly active marine community, to moonlight sails through the Great Sound, or pirate night parties on small, secluded islets. Hotel lobbies and Visitors Service Bureaux should have any leaflets you require.

Bermuda Perfumery: North Shore Road, Baileys Bay, tel: 293 0627. Open: April–October Monday–Saturday 9 a.m.–5 p.m., Sunday 10 a.m.–4 p.m. November–March Monday–Saturday 9 a.m.–4.30 p.m. Watch perfume being made in the laboratory; learn the history of local perfume and walk through fragrant gardens where many of the blossoms used in the manufacture of the scent are grown.

Crystal Caves: 8 Crystal Caves Road, Baileys Bay, tel: 293 0640. Open: daily 9.30 a.m.–4.30 p.m. Admission: BD$3. Underground lake discovered by two small boys in 1907, shimmering with reflected stalagmites and stalactites.

Amber Caves of Lemington: Harrington Sound Road, Baileys Bay, tel: 293 1188. Open: Monday–Saturday 9.30 a.m.–4.30 p.m. Admission: BD$3. Not as dazzling as the Crystal Caves, but this amber-tinted grotto is still worth a visit and is especially good on rainy days when it is not possible to go to the beach.

Bermuda Aquarium, Museum and Zoo: Flatts Village, Harrington Sound, tel: 293 2727. Open: daily 9.30 a.m.–4.30 p.m. Admission: BD$4. Over 75 species of fish and 50 types of marine invertebrates are housed in this ultra-modern aquarium. The zoo has monkeys, alligators and other tropical animals, while the museum gives an insight into Bermuda's marine and geological development.

Devil's Hole: Harrington Sound Road, Smiths, tel: 293 2072. Open: daily 9.30 a.m.–4.30 p.m. Admission: BD$5. Visitors are provided with baited but hookless lines to catch extremely large fish who feast on the food and then swim away.

(See *Sports* for athletics events)

January/February: **Regional Bridge Tournament**
Sponsored by Bermuda Unit of the American Contract Bridge League.

January/February: **Bermuda Festival**
A six-week international arts festival featuring world-renowned artists specialising in classical music, dance, jazz, drama and popular entertainment.

February: **Annual Street Festival**
Musical entertainment, crafts, fashion show, the Gombeys, Regimental Musical Display and more all on Front Street in Hamilton.

March: **All Breed Championship Dog Show**
A week of competitions featuring dogs from Bermuda and other countries.

March/April: **Bermuda College Weeks**
Several weeks featuring a weekly programme of events for visiting college students spending their spring vacations on the island.

April: **Peppercorn Ceremony**
Pomp and ceremony in St George's when the Masonic Lodge of Bermuda pays annual rent for its headquarters, the Old Station House.

April: **Agricultural Show**
A three-day exhibit of Bermuda's best fruits, flowers, vegetables and livestock, also featuring equestrian and other ring events.

April/May: **Open Houses and Gardens**
Beautiful Bermuda homes and gardens open to visitors every Wednesday afternoon.

April–October: **Beat Retreat Ceremonies**
(Excluding August) Alternating in Hamilton, St George's and the Royal Naval Dockyard, this historic military re-enactment features the Bermuda Regiment Band, the Bermuda Isles Pipe Band (with dancers), plus members of the Bermuda Pipe Band.

June: Queen's **Birthday Parade**
Public holiday with military parade on Front Street, Hamilton.

November: **Convening of Parliament**
The Governor opens Parliament amid

The Affordable Way to Enjoy Bermuda.

Enjoy Bermuda's best at the Belmont, a magnificent 100-acre resort estate. With spectacular views. One of the island's finest 18-hole championship golf courses. The island's largest hotel pool. Free daytime tennis. Nightly entertainment. Monday night swizzle party. Plus first-class accommodations, hearty American breakfast and afternoon tea daily. Private dock for ferry to city shopping and sightseeing.

Special unlimited golf and honeymoon packages available. Call 1-800-225-5843 in the U.S. Or call 081-567-3444 in the U.K.

Bermuda's Sport Resort.
BELMONT
HOTEL, GOLF AND COUNTRY CLUB

Trusthouse Forte

WE INVITE YOU TO TAKE OUR FREE TOUR AND VISIT THE HISTORIC PERFUMERY AND TROPICAL GARDENS WHICH PRODUCE OUR EXOTIC PERFUMES.

*t*here is so much to see *(so be sure to bring along your camera)*! ¶ Begin your day with a visit to our Perfumery, Discover how our natural, fragrant perfumes were first created and how today, with the advances in technology, the process has been updated and streamlined. ¶ If you wish you may purchase your favourite fragrances right there on the spot. A sweet lingering memento of your Bermuda holiday! ¶ Once you have toured the Perfumery, and our guide has answered all your questions, you may wish to venture out on your own along our beautiful Nature Trail and visit the Orchid House and Ornamental Gardens.

THE NATURE TRAIL:
is an easily laid out track which gently winds its way through the fields, gardens and jungle to the orchid House. A complimentary guide map is available, and most of the many exotic plants and flowers are clearly labelled so that you can truly appreciate the many points of interest along the trail.

THE ORCHID HOUSE:
here you will find the most extensive collection of orchids in Bermuda. Also you'll see other varieties of rare exotic species gathered from around the world.

THE TEA GARDEN:
dominated by a Royal Poinciana tree this delightful trestled garden is always alive with beautiful vibrant colours and fresh natural perfumes, including old garden Bermuda roses. There are also several "rest-spots" along the trail, where you are welcome to simply sit, relax and enjoy the beauty around you.

THE ORNAMENTAL GARDEN:
our newest garden, featuring a wide variety of exotic plants. Take a few moments to enjoy the colour and slendour of this formal garden.

APRIL THROUGH OCTOBER
Open daily,
Monday to Saturday, 9am – 5pm.
Sundays and holidays, 10am – 4pm.
NOVEMBER THROUGH MARCH
Monday to Saturday, 9am – 4.30pm.
(Closed Sundays and Public Holidays.)

NORTH SHORE ROAD
PERFUMERY
BAILEY'S BAY
SWIZZLE INN
POST OFFICE
WILKINSON AVE
BLUE HOLE HILL
ICE CREAM PARLOUR
TO AIRPORT
TO SOUTH SHORE

Perfumery AND Gardens
THE BERMUDA

TELEPHONE: 293 0627
All major Credit Cards accepted.

traditional ceremony with a military guard of honour.

November: **All Breed Championship Dog Show**
A week of competitions featuring dogs from Bermuda and other countries.

November: **Remembrance Day**
The day is marked with a parade of Bermudian, British and US military units, Bermuda Police and Veterans organisations, to honour men and women who died in the service of their country.

November-March: **Bermuda Rendezvous Time**
Daily activities throughout the winter season, including historic events in St George's, a Market Day with local artisans, a Skirling Ceremony and walking tours. Musical displays by military bands are frequently scheduled for the evenings on Front Street in Hamilton.

TOUR GUIDES

There are no organised tours of Bermuda, but taxis may be hired by the hour, the day or the mile. See the *Getting Around* section for details.

CULTURE PLUS

MUSEUMS & HISTORIC BUILDINGS

For information about historic buildings, contact the Bermuda National Trust, Waterville, Paget. Tel: 236 6483.

Verdmont: Collector's Hill, Smiths Parish, tel: 236 7369. Open: Monday–Friday 10 a.m.–5 p.m. Admission: BD$2. A fine late-17th-century mansion containing antique furniture. Vermont is the most important National Trust house on the island.

Confederate Museum: Kings Square, St George's, tel: 297 1423. Open: Monday–Friday 10 a.m.–5 p.m. Admission: BD$1.50. The former Globe Hotel (1698) was the headquarters of the principal Southern agent in Bermuda mainly concerned with procurement and blockade-running during the American Civil War.

Tucker House: Water Street, St George's, tel: 297 0545. Open: Monday–Friday 10 a.m.–5 p.m. Admission: BD$2. Home of the distinguished Tucker family of England, Bermuda and Virginia. Fine collection of furniture, portraits and silver.

The Old Rectory: Broad Alley, St George's, tel: 297 0879. Open: Wednesday and Friday 10 a.m.–5 p.m. Donations welcome. A charming Bermudian cottage built around 1705.

Palmetto House: North Shore Road, Devonshire, tel: 295 9941. Open: Thursday 10 a.m.–5 p.m. An 18th-century cruciform house, with three rooms on display.

Stewart Hall: Queen Street, St George's, tel: 297 1912. Open: Monday and Wednesday 9 a.m.–5 p.m., Saturday 10 a.m.–5 p.m. except lunchtime 1 p.m.–2 p.m. Historic building with interesting features.

Town Hall: Kings Square, St George's. Open: Monday–Saturday 9 a.m.–4 p.m. The site of many history events in Bermuda's oldest town.

The Bridge House: King Square, St George's, tel: 297 8211. Open: Monday–Saturday 10 a.m.–5 p.m. Built shortly after 1700 and a home to several governors, this very attractive house is now an art gallery.

Deliverance: St George's. Open: daily 10 a.m.–4 p.m. Admission: BD$2. This replica of one of Bermuda's founding ships is expertly built and brings to life the hardship conditions which earlier settlers faced crossing the Atlantic. All proceeds go to local charitable organisations.

State House: King Square, St George's. Open: most Wednesdays 10 a.m.–4 p.m. The oldest building in Bermuda, the State House was built in 1620. Originally the seat of government assembly meetings, it is now a Masonic Lodge whose annual Peppercorn Ceremony, when the Masons pay their rent, is an occasion full of pomp and colour.

Historical Society Museum: Featherbed Alley & Duke of Kent Street, St. George's, tel: 297 0423. Open: Monday–Saturday 10 a.m.–4 p.m. Admission: BD$1. Artefacts from Bermuda's past.

Carter House: US Naval Air Station, St David's. Open: Wednesday 11 a.m.–2 p.m. Built by the descendants of Christopher Carter, one of the island's earliest settlers, the house is now a small museum. Visitors must enter at the Main Gate of the Naval Air Station, the end of Kindley Field Road, and need to bring passports. If on a scooter, the cycle rental must be shown and you need to have goggles or a face shield for protection. Best to enquire at a Visitors Service Bureau before setting out to avoid being turned away at the gate.

Maritime Museum: Royal Naval Dockyard, Ireland Island, tel: 234 1418. Open: daily 10 a.m.–5 p.m. Admission: BD$5. A fascinating series of buildings which vividly documents Bermuda's maritime activities.

Somerset Library: Springfield, Somerset Road, tel: 234 1980. Open: Monday and Wednesday 9 a.m.–1 p.m., then 2 p.m.–5 p.m. Saturday 10 a.m.–1 p.m., then 2 p.m.–5 p.m. Restored by the National Trust, this beautiful plantation home is bordered by the Gilbert Nature Reserve.

Camden: South Shore Road, Paget, tel: 236 5732. Open: Tuesday and Friday 12 noon–2 p.m. Located deep in the grounds of the Botanical Gardens, this dignified house is now the official residence of Bermuda's premier.

FORTS

Gates Fort: St.George's. Open: daily 10 a.m.–4.30 p.m. The fort was originally a small sea battery.

Fort St Catherine: off Barry Road, St George's, tel: 297 1920. Open: daily 10 a.m.–4.30 p.m. Admission: BD$2.50. Replicas of the Crown Jewels and a series of dioramas which clearly illustrate decisive dates in Bermuda's history. Five of its big guns, which could hurl a huge projectile over half a mile (800 metres), have been restored. Admission: BD$2.50.

Fort Hamilton: Happy Valley Road, Pembroke, tel: 292 2845. Open: Monday–Friday 9.30 a.m.–5 p.m. Historic fort whose moat has now become a garden of flowers and shrubs.

Scaur Hill Fort: Somerset Road, Somerset Island, tel: 234 0908. Open: daily 9 a.m.–4.30 p.m. Picnic in the grounds of this historic fortification. The grounds stay open until sunset.

NIGHTLIFE

Most nightlife for visitors is conducted in hotels. Entertainment tends to be Big Band sounds or, increasingly and much to the dismay of local musicians, disco music. Non-residents are usually welcome, but it would be wise to check first.

Much more exciting is to go to one of the places where Bermudians themselves go. This is where the real action takes place. The music is loud, the drinks are cheap and, the later the hour, the more people arrive. The clientele is primarily black and friendly; white strangers will be welcomed and the only problem you might experience is being allowed to pay for your own drink. Three places in Hamilton where it's fun to forget that Bermuda is a formal island are: **Casey's**, next to Kentucky Fried Chicken on Queen Street, tel: 293 9549; **Place's** on Dundonald Street, tel: 293 9268; and the **Spinning Wheel** on Court Street, tel: 292 7799. If you're too shy to enter a club on your own, strike up a conversation with the bartender in your hotel, and an invitation might well be forthcoming.

SHOPPING

WHAT TO BUY

Bermudian goods: Outerbridge sherry pepper sauce; Hortons black rum cake; Bermuda spirits (Black Seal Rum, Silver Label Light Rum, Rum Swizzle, Bermuda Gold, Banana Liqueur, Bermuda Triangle); floral perfume by the Bermuda Perfumery and Royall Lyme; hand-made cedar candle-holders, lamps and book-ends.

British goods: cashmeres, linens, woollens, tartan, Liberty silk scarves, menswear and walking sticks, Wedgwood, Royal Copenhagan, Royal Crown Derby and other fine china and porcelain.

SHOPPING AREAS

Hamilton is the obvious place, from the elegant facades of Front Street to the indoor arcades behind. Many of Hamilton's shops are family-owned businesses which date back to the 1860s. Gosling's, the liquor merchants, is even older – the shop was established in 1806.

As a break from busy Hamilton, it's refreshing to look for souvenirs in both the narrow backstreets of St George's and by Mangrove Bay in the village of Somerset. Under no circumstances miss the bucolic delights of shopping at both the Irish Linen Shop and its neighbouring branch of Triminghams near Somerset. Coming across these stores from the south by accident while walking the country lanes is to feel a little like shopping in the jungle.

EXPORT PROCEDURES

Bermuda's shopping bargains are most convenient for North American visitors; less so for Europeans. As well as substantial savings on British goods, any gift of under $50 (USA) or $20 (Canada) can be posted abroad by mail without infringing on the duty-free allowance.

So how are prices kept low? Bermuda is not a "duty-free" island, but most stores buy direct from manufacturers and avoid the high distribution costs which plague US retailers. "In bond" shopping is another way the island saves money. These "in bond" goods, mainly spirits and cigarettes, are priced low because technically the merchandise has not entered the country.

There is no duty free shop at the airport. Bottles of in-bond drink are delivered directly to the airport without you seeing them at the point of purchase. In-bond spirits can be substantially less expensive than elsewhere, but be sure to arrange your purchases several days before you plan to leave the country.

SPORTS

PARTICIPANT

For a look at the athletics opportunities which Bermuda can offer, read the chapter called *Bermuda Sports* (page 109). Two booklets invaluable to sports lovers are the *Golfer's Guide* and the *Sportsman's Guide*, which are available from the Department of Tourism.

Equestrians will be interested to note there are two riding establishments, both of which offer instruction: Lee Bow Riding Centre, Tribe Road #1, Devonshire, tel: 236 4181, and Spicelands, Middle Road, Warwick, tel: 238 8212. Lee Bow tends to specialise in juniors, while Spicelands has breakfast and evening rides as well as the usual agenda.

Here is a calendar of annual sporting events:

Sailing:
International Race Week (April/May)
Heritage Trophy, Fitted Dinghies (May)
Newport-Bermuda Race (June, even years)
Marion-Bermuda Cruising Race (June, odd years)
King Edward VII Gold Cup Match Racing Regatta (November)

Golf:
Bermuda PGA Championship (January)
Bermuda Amateur Matchplay (March)
Bermuda Amateur Strokeplay (June)
Bermuda Open Championship (October)
Belmont Invitational Championships (November)
Bermuda Goodwill Championships (December)

Tennis:
USTA Mother-Daughter, Father-Son Tournament (March)
International Open (April)
Bermuda Lawn Tennis Club Invitational (November)
Coral Beach Club Invitational (November)

Cricket:
Central Counties Cup Final (July)
Cup Match (Thursday and Friday before first Monday of August)
Eastern Counties Cup Final (August)
Western Counties Cup Final (August)

Football (soccer)**:**
Diadora International Youth Cup (April)
FA Challenge Cup Final (April)
Martonmere Cup Final (November)
Dudley Eve Trophy final, two legs (Christmas Day, New Year's Day)

Rugby:
Easter Classic (Easter Sunday)
World Rugby Classic (November)

Squash:
Bermuda Open (November)

Bowling:
Annual Bermuda Invitation Rendezvous Tournament (February)

Hockey:
Bermuda Hockey Festival (September)

Powerboats:
Around the Island Race (July/August)

Cycling:
Grand Prix Aux Bermuda (April)

Triathlon:
Bermuda International Triathlon (September)
Bermuda Triathlon (September/October)

Road running:
International Race Weekend (mid-January)
Marathon Derby (May)

SPECIAL INFORMATION

Bermuda is an island for grown-ups. Although Bermudians themselves are welcoming towards children, hotel dining rooms are formal, as is the way of life. The absence of cars prevents anything resembling a "traditional family holiday", as very little can be carried on a moped, even a moped built for two.

Some of the beaches, of course, are ideal for children, with shallow waters and a gently sloping shelf. Shelly Bay on the North Shore is ideal, with public conveniences nearby; so is Somerset Long Bay. Admiralty House Park, at the junction of North Shore and Spanish Point Roads in Pembroke has a cove with an almost land-locked beach which is also suitable.

If staying in self-catering accommodation and willing to travel by ferry or bus, parents and children will no doubt have an excellent time. But you'll have to work at it.

DISABLED

An *Access Guide* for the handicapped traveller produced by The Society for the Advancement of Travel for the Handicapped is available by request from the Department of Tourism.

Further Reading

The Adventurers of Bermuda, by Henry C. Wilkinson, Oxford University Press (1933).

Architecture Bermuda Style, by David R. Raine, Pompano Publications.

As a Matter of Fact, by George Rushe, The Bermuda Press.

Bermuda, by Theodore L. Godet M.D., Smith, Elder and Co. (1860).

Bermuda a Colony, a Fortress, and a Prison, by A Field Officer, Longman, Brown, Green & Roberts (1857).

Bermuda and the Bahamas, by Darwin Porter, Prentice Hall Press.

Bermuda From Sail to Steam, by Henry C. Wilkinson, Oxford University Press (in two volumes).

Bermuda in the Old Empire, by Henry C. Wilkinson, Oxford University Press.

Bermuda Journey, by William Zuill, Coward-McCann, Inc.

Bermuda Past and Present, by Walter Brownell Hayward, Dodd, Mead and Company (1910).

The Bermudas, by William Frith Williams, Thomas Cautley Newby (1848).

Bermuda's Story, by Mrs Terry Tucker, Bermuda Bookstores (and numerous other books and booklets).

The Bermuda Triangle Mystery—Solved, by Larry Kusche.

The Early Forts of Bermuda, by Jack Arnell, Bermuda Fire & Marine Insurance Company Limited.

Endangered Birds: Management Techniques for Preserving Threatened Species, by David Wingate, The University of Wisconsin Press, Madison (reprinted for private distribution).

Gombey, by Louise A. Jackson, M.B.E.

Great Guns of Bermuda, by Dr. Edward Harris, Bermuda Maritime Press.

Held in Trust, by the Bermuda National Trust, National Trust Publications.

The Historic Towne of St George, by David F. Raine, Pompano Publications.

The Islands of Bermuda—Another World, by David F. Raine, Macmillan.

Isle of Devils, by Jean Kennedy, Collins.

Life on Old St David's, Bermuda, by E.A. McCallan, Bermuda Historical Society.

A Man Called Intrepid, by William Stevenson, Macmillan.

Memorials of the Bermudas, by Sir J.H. Lefroy, Bermuda Historical Society and Bermuda National Trust (two volumes).

Queen of the East, by John Weatherill, Morrell Wylye Head.

The Restoration of an Island Ecology, by David Wingate, Whole Earth Review.

Sir George Somers, by David F. Raine, Pompano Publications.

The Story of Bermuda, by Hudson Strode, Harcourt Brace & Co. (1946).

The Story of Bermuda and her People, by W.S. Zuill, Macmillan Caribbean.

Tom Moore's Bermuda Poems, by William Zuill, The Bermuda Bookstore.

Useful Addresses

Local Visitors Service Bureaux can help with queries, opening hours and accommodation. They also stock a large range of brochures and information leaflets.

Hamilton: tel: 295 1480.
St George's: tel: 297 1642.
Somerset: tel: 234 1388 (summer only).
Bermuda Airport: tel: 293 0736.

The Bermuda National Trust provides details of historic buildings, selected nature reserves and private gardens which are open to the public on certain days in spring. The Trust's headquarters are at Waterville, Paget, tel: 236 6483.

TOURIST INFORMATION

These are the contact addresses for Bermuda's tourist offices:

In Bermuda:
Global House
43 Church Street
Hamilton MH 12

Abroad:
Suite 201
310 Madison Avenue
New York, NY 10017, USA

Suite 1070
Randolph-Wacker Bldg.
150 N. Wacker Drive
Chicago, Illinois 60606, USA

Suite 2008
235 Peachtree Street NE
Atlanta, Georgia 30303, USA

Suite 1010
44 School Street
Boston, MA 02108, USA

Suite 1004
1200 Bay Street
Toronto, Ontario
Canada M5R 2A5

European Representative:
Bermuda Tourism
BCB Ltd
1 Battersea Church Road
London SW11 3LY
United Kingdom

Western Region Representative:
John A. Tetly Inc.
Suite 606
3075 Wilshire Blvd.
Los Angeles, CA 90010
USA

ART/PHOTO CREDITS

INDEX

Q - R

S

T

U